On This Day In Music History

"Combining fascinating asides of musical history with informative facts ranging from current collectible values to little-known recording studio collaborations, author Jay Warner has created a montage of musical interest that will hold anyone who opens the front cover."

— John Koenig, editor, *Discoveries* magazine

"Very interesting trivia that appeals to the curious mind. A great entertainment source." **— Maurice White, Earth, Wind & Fire**

"A must-have music trivia book. As a reader of rock-and-roll history, I enjoyed it. The book gives insightful background on noted artists I grew up with." **—Otis Williams, The Temptations**

Album covers, courtesy fo Record Research
Cover photos, courtesy of Photofest
Interior photos, courtesy of Photofest

On This Day in Music History

Published by Hal Leonard Corporation
7777 Bluemound Road
P.O. Box 13819
Milwaukee, WI 53213

Trade Book Division Editorial Offices
151 West 46th Street, 8th Floor
New York, NY 10036

Library of Congress Cataloging-in-Publication Data
Warner, Jay.
  On this day in music history / by Jay Warner.-- 1st ed.
    p. cm.
  ISBN 0-634-06693-5 (pbk.)
  1. Popular music--History and criticism--Miscellanea. I. Title.
  ML3470.W34 2004
  781.64'0973--dc22
                                    2003024566

Printed in the United States of America
First Edition
Book Designed by Hal Leonard Creative Services

Visit Hal Leonard online at **www.halleonard.com**

On This Day In Music History

Foreword

The fascinating thing about history is that it is essentially about people. We relate to time by the significance of certain dates. Take October 9, for example. What does it mean to you? The obvious answer is that it's the day that John Lennon was born on in 1940, and coincidentally he shared his birthday with his younger son, Sean. For me, it has an even greater significance, for on that day, my youngest son, Giles, was also born. When John heard my news he congratulated me and said, "Now you know what kind of an idiot he is going to be!"

"History is more or less bunk," said Henry Ford. Well, he may have been a genius for making cars, but I think he was wrong about that. Every day that goes by is of enormous importance to someone in our world, and I know there are many dates that are particularly significant to me—joyous days, funny days, days of achievement, days of failure, days of laughter, and days of sorrow. Who can possibly forget that terrible eleventh day in a September not that long ago? I doubt if there is anyone in the Western world who does not remember it with deep sadness and horror. It will remain for a long time to come the most significant day of the year for us all.

So it is in our world of music. One clearly remembers the day one's child is born, and I will never forget the day in 1967 when I received my first Grammy, shaking the hand of Duke Ellington as he passed me my precious award. Why should we not mark significant milestones in the development of music? Author Jay Warner has hit upon the idea of making a chronicle of all those important happenings as they appeared in one year or another, and I find it fascinating reading.

Dates are important, as any astrologer will tell you. Most people look at their horoscopes and wonder if there is anything in it. Maybe there is...

Centuries ago I produced a record with the great John McLaughlin and his Mahavishnu Orchestra along with Michael Tilson Thomas. That album is still one of my all-time favorites. Soon after we had started recording, John came to me and said, "I'll bet you were born under the sign of Capricorn!" Well, he had a one in twelve chance of getting it right. I confirmed his guess, and asked him what gave him the clue. He said he felt that we both thought exactly alike—we were in tune with each other in every way. I felt much the same, and then we discovered that our birthdays were just one day apart. Uncanny? No, it just confirms what I have always believed. The calendar, the day, and the month are important because they belong to human beings. History is not bunk; it is the result of real events taking place with real people. It records the essence of the lives of so many wonderful human beings in the past, and it is happening right now. You and I are making history as we go along. What happens today will be history tomorrow. Every day is significant—every day we live.

George Martin, April 2004

Introduction

The dictionary defines trivia as "matters or things of very slight importance, commonplace, or ordinary." Yet anyone who's ever read anything about a favorite sports star, singer, historic figure, or celebrity will find that it's often the so-called trivia that makes things memorable about that person or event.

In those instances where such trivia can peak the interest of a fan or curiosity seeker, trivia's very stark and unforgiving definition seems misleading at the least and even contradictory. Nowhere is that more apparent than in a book that subsists by using as one of its cornerstone "hooks," the constant interest and relevance of things that by themselves may seem of "little importance." However, put the book into the context of a volume based on the progression of hundreds of parallel lives through the timeline of a pseudo-calendar format can be anything but "commonplace or ordinary."

Being a collector of everything from baseball memorabilia and history books to records and music memorabilia has made me appreciate trivia in all its individual forms. When I wrote *The Billboard Book of American Singing Groups* (Decapo Press), I realized what may seem insignificant information by itself is like a spice before it is added to food. Once blended with the trivia, the stories take on a whole different flavor. When a bit of information is put on the page of a calendar, it doesn't necessarily generate excitement, but as the days unfold and one piece of a seemingly unrelated comment expands with other comments to tie together over weeks and months, the cultural coincidences take form of a fascinating series of events without the often boring set-up required in biographies and all-too-well-known histories.

At first glance, this book takes on the appearance of an entertaining reference, but a closer look will, I believe, show that it's actually a lot of connecting vignettes, telling a vast history of music.

Most people will probably flip to their birthdays or those of loved ones to see what happened on that day. That's fine, but if you delve deeper by following the day-to-day happenings you'll find the thread of popular music woven throughout and key events peppered with everything from amusing anecdotes to thought-provoking quotes.

By combining a calendar format with an elevated element of what some misdefine as trivia, this new kind of to-the-point history will hopefully set a new trend in books for the instant gratification age of the twenty-first century.

After all, on January 1, The Beatles were discovered (and rejected) and on December 31, the world learned they broke up. In between are the crib notes of music history.

—Jay Warner

January

1

#1 Song 1955: "Let Me Go Lover," Joan Weber

Born: Country Joe McDonald, 1942; Grandmaster Flash, 1958

1953 Legendary country singer Hank Williams had a career forty-two chart singles, including eleven #1s such as "Lovesick Blues," "Hey Good Lookin'," "Cold, Cold Heart," and "Jambalaya." The hard-drinking Mount Olive, Alabama, youth (he started drinking at age eleven) started out as a songwriter in Nashville and had his first hit with "Move It on Over" in 1947. Troubled by back problems most of his life, pain killers, and booze became his crutch. He died of a heart attack in the rear seat of a Cadillac en route to a concert in Ohio today. He was only twenty-nine.

1966 The Beach Boys charted with a remake of The Regents 1961 hit "Barbara Ann." The basically a capella affair started out as a party record in the studio and wound up reaching #2, becoming another Beach Boys million-selling milestone even though no one in the group sang lead. That position was filled at the insistence of the "Boys" by Dean Torrance of Jan & Dean, who just happened to drop by for the festivities and joined in!

1960 Johnny Cash played his first of many free concerts at San Quentin Prison, California. Country star-to-be Merle Haggard was a convict in the audience.

1962 Decca Records A&R head Dick Rowe established his place in history when he turned down four Liverpool musicians called The Beatles after they had auditioned for his A&R man, Mike Smith. They performed and recorded fifteen songs for him, including "Three Cool Cats," "September in the Rain," "Besame Mucho," and "Searchin'," along with several Lennon-McCartney songs, all chosen by Brian Epstein. The Beatles auditioned at Decca's studios in Broadhurst Gardens, West Hampstead, North London. Rowe told Epstein, "Groups of guitars are on the way out. You really should stick to selling records in Liverpool." Instead, he signed the Essex band Brian Poole & the Tremeloes, who had auditioned the same day, because they lived closer to London. Rowe quickly made up for his misstep by signing The Rolling Stones to Decca…on George Harrison's advice.

1964 Dusty Springfield's "I Only Want to Be with You" became the first record played on Britain's new pop-music TV show, *Top of the Pops*.

January

1957 Jackie Wilson recorded his last sides with The Dominoes (including "To Each His Own") for Decca before embarking on his tremendous solo career.

1962 The Escorts (with future Pointer Sisters and Ringo Starr's record producer, Richard Perry, singing bass) recorded their up-tempo version of "Gloria" (a $60 collectible today) as their first single.

1964 The Rolling Stones backed Cleo Sylvestre, a British singer on The Teddy Bears' 1958 hit "To Know Him Is to Love Him," written by Phil Spector.

1969 The Beatles began filming a TV movie called *Get Back* at Twickenham Studios near London. The next day, they performed new songs, including "Let It Be" and what would become the title song of George Harrison's 1970–71 album called *All Things Must Pass*.

Jackie Wilson

January

3

#1 Song 1970: "Raindrops Keep Fallin' on My Head," B.J. Thomas

Born: Maxene Andrews (Andrews Sisters), 1918; George Martin (producer of The Beatles albums), 1926; Willie Mitchell, 1928; Stephen Stills, 1945; John Paul Jones (Led Zeppelin), 1946

1946 John Paul Jones, the bass player for Led Zeppelin was born today. He was with the band (which originally called itself The New Yardbirds) from its forming in 1968 until they broke up in 1980. They're best known for the hits "Whole Lotta Love" and "Stairway to Heaven." Despite the latter's popularity, it was never issued as a commercial 45.

1950 Sun Records—future home of Johnny Cash, Roy Orbison, Carl Perkins, Jerry Lee Lewis, and Elvis Presley—opened for business by Sam Phillips in Memphis, Tennessee.

1967 Carl Wilson (The Beach Boys) refused to accept his draft notice during the Vietnam War and spent five years fighting in court until he was finally acquitted of draft evasion.

1969 Newark, New Jersey, Police confiscated an entire shipment of John Lennon and Yoko Ono's *Two Virgins* album, the highlight of which was a full frontal nude photo of the couple. The LPs were only allowed in the U.S. when the record label agreed to wrap them in plain brown paper.

1970 The Beatles recorded their last song as a group today. The George Harrison–penned lament "I, Me, Mine" wound up on the *Let It Be* album. Actually only three Beatles performed on it—George, Paul, and Ringo.

John Lennon and Yoko Ono's
Two Virgins

January

#1 Song 1964: "There! I've Said It Again," Bobby Vinton

Born: John McLaughlin (Mahavishnu Orchestra), 1942

1936 *Billboard* magazine, founded in 1894 as an entertainment periodical for circuses, published its first music chart for record sales. The first #1 record (on 78 RPM) was "Stop! Look! Listen!" by jazz artist Joe Venuti.

1964 Betty Harris's second of three Top 100 singles, "His Kiss," charted today. Betty was originally a maid for blues singer Big Maybelle. Her career started when Maybelle brought her onstage for duets.

1986 Philip Lynott was the lead singer and bass player for the Irish rock band, Thin Lizzy. Born in Dublin to a Brazilian father and an Irish mother, he started with an R&B group called the Black Eagles. Thin Lizzy evolved out of members from subsequent Lynott groups like Sugar Shack and Orphanage (an interesting name since Philip was born out of wedlock). Their biggest hit in the States was "The Boys Are Back in Town" (1976), but they were very popular in Europe. Philip died today of complications from a drug overdose in a hospital in Salisbury, England, at age thirty-four.

1992 Elton John hit the charts with "Don't Let the Sun Go Down on Me" giving him twenty-three straight years with a Top 40 chart song in each year—tying him with Elvis Presley.

January

#1 Song 1959: "The Chipmunk Song," David Seville

Born: Sam Phillips (Sun Records), 1923; George Brown (Kool & the Gang), 1949; Bryan Hitt, 1954 (REO Speedwagon)

1929 Wilbert Harrison, the man who made the Leiber-Stoller song "Kansas City," a rock 'n' roll classic, was born in Charlotte, North Carolina. Wilbert was one of twenty-three children.

1935 The Boswell Sisters topped the pop charts today with their 78 RPM hit single, "The Object of My Affection." It was the first #1 by a girl group in music history. They were also the first act in music history to have a song with the term "rock 'n' roll" in the title when their 1934 recording of "Rock and Roll" reached #7 on the pop charts. Although it preceded Alan Freed's coining of the term by some twenty years, the connotation was a bit different. The song was from the motion picture *Transatlantic Merry-Go-Round* and referred to "rocking and rolling" back and forth on a boat.

1940 The first test of FM radio was heard by the Federal Communications Commission. It would be a year before radios with FM capability belonging to the public would hear the new static-free signals.

1954 Elvis Presley recorded two country songs for a demo at Sun Records. The songs were "It Wouldn't Be the Same Without You" and "I'll Never Stand in Your Way." It would still be several months before Elvis cut his first record.

1959 Buddy Holly's "It Doesn't Matter Anymore" was issued by Coral Records. It was Buddy's last single before his death.

1966 "I Feel Fine" and "Help!" were rerecorded by The Beatles and inserted in *The Beatles at Shea Stadium* soundtrack, due to the fact that the volume of audience noise was so great that the original performances couldn't be heard clearly on the tape.

1998 Sonny Bono was the brain behind Sonny & Cher (originally known as Caesar & Cleo), the pop duo that had twenty chart hits between 1965 and 1973, including "I Got You Babe." He went on to be mayor of Palm Springs, California and was then elected to Congress in 1994. He died in a skiing accident near Lake Tahoe today. He was sixty-two.

January

#1 Song 1958: "At the Hop," Danny & the Juniors

Born: Nino Tempo, 1935; Van McCoy, 1944; Syd Barrett (Pink Floyd), 1946; Mark O'Toole, 1964 (Frankie Goes to Hollywood)

1947 Sandy Denny, the lead singer of the British folk rock pioneers Fairport Convention, was born today. She sang with the band from 1968 through 1970, went solo, and then returned from 1973 through 1976. Sandy did the original version of "Who Knows Where the Time Goes," later made popular by Judy Collins.

1957 Elvis Presley made his last of seven appearances on *The Ed Sullivan Show*, wearing a velvet shirt with a gold vest. He performed "Don't Be Cruel" in the style of former Dominoes lead singer Jackie Wilson, whom he had heard performing it in Las Vegas the previous year. This was the famous Sullivan show performance where he was shot mostly from the waist up. He also sang "Hound Dog," "Love Me Tender," "Heartbreak Hotel," and his new single, "Too Much."

1962 Danny & the Juniors seventh hit, "Twistin' All Night Long," charted with guest vocals by Freddie Cannon and the uncredited Four Seasons.

1973 Dolly Parton reached the country hit list with "My Tennessee Mountain Home" (#15), one of ninety-nine charters for the country charmer through 1990.

Dolly Parton

January

7

#1 Song 1956: "Memories Are Made of This," Dean Martin

Born: Paul Revere, 1942; Kenny Loggins, 1948

Died: Larry Williams, 1980

1963 Chubby Checker's fifteenth hit "Dancin' Party" (#12) earned him a plagiarism suit by Gary "U.S." Bonds, who felt the "Chubster's" single was too similar to Bonds's 1961 hit "Quarter to Three."

1964 Cyril Davies, a pioneering British blues harpist, died today. He started with Chris Barber's Jazz Band and by 1957 had opened the Roadhouse Blues Club, where the likes of Mick Jagger, Eric Clapton, and Brian Jones got their start. His band, Blues Incorporated, had a revolving door of later-to-be legends, like Robert Plant, Ginger Baker, Charlie Watts, and Jack Bruce in the early '60s.

1967 The Young Rascals and The Doors played a concert at Winterland.

1992 Debbie Gibson (managed by her mother) made her Broadway debut in *Les Misérables*, playing Eponine.

2000 Bernice Petkere, known as the "Queen of Tin Pan Alley" in the 1930s, died at the age of ninety-eight. Her first song, "Starlight," was recorded by Bing Crosby. Others who recorded her songs included Kate Smith, Tony Bennett, and Nancy Wilson. She also wrote music for radio shows and the score for the MGM musical *Ice Follies of 1939*, starring Joan Crawford and James Stewart.

January

#1 Song 1994: "Hero," Mariah Carey

Born: Elvis Presley, 1935; Little Anthony, 1940; Robbie Krieger (The Doors), 1946; David Bowie, 1947; Mike Reno (Loverboy), 1955

1944 Jo Stafford, formerly of The Pied Pipers, had her first of seventy-eight Top 100 singles, "Old Acquaintance," which reached the popularity list on its way to #14. Her seventy-eight hits were compiled in only thirteen years (1944–57).

1946 Elvis Presley's parents bought him a guitar for his eleventh birthday at a Tupelo hardware store. Elvis wanted a bicycle, but his mother was afraid he might get hurt.

1960 Eddie Cochran recorded his last session at Goldstar Studios in Hollywood backed by members of The Crickets. Soon after, he died. Ironically, the last song he recorded was called "Three Steps to Heaven" and became his only #1 in England. It never charted in the U.S.

1966 The Beatles album *Rubber Soul* and the 45 "We Can Work It Out" both reached #1 on the *Billboard* charts. While this was happening, Ringo, John, and George partied at the home of friend Mick Jagger.

The Beatles' Rubber Soul

2001 Laura Webb Childress, tenor vocalist for The Bobbettes, died. She and her four school-mates were barely in their teens when they formed the Harlem Queens and soon became the rage with their classic, "Mr. Lee," a song they wrote about their fifth-grade teacher that went to #1 R&B and #6 pop in 1957. It made them the first all-girl rock 'n' roll group to have a Top 10 hit (and a #1 R&B record).

January

9

#1 Song 1961: "Wonderland by Night," Bert Kaempfert

Born: Joan Baez, 1941; Jimmy Page, 1944 (Led Zeppelin); Scott Engel (The Walker Brothers), 1944

1968 Elvis Presley's "Guitar Man" was released. From the soundtrack of the film *Clambake*, it was Presley's ninety-ninth chart 45, eventually reaching #43 on the Top 100. Also issued today, *Elvis' Gold Records, Vol. 4* (#33). Only "The King" could justify four albums' worth of million-sellers.

1979 Rod Stewart performed "Do Ya Think I'm Sexy" at the Music for UNICEF concert at the United Nations in New York.

1990 Sinead O'Connor topped Mr. Blackwell's annual list of worst dressed women. He called her "the bald-headed banshee of MTV."

2001 Lynne Nixon Denicker, lead of The Aquatones, passed away. The group, formed in Valley Stream, Long Island, New York, in 1957, had a hit with their first single, "You" (#21 pop, #11 R&B), but couldn't chart again despite seven excellent follow-up singles. They disbanded in 1960. They were the first male group with a female lead to have a hit, both pop and R&B, in the rock 'n' roll era. Lynn was trained as an operatic soprano.

January 10

#1 Song 1981: "Just Like Starting Over," John Lennon

Born: Jerry Wexler (producer of Aretha Franklin), 1918; Johnnie Ray, 1927; Ronnie Hawkins, 1935; Rod Stewart, 1945; Jim Croce, 1943; Donald Fagen (Steely Dan), 1948; Pat Benatar, 1953; Shawn Colvin 1956

1956 Elvis Presley recorded his first sides for RCA at their Nashville studio. The band included Floyd Cramer (piano), Chet Atkins (guitar), and D.J. Fontana (drums). The songs were The Drifters' "Money Honey," Ray Charles's "I Got a Woman," and publicist Mae Axton's original "Heartbreak Hotel."

1956 Rock 'n' roll took an exciting turn with the release of Frankie Lymon & the Teenagers, "Why Do Fools Fall in Love" (#6 pop, #1 R&B).

1958 New York's St. Nicks Arena hosted a rock 'n' roll show and dance, featuring The Five Satins, The Dubs, The Chantels, and The Deltairs.

1959 Rod Stewart received a guitar for his fourteenth birthday from his parents. They obviously had no idea they were giving him a monumental career direction.

1969 While filming the TV show *Get Back*, George Harrison announced he was quitting The Beatles. Ringo summed it up by saying, "George had to leave because he thought Paul was dominating him. Well, he was." Adding to George's displeasure was the constant intrusive behavior of the ever-present Yoko Ono.

January

11

#1 Song 1969: "I Heard It Through the Grapevine," Marvin Gaye

Born: Slim Harpo, 1924; Chuck Barksdale (The Dells), 1935; Bill Reed (The Diamonds), 1936; Janice Pought (The Bobbettes), 1945; Vicki Peterson, 1960 (The Bangles)

1964 The Beatles "I Want to Hold Your Hand" debuted on the American charts (in *Cashbox* magazine) at #80 from advance orders and airplay, even though it was still two days away from its U.S. release.

1965 While The Righteous Brothers were in London, their new single, "You've Lost That Lovin' Feelin'," was featured on the TV show *Juke Box Jury*. All four panelists voted it a miss and one questioned if it was being played at the right speed! By February 4, it was #1 in England and the U.S.

1967 Ringo Starr and Paul McCartney saw Jimi Hendrix perform at the Bag O'Nails Club in London. Earlier, McCartney had seen a BBC2 program of Bach's Brandenburg Concerto No. 2 in F major, featuring a piccolo trumpet solo, which gave him the idea for using the instrument in "Penny Lane."

1992 A tribute album to Elton John peaked at #18 on the U.S. Top 200. It featured versions of Elton's songs sung by The Beach Boys, Joe Cocker, Jon Bon Jovi, Phil Collins, George Michael, The Who, and Tina Turner, among others.

January

#1 Song 1963: "Go Away Little Girl," Steve Lawrence

Born: Long John Baldry, 1941; Cynthia Robinson (Sly & The Family Stone), 1946; Maggie Bell (Stone the Crows), 1946

1939 Songwriter Jack Lawrence brought a tune he'd written to an Ink Spots recording session. The song was the standard-to-be "If I Didn't Care."

1957 Elvis Presley recorded in Nashville at Radio Recorders. Among the songs were "Don't Be Cruel," "All Shook Up," and "I Believe."

1963 Bob Dylan, eight months before his first album (*The Freewheelin' Bob Dylan*, #22) charted, appeared in a BBC radio play, *Madhouse on Castle Street* in the part of (what else!) a folksinger.

1963 Recorded in November 1962, The Beatles' "Please Please Me" was issued in England as their second single and became their first Top 5 (#2) U.K. hit. It reached #3 in the U.S. fourteen months later.

1965 The rock 'n' roll teen show *Hullabaloo* first aired on NBC-TV.

January

13

#1 Song 1962: "The Twist," Chubby Checker

Born: Bobby Lester (The Moonglows), 1930; Trevor Rabin (Yes), 1955; Fred White (Earth, Wind & Fire), 1955

1958 The original version of "Dedicated to the One I Love" by The Five Royales was released. Three years later it became a hit (#3) for The Shirelles and again in 1967 for The Mamas & the Papas (#2). The song was written by Lowman Pauling of The Five Royales, who went on to be a hit producer for Motown records in the 1960s.

1964 The Beatles single "I Want to Hold Your Hand"/"I Saw Her Standing There" was issued in the U.S. on Capitol Records, the American affiliate of Europe's EMI.

1969 Fourteen years after his last recording session in Memphis as an artist on Sun Records, Elvis Presley returned to record for RCA.

1979 The YMCA filed a libel suit against the Village People for their "Y.M.C.A." hit single. It considered the song defamatory. The suit was later dropped.

1980 The Beach Boys, Jefferson Starship, and The Grateful Dead headlined a Los Angeles benefit concert to aid the victims of the Khmer Rouge in Kampuchea.

Village People

January

#1 Song 1967: "I'm a Believer,"
The Monkees

Born: Clarence Carter, 1936;
Allen Toussaint, 1938

1955 Alan Freed's first Rock 'n' Roll Ball in New York at St. Nick's Arena included The Drifters, The Moonglows, The Harptones, and The Clovers.

1967 Janis Joplin and Big Brother & the Holding Company performed at the first "Human Be-In" in Golden Gate Park, along with The Jefferson Airplane and The Grateful Dead.

1967 According to the British press, Paul McCartney was offered the opportunity to write the music for a new play production of Shakespeare's *As You Like It*, which was to star Sir Laurence Olivier. He turned it down, reportedly saying something to the effect that he couldn't create contemporary music that would work with Elizabethan words.

1973 Elvis Presley's *Aloha from Hawaii* performance was broadcast live via satellite from the International Convention Center Arena in Honolulu to most of the Far East, including Japan, Hong Kong (where Presley is affectionately known in Chinese as "King Cat"), Korea, and more than twenty European nations. The concert was seen by the largest audience ever—over one and a half billion people.

1992 When not hanging with a New York street gang, Jerry Nolan was the drummer for the glam-rock, punk band, the New York Dolls, having replaced original and deceased member, Billy Murcia. Best known for their trash-rock version of The Cadets classic "Stranded in the Jungle," the Dolls disintegrated in the mid 1970s (the Dolls influenced The Sex Pistols). Jerry formed The Heartbreakers in England, often sharing the bill with The Clash. Nolan's heroin addiction led to pneumonia and an eventual stroke today. He was forty-six.

January

15

#1 Song 1983: "Down Under," Men at Work

Born: Edward "Sonny" Bivins (The Manhattans), 1942; Joan Johnson (The Dixie Cups), 1945; Martha Davis (The Motels), 1951

1955 LaVern Baker charted with "Tweedlee Dee" (#14), her first of twenty pop Top 100 45s between 1955 and 1966. She also had twenty-one R&B hits and was inducted into the Rock and Roll Hall of Fame in 1991.

1965 The first single by The Who, "I Can't Explain," was released. It reached #8 in the U.K. (#93 U.S.).

1992 On TV's *Entertainment Tonight*, Brenda Lee, the diminutive dynamite damsel, suggested that the all-male lineup of inductees into that night's Rock and Roll Hall of Fame should have included the likes of The Shirelles, Mary Wells, Dionne Warwick, Connie Francis, and herself. "The women who pioneered rock 'n' roll…were just as important as the males," she stated.

Brenda Lee

January

16

#1 Song 1965: "Come See About Me," The Supremes

Born: Hal Miller (The Rays), 1931; Bob Bogle (The Ventures), 1937; Barbara Lynn, 1942; Sade, 1959; Maxine Jones (En Vogue), 1966

1953 R&B collectors' favorite "Keep It a Secret" by The 5 Crowns (Rainbow) was released. Purchase price: 79¢. Today it's a $2,000 rarity!

1957 Elvis Presley worked on the *Loving You* film soundtrack with New York songwriter Ben Weisman in attendance. Weisman wrote "Got a Lot O' Livin' to Do" for the film and would go on to have fifty-six additional songs recorded by Presley in the coming years, more than any other songwriter.

1980 Paul McCartney spent the first of ten days of a trip to Japan in prison for possession of a half pound of marijuana found in his suitcase at Tokyo Airport. He was immediately deported back to England after his ten-day stay.

1988 Tina Turner performed before 180,000 fans at Rio de Janeiro's Maracan Stadium—a box office record for a single artist.

1991 Tina Turner and ex-hubby Ike Turner were inducted into the Rock and Roll Hall of Fame at its sixth annual induction ceremonies. Producer Phil Spector accepted the award in their absence.

January

17

1948 Mick Taylor, who replaced Brian Jones, in The Rolling Stones was born today. The guitarist, formerly with John Mayall's Blues Band, came on board in 1969 and was replaced in 1974 by ex-Faces member Ron Wood. Taylor went on to join Jack Bruce's group and played backup for Bob Dylan in the '80s.

1964 The Beatles performed at the opulent French showplace The Olympia Theater in Paris. The age-old music hall was not prepared for contemporary music and its power supply blew out three times during the concert. A back-stage argument involving a French photographer added to the turmoil, resulting in an onstage fistfight that nearly claimed George's guitar as a casualty.

1969 Led Zeppelin's self-titled debut album was released eventually, reaching #10. With it would begin the era of "heavy metal."

1972 Bellvue Street in Memphis was renamed Elvis Presley Boulevard.

1990 The Four Seasons, The Platters, The Four Tops, Hank Ballard, Bobby Darin, Simon and Garfunkel, The Kinks, and The Who were inducted into the Rock and Roll Hall of Fame at their fifth annual awards presentation in New York City.

Led Zeppelin

January

18

1961 Elvis Presley signed a movie contract for five more years with film producer Hal Wallis that would include *Blue Hawaii* and *Fun in Acapulco*. Wallis previously had Presley under contract for the films *Loving You* and *King Creole*.

1964 "I Want to Hold Your Hand" became The Beatles' first U.S. chart single (#1). It was already their sixth 45 in the U.K. (#1). It also became their first of seventy-two career American single hits on the pop charts and stayed at #1 for seven weeks.

1978 Neil Sedaka (with twenty-nine chart singles, to date) was given a star on Hollywood's Walk of Fame. Neil started his career with the original Tokens in 1956, the precursor to "The Lion Sleeps Tonight" group.

1989 Dion, The Temptations, The Ink Spots, The Rolling Stones, Stevie Wonder, The Soul Stirrers, Otis Redding, and Bessie Smith were inducted into the Rock and Roll Hall of Fame at its fourth annual awards ceremony in New York City. The only non-performer inducted was legendary record producer Phil Spector, who was given his award by Tina Turner. Spector produced and co-wrote Tina's epic single "River Deep, Mountain High."

January 19

#1 Song 1959: "Smoke Gets in Your Eyes," The Platters

Born: Phil Everly (The Everly Brothers), 1939; Janis Joplin, 1943; Shelly Fabares, 1944; Dolly Parton, 1946; Robert Palmer, 1949; Dewey Bunnell (America), 1952

1957 Pat Boone sang at President Dwight D. Eisenhower's inaugural ball.

1977 The Charlie Daniels Band performed at President Jimmy Carter's inaugural ball.

1981 Frank Sinatra, Donny & Marie Osmond, and Dean Martin performed at President Ronald Reagan's inaugural ball.

1994 Elton John, John Lennon, The Band, The Grateful Dead, Duane Eddy, Willie Dixon, Bob Marley, Johnny Otis, and Rod Stewart (whose former occupation was that of a grave digger) were inducted into the Rock and Roll Hall of Fame in New York. Stewart was to have received his award from Jeff Beck, but couldn't make it to the ceremony as he was stuck in Los Angeles due to the infamous earthquake of 1994 two days prior to the induction.

1998 Pioneering rockabilly artist Carl Perkins was best known for his #1 country hit "Blue Suede Shoes" and for being one of the first artists to break out on Sun Records. Carl was a major influence on many rock 'n' rollers of the '60s, including The Beatles. He was inducted into the Rock and Roll Hall of Fame in 1987. He died of a series of strokes today at the age of sixty-five.

Carl Perkins

January

#1 Song 1973: "You're So Vain", Carly Simon

Born: Leadbelly, 1888; Ron Townson (The 5th Dimension), 1941; William Powell (The O'Jays), 1942; Dave Libert (Happenings), 1943; Eric Stewart (10cc), 1945; Paul Stanley (Kiss), 1952

1953 The McGuire Sisters' first of fifty-nine singles, "Pickin' Sweethearts," was released.

1958 The Chantels' classic, "Maybe," charted, eventually reaching #15.

1964 The album *Meet the Beatles* was issued in America two days after "I Want to Hold Your Hand" charted. The album contained twelve tracks (the British pressing called *With the Beatles* had thirteen), nine of which were on the U.K. release. It excluded "Money," "Please Mister Postman," "Devil in Her Heart," "Roll Over Beethoven," and "You Really Got a Hold on Me" (not so coincidentally, all cover songs)—replaced by "I Want to Hold Your Hand," "I Saw Her Standing There," "This Boy," and "Hold Me Tight." By the end of the year, The Beatles would have thirty-three singles issued in the U.S. on three different labels.

1965 The founding father of rock 'n' roll, Alan Freed coined the term in 1946 and became an overnight disc jockey sensation at Cleveland's WJW radio in 1951 when he began playing original rock and R&B records instead of the pasteurized pop covers by white acts. On March 23, 1952, Freed held the first rock 'n' roll concert, which attracted more than 10,000 teen fans. He also oversaw and starred in two of the '50s most successful rock-'n'-roll movies, *Rock, Rock, Rock* and *Mister Rock and Roll*. The payola scandal of the '60s made Freed a target and scapegoat as America's most popular dee-jay was fired by WINS in New York. Alan Freed died, out of work at the age of forty-three today.

1988 The Beach Boys, Bob Dylan, The Beatles, The Drifters, The Supremes, and Berry Gordy, Jr. (founder of Motown) were inducted into the Rock and Roll Hall of Fame at their third annual induction ceremonies. Also inducted as early influences were bluesman Leadbelly, folk artist Woody Guthrie, and jazz musician Les Paul— pioneers all. Coincidentally, Leadbelly had been born 100 years earlier on this day.

January

21

1957 Patsy Cline performed on *Arthur Godfrey's Talent Scouts*, winning with "Walkin' After Midnight." Godfrey told her, "You are the most innocent, the most nervous, most truthful, and honest performer I have ever seen." Soon after, she became a regular on his weekly TV show.

1961 Patsy Cline performed at the Grand Ole Opry, only two weeks before giving birth to a son, Randy.

1966 George Harrison married Patti Boyd, an actress he met on the set of The Beatles film *Help*.

1984 Legendary vocalist Jackie Wilson died. He began as an amateur boxer in Detroit. In 1953, he joined Billy Ward's Dominoes as replacement for another legendary lead singer, Clyde McPhatter. He left in 1957 for a solo career that included fifty-four pop and forty-seven R&B hits, like "Higher & Higher" and "Baby Workout." He died after an eight-year coma brought on by a heart attack while onstage (September 25, 1975). He was singing his biggest hit, "Lonely Teardrops," at the time.

1987 Aretha Franklin was inducted into the Rock and Roll Hall of Fame by Rolling Stones member Keith Richards during the second annual awards presentation in New York City. Also inducted were Roy Orbison, The Coasters, Marvin Gaye, Carl Perkins, Smokey Robinson, Eddie Cochran, Bo Diddley, Ricky Nelson, B. B. King, Big Joe Turner, and Muddy Waters. Clyde McPhatter, Bill Haley, and Jackie Wilson were posthumously inducted. Today also happened to be the third anniversary of Wilson's death.

January

#1 Song 1966: "Sounds of Silence," Simon & Garfunkel

Born: Sam Cooke, 1935; Addie ("Micki") Harris (The Shirelles), 1940; Steve Perry (Journey), 1949

1959 Buddy Holly made his final demos in his New York apartment. The six rough solo voice-guitar tracks included "Bo Diddley," "Love Is Strange," Little Richard's "Slippin' & Slidin'," and Leiber & Stoller's "Smokey Joe's Cafe." He died twelve days later.

1966 Frank Sinatra's daughter Nancy hit the Top 100 with "These Boots Are Made For Walkin'." The song "walked" all the way to #1.

1969 The Beatles worked on their *Get Back* album and TV show, filming The Drifters' "Save the Last Dance for Me," Canned Heat's "Going Up the Country," and originals "She Came in Through the Bathroom Window," "Don't Let Me Down," and "I've Got a Feeling."

1969 In a session at Memphis's American Studios, Elvis Presley met his longtime idol, R&B great Roy Hamilton of "Unchained Melody" fame. Elvis then recorded one of his most enduring future hits, "Suspicious Minds."

Nancy Sinatra

January

23

#1 Song 1965: "Downtown"
Petula Clark

Born: Jerry Lawson (The Persuasions), 1944; Patrick Simmons (The Doobie Brothers), 1950; Robin Zander (Cheap Trick), 1953

1959 Dion began the infamous "Winter Dance Party" tour with Ritchie Valens, Buddy Holly, and The Big Bopper. He would become the only headliner to survive as the latter three all died in a small plane crash midway through the tour.

1963 While driving in their van from London to Liverpool in a freezing wind, The Beatles' front windshield shattered. The group lay huddled in the back while their roadie drove with a paper bag over his head with slits for his eyes affording him little protection from the terrible temperatures. John Lennon later said the roadie looked like a bank robber.

1965 Petula Clark became the first British female to reach the top of the U.S. pop charts since Vera Lynn (1952) when "Down Town" hit #1. The Jackie Trent–Tony Hatch-penned million-seller was originally written for The Drifters.

1970 Judy Collins, testifying at the trial of the "Chicago Seven," was denied permission to *sing* her testimony!

1976 The *Donny & Marie Show* debuted on ABC-TV tonight. It ran for three years and fifty-seven episodes.

January

#1 Song 1976: "Do You Know Where You're Going to," Diana Ross

Born: Zeke Carey (The Flamingos), 1933; Neil Diamond, 1941; Ray Stevens, 1939; Tammi Terrell, 1946; Warren Zevon, 1947

1948 Peggy Lee hit the charts with the rhythmic "Mañana (Is Good Enough for Me)." The Latin-flavored smash stayed at #1 for nine weeks.

1957 In Hollywood, Elvis recorded his soon-to-be standard "(Let Me Be Your) Teddy Bear." It was about this time he answered an interviewer's question as to why he became a singer by saying, "I wanted to be a singer because I didn't want to sweat."

1962 The Beatles signed a management contract with Brian Epstein at Brian's office. He would receive twenty-five percent of their gross earnings at a time when the standard arrangement was for a manager to receive ten percent. Although all four members signed, Epstein refused as he had not yet fulfilled his promise to get them a record deal and withheld his signature until he had proven himself.

1970 The Mini-Moog Synthesizer was introduced by its inventor, Dr. Robert Moog.

Peggy Lee

January

25

#1 Song 1997: "Un-Break My Heart," Toni Braxton

Born: Etta James, 1938; Malcolm Green (Split Enz), 1953; Andy Cox (The English Beat), 1956

1953 The Flamingos signed with Chicago's Chance Records. It would be the start of a legendary career that encompassed eleven pop and nine R&B chart hits, including "I Only Have Eyes for You" in 1959. Many historians consider The Flamingos the greatest vocal group of all time.

1956 Elvis Presley's first RCA single, "Heartbreak Hotel," was released. By April 21, it was #1.

1963 Janis Joplin began singing in North Beach (San Francisco) coffee houses, passing her hat for beers.

1964 Dusty Springfield charted with "I Only Want to Be with You" (#12). It became her first of nineteen hits through 1987.

1983 Lamar Williams was the bass player for The Allman Brothers Band during 1973 when it hit with "Rambling Man" and "Jessica." He later joined the R&B–jazz band Sea Level for five albums through 1980. Lamar died today of cancer brought on by his exposure to Agent Orange while he was fighting in Vietnam.

Etta James

January

26

1963 Skeeter Davis hit the Top 100 with "The End of the World" (#2), her biggest of eight career charters.

1970 Elvis began a month-long stay at the Showroom of the International Hotel in Las Vegas. Garnering enthusiastic reviews, this was the first time Elvis wore his now famous one-piece jumpsuit.

1970 Phil Spector and John Lennon wrote and recorded Lennon's "Instant Karma" in one day. It charted thirty-three days later (February 28), eventually reaching #3.

1977 Peter Green, one of the founding members of Fleetwood Mac, was committed to a mental institution after he attacked his accountant with an air rifle when the latter was attempting to deliver a $30,000 royalty check. Green didn't want it!

1992 Gloria Estefan performed during halftime at Superbowl XXIV between the Washington Redskins and the Buffalo Bills in Minneapolis.

January

27

#1 Song 1962: "Peppermint Twist," Joey Dee & the Starliters

Born: Elmore James, 1918; Bobby "Blue" Bland, 1930; Nick Mason (Pink Floyd), 1945; Nedra Talley (Ronettes), 1947; Brian Downey (Thin Lizzy), 1951; Seth Justman (The J. Geils Band), 1951

1956 The Platters, The Drifters, The Five Keys, and The Turbans began a tour in Pittsburgh while The Flamingos, The Orioles, The Charms, and The Sweethearts toured the South starting in Richmond, Virginia.

1962 Rock 'n' roller Chubby Checker achieved a first when he put four albums in the U.S. Top 10. Prior to that, only middle-of-the-road–pop artists had reached such a milestone.

1967 Aretha Franklin recorded her first sides for Atlantic Records at Rick Hall's Florence Alabama Music Emporium (FAME) studios in Muscle Shoals. The day's work produced the classic "I Never Loved a Man (The Way I Love You)."

1990 Kylie Minogue's remake of Little Anthony & the Imperials 1958 standard "Tears on My Pillow" hit #1 in England becoming her fourth chart topper.

1991 Whitney Houston performed "The Star-Spangled Banner" at Superbowl XXV in Miami. Response was so great that a single and video were rush released. Talk about patriotism: The single reached the national charts, peaking at #20.

Chubby Checker

28

January

#1 Song 1984: "Owner of a Lonely Heart," Yes

Born: Corky Laing (Mountain), 1948

1950 When The Robins' single "If It's So, Baby" charted (#10 R&B), they became the first West Coast vocal group to make the Top 10. Seven years later, they would become the nucleus of The Coasters.

1956 Elvis Presley made his national TV debut on *Stage Show*, the Tommy and Jimmy Dorsey CBS-TV show in New York, singing "Shake, Rattle, and Roll" and "I Got a Woman." He was introduced by Cleveland deejay Bill Randle, who had discovered The Diamonds and The Crewcuts, among others.

1970 A cross section of musical messengers—including The Rascals; Blood, Sweat & Tears; Judy Collins; Dave Brubeck; Harry Belafonte; and the cast of the Broadway musical *Hair*—performed in an anti-war benefit concert at New York's Madison Square Garden.

1983 Billy Fury (Ronald Wycherly) was a British rock 'n' roller briefly considered the "British Elvis." He was signed to Decca in 1959 and had a series of hits including "Halfway to Paradise" and "Jealousy." He starred in the British film *Play It Cool* (1962) and had his own TV show in 1964. Due to ill health, he retired prematurely from performing in the mid '70s and died of a heart attack at his London home. He was forty-one and bankrupt.

1993 Hit British artist Lulu, who began her career in 1963 as lead of Lulu & The Lovers performed on BBC1-TV's *Top of The Pops*, the only female vocalist to appear on that long running show in each of the last four decades.

January

29

#1 Song 1977: "Car Wash," Rose Royce

Born: David Byron (Uriah Heep), 1947; William King (The Commodores), 1949; Tommy Ramone (The Ramones), 1952

1957 The world-famous Platters made their first appearance in New York at Ben Maksik's Town & Country Club after a tour of Australia. They had eleven chart hits in little over a year, including "Only You," "The Great Pretender," and "My Prayer."

1965 Houston-born British rocker P.J. Proby split his pants onstage at Croydon, London. He liked the reaction so much, it became a part of his act.

1964 The Beatles rerecorded "I Want to Hold Your Hand" and "She Loves You" at the Pathé Marconi Studios in Paris. They sang in German, the only time they ever recorded in a foreign language (unless you count "Michelle"). That session turned out to be their only session outside of the U.K., despite the fact they often talked of wanting to record in America.

1965 The Who made its debut appearance on *Ready, Steady Go*, Britain's answer to *American Bandstand*. Also on the show that evening were The Hollies, Goldie & the Gingerbreads, Donovan, and The Animals.

1985 Forty-six rock stars gathered in Los Angeles to record "We Are the World" to raise money for charity. Among the artists: Ray Charles, Bob Dylan, Michael Jackson, Bruce Springsteen, and Quincy Jones.

The Platters

January

#1 Song 1961: "Will You Love Me Tomorrow," The Shirelles

Born: Ruth Brown, 1928; Joe Terry (Danny & the Juniors), 1941; Sandy Yaguda (Jay & the Americans), 1943; Marty Balin (Jefferson Airplane), 1943

1956 Elvis Presley recorded four songs at RCA's New York studio, including a cover of Carl Perkins's current Sun Records hit, "Blue Suede Shoes." At this time, there was great fear emanating from the RCA executives that they might have been mistaken in signing Elvis.

1958 The Silhouettes standard rocker, "Get a Job," charted en route to #1. The '70s group Sha Na Na named themselves after a line in the song.

1961 Carole King and husband Jerry Goffin had their first songwriting #1 when The Shirelles' "Will You Love Me Tomorrow" reached the top spot (with Carole playing drums). It would be almost ten years before she would have a #1 as an artist ("It's Too Late").

1969 The Beatles performed their now famous "Rooftop Concert" on top of their London office. It would become the final live Beatles concert. They played "Don't Let Me Down," "Dig a Pony," "The One After 909," "I've Got a Feeling," "God Save the Queen," and "Get Back." Lennon ended the era by saying flippantly, "I'd like to say thank you on behalf of the group and ourselves and I hope we passed the audition."

1973 Kiss appeared at the Country Popcorn Pub in Queens, New York, for their first-ever live performance. Through 2002 they would perform live another 1,809 times!

January

31

#1 Song 1970: "I Want You Back," The Jackson 5

Born: Chuck Willis, 1928; Phil Collins (Genesis), 1951; Harry Casey (K.C. & the Sunshine Band), 1951; Phil Manzanera (Roxy Music), 1951; John Lydon (Public Image Ltd.), 1956

1958 Little Richard retired at the peak of his career to become an evangelist. He made the decision when on a plane trip to Australia, the plane suffered engine trouble and Richard swore that if he landed alive he would devote himself to God. His conversion lasted all of four years.

1967 Janis Joplin performed at the Matrix in San Francisco doing her "Amazing Grace/High Heel Sneakers" medley.

1967 John Lennon bought a circus poster from 1843 in an antique shop in London. The poster gave him and Paul McCartney almost the entire lyric for "Being for the Benefit of Mr. Kite." Meanwhile, Radio London, a pirate station, had the distinction of being the first radio outlet to play The Beatles' new single, "Penny Lane."

1985 Barbara Cowsill was the mom and background singer in the popular '60s folk-rock group, The Cowsills, which was actually made up of her children. The Rhode Island mom and her crew were discovered by record producer Wes Farrell and subsequently charted eight times between 1967 and 1969, including the million-sellers "Hair," "Indian Lake," and "The Rain, the Park, and Other Things." ABC-TV chose them to sing the theme from the *Love Boat*, but they balked at performing in a sitcom about themselves when told that the mother would be played by actress Shirley Jones. Instead, ABC, with Farrell producing the music, made its own Cowsills sitcom called *The Partridge Family* and the rest, as they say, is history. By 1972, Barbara and the family were bankrupt. Barbara died today while working the graveyard shift at a Tempe, Arizona, nursing home from emphysema. She was fifty-six. Note: If Barbara had agreed to let Shirley Jones play her part we might never have heard of David Cassidy and Danny Bonaduce!

February

#1 Song 1945: "Rum & Coca Cola," The Andrews Sisters

Born: Bob Shane (The Kingston Trio), 1934; Don Everly (The Everly Brothers), 1937; Joe Sample (The Crusaders), 1939; Tommy Duffy (The Echoes), 1944; Rick James, 1948

1960 Actress-singer Connie Stevens charted with "16 Reasons," which eventually rose to #3. She was starring in TV's *Hawaiian Eye* at the time.

1964 The album *Meet The Beatles* debuted on the U. S. charts, rising to #1 and staying on top for an amazing eleven weeks. The Beatles would go on to have forty American chart albums through the mid '90s and would place almost half of them (seventeen) on the Top 100 after they broke up.

1964 The quintessential party record "Louie, Louie" by The Kingsmen was declared pornographic by the Governor of Indiana but an FCC investigation concluded, "the record to be unintelligible at any speed we played it!"

1969 Joni Mitchell performed at Carnegie Hall in New York City.

1978 Elvis Presley was inducted into *Playboy* magazine's Musical Hall of Fame.

1986 A British pop-crooner with the Stargazers, Dick James (Reginald Vapnick) was signed as a solo act to Parlophone Records by George Martin in 1956. His real career began when he decided to open a music publishing company, and whom did Martin bring him as a client? Why, The Beatles, of course! As if that didn't secure James's place in music history, he also wound up representing The Hollies, The Spencer Davis Group, and many other British '60s and '70s rock 'n' rollers, including Elton John. James died of a heart attack while playing cards at his London home.

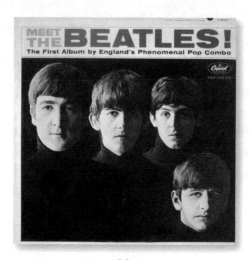

February

2

#1 Song 1959: "Smoke Gets in Your Eyes," The Platters

Born: Clarence Quick (Dell Vikings), 1937; Graham Nash, 1942

1956 The Coasters signed to Atco Records and went on to have nineteen hits over a fifteen-year period.

1963 The Beatles began a British tour in Gaumont Cinema, Bradford, England. Sixteen-year-old Helen Shapiro, The Honeys, The Kestrals, Kenny Lynch, and The Red Price Orchestra were on the bill, where The Beatles name was listed last. Their set included "Keep Your Hands Off My Baby" (Little Eva), "A Taste of Honey" (Herb Alpert), "Chains" (The Cookies), and their own "Please Please Me." John and Paul wrote "Misery" on the bus for Helen, but it was Kenny Lynch who showed interest and would become the first non-Beatle to record a Lennon and McCartney song. While on the bus John and Paul came up with the idea of rushing the microphone together and shaking their heads singing, "Whooooo," but it wouldn't be used on record until "She Loves You" was released. While all that was going on, "Please Please Me" hit the British charts at #16.

1973 *The Midnight Special*, the first rock concert TV series, debuted today with announcers disc jockey Wolfman Jack and Mike Carruthers. Each weekly show had a different guest host for the NBC show that aired through May 1981.

1974 Carly Simon and James Taylor charted with "Mockingbird," which peaked at #5. The song was adapted from the same traditional folk lyrics as the song "Bo Diddley."

1979 Sid Vicious (John Ritchie) was a totally awful bass player whose surly and violent nature made him a perfect fit for the London-based Sex Pistols, featuring Johnny Rotten. The neurotic, ultra heavy drug user with a penchant for self-mutilation was such a bad dancer that his spastic gyrations onstage were taken as a new dance fad by the group's following, which became known as "slam dancing." When Rotten disbanded the group in the middle of a show, Vicious recorded an album in London and then moved to New York, where—in a violent heroin-induced free-for-all with his girlfriend, Nancy Spungen—he awoke to find her dead. Jailed, he managed to get out, attempt to slit his wrists, be sent to a psychiatric ward, be released on bail, and overdose—all in two weeks. He died today at the age of twenty-one.

February

#1 Song 1968: "Green Tambourine," The Lemon Pipers

Born: Johnny "Guitar" Watson, 1935; David Lerchey (Dell Vikings), 1937; Angelo D'Aleo (The Belmonts), 1940; Eric Haydock (The Hollies), 1943; Johnny Cymbal, 1945; Dave Davies (The Kinks) 1947; Melanie, 1947

1900 Arthur Collins's "Mandy Lee" reached #1 today. It was the first chart topper of the twentieth century. In those days, hit status was calculated by sheet music and 78-RPM record sales as radio did not become a factor until the 1920s.

1958 The Blossoms—a girl group of professional backup singers who had worked with literally hundreds of artists from Elvis Presley, Paul Anka, and Dionne Warwick to Bobby Darin, The Beach Boys, and The Mamas & the Papas—finally had their own single released called "Have Faith in Me." When it didn't chart, they went back to the lucrative world of session singing.

1959 "The day the music died." Buddy Holly, Ritchie Valens, and The Big Bopper (J.P. Richardson) died when their plane went down in a cornfield in Clear Lake, Iowa, while they were on tour in what was called, "The Winter Dance Party." Holly had thirteen charters under his belt by the time of his demise, including "That'll Be the Day" and "Peggy Sue." The Big Bopper, who was actually a Texas deejay and rock 'n' roll vocalist, hit with the immortal "Chantilly Lace," and on this fateful day had talked his then unknown bass player, Waylon Jennings, into giving up his spot on the plane. Richie Valens, the first successful Mexican-American rocker with hits like "Donna" and "La Bamba," won a coin toss with his guitarist, Tommy Allsup, for the last seat on the plane. He remarked at the time that he'd never won anything before.

1966 Stevie Wonder performed at the Scotch of St. James Club in London and was visited back-stage by Paul McCartney, who was a big fan of the Motown superstar.

"The day the music died." The Big Bopper

35

February

#1 Song 1978: "Stayin' Alive," The Bee Gees

Born: Bernie West (The Five Keys), 1930; John Steel (The Animals), 1941; John Gambale (The Classics), 1942; Florence LaRue (The 5th Dimension), 1944; Alice Cooper, 1948

Died: Louis Jordan, 1975; Karen Carpenter, 1983

1954 The Drifters recorded "Honey Love" (#1 R&B, #21 pop), their first single at Fulton Recording Studio in New York City, along with their legendary versions of "White Christmas," "Bells of St. Mary's," and the forerunner of "The Twist," "Whatcha Gonna Do" (#2 R&B).

1978 The Bee Gees charted with "Night Fever," a song that would go on to be # 1 for eight weeks. This same day, the #1 single in America was their signature song, "Stayin' Alive."

1983 Karen Carpenter was the epitome of the soft rock–pop sound of the '70s. She (a rare case of a solo vocalist–drummer) and her brother, Richard, fashioned twenty-nine national hits between 1970 and 1982, including "Close to You," "We've Only Just Begun" and "Rainy Days and Mondays." Karen was found unconscious in her parents Downey, California, home and was rushed to Downey Community Hospital where she died of cardiac arrest today. She was only thirty-two years old.

1984 The Eurythmics reached #8 U.K. on their way to #7 U.S. with "Here Comes the Rain Again." The song was recorded in a little used church in Crouch End, London.

2000 ABBA turned down more than £60 million (almost $100 million U.S.) to reunite for a world tour of a hundred concerts. The group, which had split up seventeen years earlier, was the most commercially successful pop act of the '70s.

February

#1 Song 1955: "Hearts of Stone,"
The Fontane Sisters

Born: Barrett Strong, 1941; Cory Wells
(Three Dog Night), 1942; Al Kooper (Blood,
Sweat & Tears), 1944

1957 Bill Haley was mobbed by British fans at London's Victoria Station upon his first time arrival in England.

1962 The Beatles performed at The Cavern Club for lunchtime and The Kingsway Club, Southport, during the evening with Rory Storm and the Hurricanes' drummer, Ringo Starr, filling in for an ill Peter Best.

1966 Although Petula Clark disliked and tried to sabotage the release of "My Love," her label prevailed and the single reached #1. It became her second American million-seller and made her the first British female artist to have two U.S. #1s.

1981 Canadian Prime Minister Pierre Trudeau inducted Joni Mitchell into Canada's Juno Hall of Fame.

1998 A heavy-metal guitarist, Tim Kelly, joined the group Slaughter while attending a backyard barbecue. Influenced at age thirteen after hearing a Kiss album, his first live performance in 1990 with the group was as the opening act for, you guessed it, Kiss. The band's biggest hit was "Fly to the Angels" from its three million–selling album, *Stick It to Ya*. The ride was short, however, when Kelly was jailed, fined, and eventually put on three years' probation for transporting cocaine as part of a nationwide smuggling gang. He died in a car crash near Baghdad, Arizona, when an eighteen-wheeler hit his car "dead" on.

Slaughter's Stick It to Ya

February

6

#1 Song 1965: "You've Lost That Lovin' Feelin,'" The Righteous Brothers

Born: Bill Doggett, 1916; Fabian, 1943; Bob Marley, 1945; Natalie Cole, 1950; Axl Rose (Guns N' Roses), 1962; Rick Astley, 1966

1958 While riding a bus in Liverpool with John Lennon and Paul McCartney, fourteen-year-old George Harrison ran down the Bill Justis instrumental hit "Raunchy." John and Paul thought he was great and asked him to join their group, The Quarrymen. The lineup now consisted of John, Paul, George, Len Garry, Eric Griffiths, and sometimes John Lowe on piano. George still played for a while with his own band, The Rebels, and also sat in with Rory Storm & the Hurricanes.

1982 Joan Jett & the Blackhearts charted with "I Love Rock 'n' Roll," an eventual #1 and the first of her ten Top 100 hits through 1990.

1988 George Harrison's sixteenth and last American chart single debuted on the Top 100 today. "When We Was Fab" was a tribute to The Beatles days. Thirty years earlier to the day, George was asked to join John and Paul in The Quarrymen, the forerunner of The Beatles.

1998 The legendary Beach Boys lasted as long as they did in large part because of the youngest of the group's three brothers, Carl Wilson. The sanest member, he was often the glue that kept them on track through a career of fifty-nine hits from 1962 to 1989. A self-taught guitarist, he was an excellent falsetto vocalist who sang lead on their classics "God Only Knows" and "I Can Hear Music," and their comeback hit, "Kokomo." He died of complications from lung cancer in Los Angeles today.

Joan Jett

February

#1 Song 1976: "50 Ways to Leave Your Lover," Paul Simon

Born: King Curtis, 1934; Steve Bronski (Bronski Beat), 1960; Garth Brooks, 1962

1959 Buddy Holly's funeral in Lubbock City Cemetery (Texas) was attended by over a thousand mourners.

1962 Country music great Garth Brooks was born today in Luba, Oklahoma. His mother, Colleen Carroll, was a regular performer on Red Foley's Ozark Jubilee TV show and recorded for Capitol Records.

1964 The Beatles flew to New York City for their first visit. Five thousand placard-waving truant fans (mostly teenage girls) were huddled in the cold at JFK Airport, some since the day before. The group's entourage included the legendary and eccentric record producer Phil Spector. Spector, who had a mortal phobia about flying, was convinced The Beatles were going to be huge stars and so his logic was that it was safe to fly with them. The Beatles actually thought that the president's plane was about to land, until they realized the chaos was in their honor. Over two hundred reporters showed up for their airport press conference, which was riddled with the Mop Tops' signature sarcastic sense of humor. One unsuspecting reporter asked, "How did you find America?" John replied, "Turn left at Greenland." When Paul was told there was a campaign in Detroit to stamp out The Beatles, he responded, "We have a plan to stamp out Detroit."

1987 Madonna's "Open Your Heart" became her fifth #1 and her third from the album *True Blue*.

2001 Dale Evans, known as the "Queen of the West," died today. She was the wife of country-and-western singer and western movie star Roy Rogers. She wrote their biggest hit, "Happy Trails to You," and sang it with Roy for almost fifty years. She originally sang with The Jay Mills Orchestra and is in the National Cowgirl Hall of Fame.

February

8

#1 Song 1960: "Teen Angel," Mark Dinning

Born: Tom Rush, 1941; Creed Bratton II (Grass Roots) 1943; Vince Neil (Mötley Crüe), 1961

1957 The Diamonds' now legendary "Little Darlin'" was released (Mercury #2 pop and R&B). The popular quartet was a favorite of Dick Clark and appeared on his *American Bandstand* TV show thirty-three times during the next decade.

1962 The Beach Boys (with Jaguars member Val Poliuto in for Al Jardine) recorded six demos, including what would become the basic tracks and vocals for their first two singles, "Surfin'" (#75) and "Surfin' Safari" (#14).

1967 Peter & Gordon (of "A World Without Love" fame) broke up. Peter Asher went on to manage Linda Ronstadt, among others.

1990 Del Shannon (Charles Westover), a terrific rock 'n' roll talent of the early '60s who had seventeen hits through 1981 ("Runaway," "Hats Off to Larry"), committed suicide, shooting himself in his Santa Monica, California, home. He had recently remarried and had just finished his first album in almost nine years. Five days earlier, he performed in the annual Buddy Holly Memorial Concert in Fargo, North Dakota.

Del Shannon

February

#1 Song 1963: "Hey Paula," Paul & Paula

Born: Billy Williamson (Bill Haley & the Comets), 1925; Barry Mann, 1939; Carole King, 1942; Major Harris (The Delfonics) 1947

1961 The Beatles made their first performance appearance at The Cavern Club in Liverpool when they played an unadvertised lunch show. John Lennon had played The Cavern in August 1957 when his original group and The Beatles forerunner, The Quarrymen, were a skiffle band. The tiny club (it was only five chairs wide in most places) would forever be linked to The Beatles' beginning.

1964 The Beatles performed live on *The Ed Sullivan Show*. Sullivan had received 50,000 requests for tickets for the show. The Studio on West 53rd Street in New York City only held 728. The Fab Four performed, in order, "All My Loving," "Till There Was You," "She Loves You," "I Saw Her Standing There," and "I Want to Hold Your Hand." American popular music would never be the same. Sullivan's show had the largest TV audience in history to that time, capturing over 73 million viewers. Future Monkee Davy Jones also appeared singing a song from the Broadway musical *Oliver*.

1981 Bill Haley, the father of rock 'n' roll, started out as a hillbilly and country-western singer under the name Silver Yodeling Bill. He first sang with The Downhomers in 1943, graduated to The Four Aces of Western Swing, and by 1950, The Saddlemen. Combining aspects of R&B with his country style, he developed what he called "Cowboy Jive." The Saddlemen became The Comets, who were signed to Decca in 1954. Their classic recording of "Rock Around the Clock" was only a modest chart maker in 1954, but its use in the 1955 film *Blackboard Jungle* made its reissue #1 for eight weeks. Haley and company went on to have twenty-seven hits through 1974. Bill died in his sleep at home in Harlingen, Texas, at fifty-five of a brain tumor today.

1985 Madonna's *Like a Virgin* began a three-week stay at #1, becoming her most successful album and selling more than 7 million copies.

1991 Wilson Phillips's "You're in Love" hit the Top 100 rising to #1. It was their fourth Top 5 single and third chart topper in less than a year.

February

10

#1 Song 1958: "Don't," Elvis Presley

Born: Don Wilson (The Ventures), 1933; Roberta Flack, 1939; Jimmy Merchant (Frankie Lymon & the Teenagers), 1940; Ral Donner, 1943; Nathaniel Mayer (Nathaniel Mayer & the Fabulous Twilights), 1944

1942 Glenn Miller received the first gold record ever presented for his hit "Chattanooga Choo-Choo."

1958 The Chesters debut, "The Fires Burn No More," was released. The group went on to become Little Anthony & the Imperials.

1958 The Shirelles (originally called The Poquellos) had their first single issued today. The song, "I Met Him on a Sunday," reached #49 and was also their first of twenty-nine hits over the next nine years.

1973 After composing the song "The Nights the Lights Went Out in Georgia," Bobby Russell offered the tune to Cher, who turned it down. Russell then gave it to his wife, Vicki Lawrence, who had the #1 hit.

February

#1 Song 1984: "Karma Chameleon," Culture Club

Born: John Mills, Sr. (The Mills Brothers), 1889; Raoul Cita (The Harptones), 1928; Gene Vincent, 1935; Bobby "Boris" Pickett, 1940; Gerry Goffin, 1939

1963 The Beatles recorded their first album, including ten songs at Abbey Road Studios in London. All the recordings were done in one session, lasting ten hours at a cost of £400 (about $600). To make the event even more extraordinary, all the members had colds and John was losing his voice as they finished the tenth song, "Twist & Shout." All the songs recorded were from their shows at The Cavern Club as producer George Martin wanted to capture their live feel. The album would eventually be released in the U.S. as *Introducing...The Beatles*. In England, it would be known as the *Please, Please Me* album.

1964 The Beatles (along with The Chiffons and Tommy Roe) performed at the Washington Coliseum in Washington, D.C., in front of 8,092 fanatic female fans. It was their first U.S. concert. One of the more than 300 policemen found the volume so loud, he decided to stick a bullet in each ear. Their set included "I Want to Hold Your Hand," "All My Loving," "Please Please Me," "Roll Over Beethoven," "I Saw Her Standing There," "From Me to You," "She Loves You," "This Boy," "I Wanna Be Your Man," "Twist & Shout," "Long Tall Sally," and "Till There Was You." They came to Washington in a special train car since New York was socked in by a snowstorm. The same storm dumped eight inches of snow in Washington, but it didn't stop 2,000 girls from coming out to meet them.

1985 Sade's *Diamond Life* won the Best British Album at the fourth annual BRIT Awards at London's Grosvenor House Hotel.

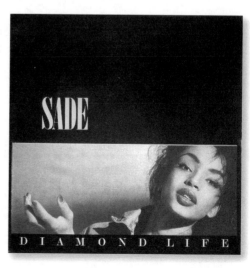

February

12

#1 Song 1977: "Torn Between Two Lovers," Mary MacGregor

Born: Ray Manzarek (The Doors), 1935; Rick Frank (Elephant's Memory), 1942; Steve Hackett (Genesis), 1950; Michael McDonald, 1952; Chynna Phillips (Wilson Phillips), 1968

1955 The McGuire Sisters biggest hit, "Sincerely," reached #1. The song was a "cover" of The Moonglows R&B hit.

1962 The Beatles auditioned for the BBC for teen audience broadcasts doing two songs led by John Lennon ("Hello Little Girl" and Chuck Berry's "Memphis, Tennessee") and two led by Paul McCartney (Peggy Lee's "Till There Was You" and "Like Dreamers Do," his own song). The producer, Peter Pilbeam, liked John, but not Paul, and concluded they were more country-western than rock 'n' roll. Still, he decided to book them for a March 7 broadcast, which would become their first on radio.

1964 The Beatles performed at the legendary Carnegie Hall in New York City after abandoning their limo for city cabs at Penn Station where 10,000 screaming fans chased after them. The historical performance was never recorded due to red tape, even though George Martin had requested that EMI arrange a taping.

1965 The Who auditioned for the *BBC Light Programme*, singing "Baby Don't You Do It" and "Shout and Shimmy." They were not universally well received, as one of the judges commented, "Overall not very original and below standard." Another said they were "ponderous and unentertaining." By a vote of four to three they passed the audition.

1967 Britain's Bobbies raided Rolling Stone Keith Richards's home, jailing him for one night and co-Stone Mick Jagger for two nights on drug possession charges. The raiding party consisted of fifteen police to arrest two half-stoned Stones!

February

13

#1 Song 1993: "I Will Always Love You," Whitney Houston

Born: Gene Ames (The Ames Brothers), 1925; Dorothy McGuire (The McGuire Sisters), 1930; Peter Tork (The Monkees), 1944; Peter Gabriel (Genesis), 1950

1956 Deejay Alan Freed, who couldn't sing or play an instrument, signed with Coral Records to compile and promote (using his name) four R&B dance party LPs in a year. None of the four charted, and all are valuable collector's items today. The only album Freed did chart with was a compilation he lent his name to for End Records in 1962 titled *Alan Freed's Memory Lane*, comprising some of the greatest singles of the '50s. It reflected the times and his love for vocal groups, as thirteen of the fourteen cuts were by groups, including "In the Still of the Night" by The Five Satins, "Sincerely" by The Moonglows, "16 Candles" by The Crests, "I'll Be Home" by The Flamingos, and "Oh, What a Night" by The Dells. The album reached #99.

1959 The Skyliners performed their first single, "Since I Don't Have You," on Dick Clark's *American Bandstand*. Three days later orders for 100,000 copies came in.

1964 While in Miami, The Beatles went to the Mau Mau Lounge specifically to see The Coasters. Later, New York disc jockey Murray the K brought them to Miami's Peppermint Lounge, where Hank Ballard & the Midnighters were performing.

1967 Davy Jones of The Monkees escaped his fanatical fans while visiting his parents' home in Manchester, England, by dressing as a girl and climbing over the back fence.

1981 Pink Floyd's *Dark Side of the Moon* LP became rock's longest running chart album at 402 weeks. It went on for another 158 weeks (560 total)! That's almost eleven years!

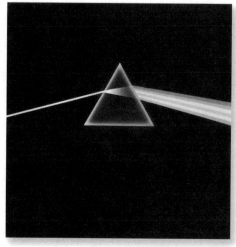

Pink Floyd's
Dark Side of the Moon

February

14

#1 Song 1981: "Celebration," Kool & the Gang

Born: Phyllis McGuire (The McGuire Sisters), 1931; Eric Andersen, 1943; Tim Buckley, 1947

1970 The Carpenters' "Ticket to Ride" charted. Although it only reached #54, it was the first of twenty-nine hits for Karen and Richard over the next twelve years.

1974 Toni Tennille and Daryl Dragon married in Virginia City, Nevada, while driving through twenty-two states promoting their debut disc, *The Way I Want to Touch You*. It was also Valentine's Day.

1977 Janis Ian received 461 Valentine's Day cards after indicating she had never received any in the lyrics to her million-seller "At Seventeen."

1981 Sheena Easton's "Morning Train" debuted on the Hot 100 on its way to #1. The song was originally called "9 to 5," but was changed to avoid confusion with Dolly Parton's hit.

1999 An early country rocker, Buddy Knox was best known for his 1957 pop hit "Party Doll," which was really an unabashed country swing tune with a pseudo-rock rhythm. Friend Roy Orbison influenced Buddy to record at Norman Petty's Clovis, New Mexico, studio, where he cut "Party Doll." Buddy formed a group called The Rhythm Orchids at West Texas State University, which birthed two other hit artists, Jimmy Bowen and Dave Alldred, later leader of Dickey Doo & the Don'ts. After the single success, Knox urged another Buddy to record at Petty's studio. That Buddy was Holly. Knox went on to have ten pop chart hits all told, and wound up living in Canada and doing the Canadian oldies circuit. He died of cancer in Bremerton, Washington, today.

February

#1 Song 1969: "Everyday People" Sly & The Family Stone

Born: Denny Zager (Zager & Evans), 1944; Melissa Manchester, 1951

Died: Nat King Cole, 1965; Michael Bloomfield (Electric Flag), 1981

1944 Mick Avory, drummer for The Kinks, was born today. He joined the band in 1963 and stayed through the late '80s, having recorded on all of the group's 23 U.S. chart hits, including "You Really Got Me" and "Lola."

1954 Joe Turner recorded the classic "Shake, Rattle & Roll," six months before Bill Haley's hit version.

1957 The Five Satins, Chuck Berry, LaVern Baker, and Fats Domino began a U.S. tour in Irving Feld's "Greatest Show of 1957" rock package.

1963 In an interview with *The New Musical Express*, John Lennon and Paul McCartney noted their mutual aspiration was "to write a musical."

1969 Vickie Jones was arrested on fraud charges after impersonating Aretha Franklin at a concert in Fort Myers, Florida. Apparently the charade was impressive. No one in the audience asked for their money back.

Joe Turner

February

16

#1 Song 1959: "Stagger Lee," Lloyd Price

Born: Patty Andrews (The Andrews Sisters), 1920; Otis Blackwell, 1932; Sonny Bono, 1935; Lynn Paul (New Seekers), 1949; Pete Willis (Def Leppard), 1960; Andy Taylor (Duran Duran), 1961

1952 Kay Starr landed on the Top 100 with "The Wheel of Fortune," her biggest record (#1 for ten weeks), in a fourteen-year chart career.

1959 The Skyliners standard "Since I Don't Have You" (#12) charted.

1959 Dodie Stevens became a one-hit wonder when "Pink Shoe Laces" charted and charged up the charts to #3. She was thirteen at the time and was discovered while singing on the Art Linkletter television show at age eight.

1964 Beatles' second *The Ed Sullivan Show* appearance was at the Deauville Hotel in Miami Beach. CBS-TV gave away 4,500 tickets. So what if no one at CBS could count? The hotel could only hold 2,600. Mitzi Gaynor topped the bill and more than 70 million viewers tuned in. Boxers Joe Louis and Sonny Liston were both in attendance (You think they were actually fans or curiosity seekers?).

1975 The CBS-TV series *Cher* debuted with guests Bette Midler, Elton John, and Flip Wilson. It was her second starring variety series in four years and would run for twenty-six episodes.

February

17

#1 Song 1962: "Duke of Earl," Gene Chandler & the Dukays

Born: Orville "Hoppy" Jones (The Ink Spots), 1905; Tommy Edwards, 1922; Bobby Lewis, 1933; Mickey McGill (The Dells), 1937; Gene Pitney, 1941; Dodie Stevens, 1947; James Ingram, 1956

1958 The Monotones rocker "Book of Love" was released. Although the hit was out on Argo Records, the first release was issued in 1957 on its original label, Mascot. That 45 is a $225 collectible today.

1958 Chuck Berry's "Sweet Little 16" charted on its way to #2.

1962 The Beach Boys first single, "Surfin'" (Candix $300), hit the national charts, reaching #75.

1968 Janis Joplin appeared in New York for the first time, playing at The Anderson Theater.

1979 Debbie Harry and Blondie hit the charts with "Heart of Glass" (#1), her first of nine hits in a little over three years. Not bad for a former *Playboy* bunny!

Blondie

February

18

#1 Song 1956: "The Great Pretender," The Platters

Born: Herman Santiago (Frankie Lymon & the Teenagers), 1941; Dennis DeYoung (Styx), 1947; Randy Crawford, 1952; John Travolta, 1954; Robbie Bachman (Bachman-Turner Overdrive), 1953

1942 The Mills Brothers recorded what would become their biggest hit, "Paper Doll." Released in May, it took fourteen months to reach #1, but when it did, it stayed there for twelve weeks, selling 6 million copies!

1956 Bill Haley & the Comets album *Rock Around the Clock* (#12) became the first rock LP to make the pop album charts.

1956 The Bonnie Sisters charted with "Cry Baby." The trio was not sisters, but they were all nurses at New York's Bellevue Hospital.

1982 Cher's Broadway acting debut came in *Come Back to the Five and Dime, Jimmy Dean, Jimmy Dean*.

1990 Annie Lennox won her fourth Best British Female Artist award at the ninth annual BRIT Awards in London. Pretty good for a girl whose pre-music days had her working in a factory filleting fish.

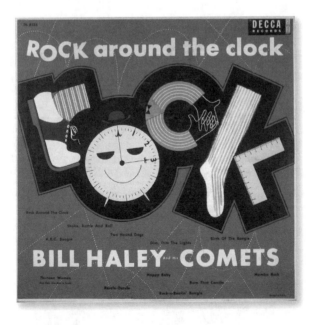

February

#1 Song 1977: "Blinded by the Light," Manfred Mann's Earth Band

Born: Bob Engemann (The Lettermen), 1936; William McClain (The Cleftones), 1938; Smokey Robinson (The Miracles), 1940; Bobby Rogers (The Miracles), 1940; Lou Christie, 1943

1966 Lou Christie's "Lightnin' Strikes" reached #1. It was quite a birthday present for the twenty-three-year-old.

1972 Three Dog Night's "Never Been to Spain" became the group's eighth Top 10 record when it peaked at #5 today.

1977 Linda Ronstadt won the Best Female Pop Vocal Performance for "Hasten Down the Wind" at the nineteenth annual Grammy Awards.

1977 Fleetwood Mac's *Rumours* album was released. It went on to spend an amazing thirty-one weeks at #1.

1980 Ron Belford "Bon" Scott was the gruff-voiced lead singer of the hard rock group AC/DC. He started in Australia with the pop group The Valentines and had a 1969 hit with "My Old Man's a Groovy Old Man." He later joined Fraternity and The Mount Lofty Rangers before coming onboard with AC/DC. He died in the backseat of his car after just another night of booze and drugs. He was 50.

1994 Bruce Springsteen's "Streets of Fire" charted on its way to #9, his first Top 10 hit in six years.

February

20

#1 Song 1965: "This Diamond Ring," Gary Lewis & the Playboys

Born: Nancy Wilson, 1937; Barbara Ellis (The Fleetwoods), 1940; J. Geils, 1946; Walter Becker (Steely Dan), 1950; Kurt Cobain (Nirvana), 1967

1968 Mike Love of The Beach Boys, Mia Farrow, Donovan, and The Beatles began their transcendental meditation course at the Maharishi Mahesh Yogi's academy in India.

1971 Helen Reddy reached the Top 100 today with "I Don't Know How to Love Him" from the rock-opera *Jesus Christ Superstar*. It was the first of twenty-one hits for the Australian vocalist.

1974 Cher filed for divorce from husband–former singing partner, Sonny Bono.

1996 Involved in a five-car crash on the I-10 freeway in Los Angeles, Barry Manilow signed autographs for police, accident victims, and fans while waiting for his Range Rover to be towed.

1998 Lead singer of the Toronto rock band Lighthouse, Bob McBride was a raspy-voiced powerhouse vocalist. The group formed in 1968 in the style of Chicago and Blood, Sweat & Tears. They were invited to perform at Woodstock, but declined. The thirteen-piece aggregation hit the U. S. charts with "One Fine Day" (#24) and four other lesser successes, but their pièce de résistance was the epic album cut "1849." McBride died of diabetes in Toronto today. He was sixty.

Maharishi Mahesh Yogi

February

#1 Song 1981: "9 to 5," Dolly Parton

Born: Nina Simone, 1933

Died: Janet Vogel (The Skyliners), 1980; Murray "The K" Kaufman (legendary New York disc jockey), 1982

1965 Keith Moon of The Who broke his manager's dishwasher when he used it to wash fruit! The raucous drummer may have spent too much time inhaling the smell of asbestos when he was a plaster salesman in his pre-Who days.

1976 Willie Nelson & Waylon Jennings album, *The Outlaws*, became the first country music album to go platinum.

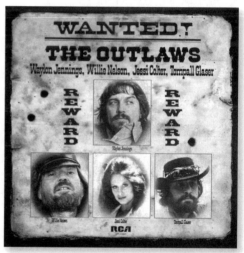

1980 Janet Vogel was the queen of soprano vocal group vocalists in the late '50s. The Pittsburgh native first sang with The Crescents and then the legendary Skyliners. Anyone remembering their classic hit "Since I Don't Have You" will recall her amazing ultra-high note finale that always brought the house down. The group charted pop six times, including "This I Swear" and "Pennies

Willie Nelson and Waylon Jennings' The Outlaws

from Heaven," but by 1961, Vogel tired of touring and retired, although she did return for oldies concerts in the '70s. Sadly, Janet committed suicide today by inhaling carbon monoxide fumes in the garage of her home in Pittsburgh.

1990 Carly Simon's "Let the River Run" won the Best Song Written Specifically for a Motion Picture category at the thirty-second annual Grammy Awards. Later that evening, it won an Oscar for Best Song.

1992 Natalie Cole performed at the famed Apollo Theatre in New York. She then donated her receipts to help save the financially strapped landmark.

February

#1 Song 1960: "Theme from a Summer Place," Percy Faith

Born: Ernie K-Doe, 1936; Bobby Hendricks (The Drifters), 1938; Robert Edwards (The Intruders), 1942; Oliver (William Swofford), 1945

1951 The Clovers recorded "Don't You Know I Love You," their first of twenty-one R&B hits over the next nine years. Written by Atlantic Records President Ahmet Ertegun, he recorded the song demo by singing into a Times Square recording booth microphone as Ertegun could neither play an instrument nor write music.

1956 Elvis Presley entered the pop charts for the first time with his RCA debut, "Heartbreak Hotel."

1965 The Beatles left London for the Bahamas to begin filming *Help*. Although customs officials in New York wanted them to deplane for inspection, the group refused, but made sure to show their respect for the officials by lighting up the minute the plane took off for the Bahamas.

1976 Florence Ballard, the original lead singer of The Supremes, died of a heart attack nine years after being forced out of the trio. Although she sang on numerous hits, including nine #1 singles, Flo passed away penniless while living on welfare with her three children. She was only thirty-two.

February

#1 Song 1974: "The Way We Were," Barbra Streisand

Born: Johnny Winter, 1944

Died: Melvin Franklin (The Temptations), 1995

1957 Patsy Cline moved onto the Top 100 with "Walkin' After Midnight," an eventual #12 hit and the first of thirteen pop winners over six years (1957–1963).

1957 The original version of "Little Darlin'" by The Gladiolas was released (Excello, #41 pop, #11 R&B). Three years later, the group would have the #1 record in the U.S. as Maurice Williams and The Zodiacs singing "Stay."

1963 The Chiffons mega-hit "He's So Fine" was the first vocal group #1 in rock history to be produced by another vocal group, The Tokens.

1991 Whitney Houston reached #1 with "All the Man that I Need"—amazingly, her ninth chart topper in five years.

1974 Billy Joel charted with "Piano Man," his first of forty-one Top 100 hits through 1994.

Billy Joel

February

1958 #1 Song: "Get a Job," The Silhouettes

Born: Joanie Sommers, 1941; Paul Jones (Manfred Mann), 1942; Rupert Holmes, 1947

Died: Johnnie Ray, 1990

1951 Rosemary Clooney's "You're Just in Love" charted, peaking at #24. It was the first of twenty-eight hits for the Maysville, Kentucky, miss between 1951 and 1960.

1956 Bill Haley & the Comets received the then unheard of guarantee of $250,000 for a twenty-one-show tour.

1962 The Beatles performed at the YMCA at Wirral, England, and were booed off the stage due to the band's long chatter between songs, which had a tendency to bore the audience.

1967 After seeing them perform at London's Saville Theatre, British manager Robert Stigwood signed a new group who called themselves The Bee Gees.

1990 Known as "The Prince of Wails" for his passionate "crying" vocal style, Johnnie Ray was a popular '50s-era balladeer. All the more amazing because he was partially deaf and wore a hearing aid most of his life, the crooner combined pop ballads with an R&B flair to create a Sinatra-like frenzy among his fans. In fact, many fans thought he was black. Known for hits like "Just Walking in the Rain" and "Cry," the heavy drinker died of cirrhosis of the liver at age sixty-three today.

February

#1 Song 1967: "Kind of a Drag,"
The Buckinghams

Born: George Harrison, 1943

1957 Buddy Holly recorded "That'll Be the Day" in the Clovis, New Mexico, studio of his producer, Norman Petty.

1963 The Beatles 45 *Please Please Me/Ask Me Why* was issued in America on Vee Jay records, the same label as The Four Seasons, who would become their biggest competition in the U.S. during the mid '60s. It was their first U.S. release under The Beatles name and it went totally unnoticed.

1976 Joni Mitchell participated in The Band's farewell concert, "The Last Waltz" in San Francisco, singing "Helpless" with Neil Young.

1989 Garth Brooks had his first country hit when "(Much Too Young) To Feel this Damn Old" hit the charts on its way to #8. During the next four years, Garth would have twenty-five Top 100 singles, including thirteen #1 smashes.

1999 Patricia Holt, Sarah Dash, Nona Hendryx, and Cindy Birdsong—better known as Patti LaBelle & the Bluebelles—appeared together for the first time in thirty-one years singing a stirring "You'll Never Walk Alone" at The Rhythm & Blues foundation's Pioneer Awards in Los Angeles. The group was presented its award by five-time Grammy winner Lauren Hill.

Garth Brooks

February

26

#1 Song 1983: "Baby Come to Me," Patti Austin and James Ingram

Born: Fats Domino, 1928; Johnny Cash, 1932; Mitch Ryder, 1945; Michael Bolton, 1953

1968 Janis Joplin signed with Columbia Records. Her manager, Albert Grossman, tactfully informed Columbia President Clive Davis of Janis's offer to sleep with him in order to seal the deal. Clive politely abstained.

1983 Michael Jackson's *Thriller* album reached #1 and stayed there for thirty-seven weeks, selling over 40 million copies. It was #1 in every Western nation.

1984 Tina Turner won Record of the Year, Song of the Year, and Best Female Vocal Performance, all with the million-seller "What's Love Got to Do With it" at the twenty-seventh Grammy Awards.

1990 Cornel Gunter of The Coasters was shot and killed while in his car in Las Vegas. He was scheduled to perform at The Lucky Lady Hotel that night. Thirty years earlier to the day, Cornel and The Coasters recorded their thirteenth hit, "Wake Me, Shake Me" (#51 pop, #14 R&B), in New York City.

Michael Jackson's Thriller

February

27

#1 Song 1961: "Pony Time," Chubby Checker

Born: Neal Schon (Journey), 1954

1955 The seven-inch single took the lead in sales for the first time over the ten-inch 78 RPM single. The 45, as it was called, was introduced in 1949.

1961 Aretha Franklin made her pop-chart debut with "Won't Be Long" on Columbia Records. It reached #76 and became the first of seventy-four hits for the "Queen of Soul" over the next thirty-three years.

1961 Cathy Jean & the Roommates "Please Love Me Forever" charted en route to #12.

1967 Paul McCartney read a story in the *Daily Mail* newspaper about a missing teenager that gave him the idea for the song "She's Leaving Home."

1993 After fourteen weeks at #1, Whitney Houston's "I Will Always Love You" became the longest-running chart topper, eclipsing Boys II Men's 1992 smash, "End of the Road." Additionally, the 4 million–selling single was #1 in more than a dozen countries.

February

28

#1 Song 1970: "Bridge over Troubled Waters," Simon & Garfunkel

Born: Joe South, 1940; Marty Sanders (Jay & the Americans), 1941; Don Ciccone (The Critters), 1946

Died: Frankie Lymon, 1968

1942 Brian Jones, original second guitarist for The Rolling Stones, was born today. He joined the band in 1962 and played on all of their hits through 1969 when he left due to poor health. He died in his swimming pool twenty-six days after quitting the group.

1964 The Carolons recorded their classic "Let It Please Be You" (Mellomood). The Brooklyn quintet consisted of four Jews and a Puerto Rican lead singer.

1966 The famous Cavern Club in Liverpool, home to The Beatles for over 280 performances between 1961 and 1963, closed due to bankruptcy. Overzealous fans barricaded themselves inside and had to be evicted by police.

1967 John Lennon borrowed a title idea from his three-year-old son, Julian, after seeing a picture he drew that had the title, "Lucy in the Sky with Diamonds." Julian's teacher wrote it there after asking the child what his drawing was called. The Beatles began rehearsing the song today.

1968 Frankie Lymon was the yardstick by which all '50s rock 'n' roll vocal group lead singers were measured. The pioneering lead singer of Frankie Lymon & the Teenagers, Frankie established the "Kiddie" lead sound that was copied by hundreds of artists through the '60s. Known for classics like "Why Do Fools Fall in Love" and "I Want You to Be My Girl," Lymon and company were the first rock 'n' roll singing group to have a #1 hit in England. They were inducted into The Rock and Roll Hall of Fame in 1993. Lymon died of a drug overdose at his grandmother's house today. He was only twenty-five.

February

#1 Song 1964: "I Want to Hold Your Hand," The Beatles

Born: Gretchen Christopher (The Fleetwoods), 1940

1964 Betty Everett charted with "The Shoop Shoop Song," which rose to #6.

1980 Buddy Holly's glasses and The Big Bopper's watch were found in a dust-covered file in the precinct of the Mason City, Iowa, police. They'd been misplaced twenty-one years earlier after the plane crash that killed them and rocker Ritchie Valens.

1996 Known as the "Boy Wonder of the Record Business," Wes Farrell (Wes Fogel) started as a hit songwriter ("Hang on Sloopy," for The McCoys, "Boys" for The Shirelles and The Beatles, and "Come A Little Bit Closer" Jay & the Americans) and became the preeminent music business entrepreneur with record labels (Chelsea/Roxbury) and publishing company (Pocket Full of Tunes) in the mid '60s through the mid '70s. farrell produced hits for The Partridge Family, The Cowsills, and Wayne Newton while his publishing company handled the music of Bruce Springsteen, Barry Manilow, and The Rascals, among others. He died of cancer while vacationing near his home in Florida. He was fifty-six.

Buddy Holly

61

March

1

#1 Song 1975: "Best of My Love," The Eagles

Born: Harry Belafonte, 1927; Jim Ed Brown (Browns), 1934; Roger Daltrey (The Who), 1944; Mike Dabo (Manfred Mann), 1944

1949 RCA Records introduced the first 45-rpm record.

1957 Frankie Lymon & the Teenagers received $7,500 to perform at a carnival in Panama. In 1957, that was an enormous sum for a one-night stand, especially for a black, teen act.

1970 *The Ed Sullivan Show* honored The Beatles with various artists singing tributes, including Dionne Warwick who warbled "We Can Work It Out" and "A Hard Day's Night," along with a duet by Paul McCartney and Peggy Lee on "Yesterday."

1974 Olivia Newton-John won Record of the Year and Best Pop Female Vocal Performance at the seventeenth Grammy Awards for "I Honestly Love You." Album of the Year was *Fulfillingness' First Finale* by Stevie Wonder.

1991 Frank Esler-Smith was the keyboard player for the Australian pop group, Air Supply. Born in London, Frank became the music director for the Australian production of *Jesus Christ Superstar*. It was there he met Russell Hitchcock and formed the band that went on to have hits like "Lost in Love" and "Here I Am." He died of pneumonia in Melbourne, Australia, on this day.

Harry Belafonte

March

#1 Song 1963: "Walk Like a Man," The Four Seasons

Born: Lawrence Payton (The Four Tops), 1938; Lou Reed, 1942; Eddie Money, 1949; Karen Carpenter, 1950; Jay Osmond (The Osmonds), 1955; John Bongiovi, 1962

1960 After serving his military time in Germany, Elvis Presley touched down at Prestwick Airport, Scotland, to refuel en route to America. Elvis disembarked to talk with waiting fans and then returned to the plane. It was the only time he ever set foot on British soil, as Elvis never performed outside of North America.

1964 While their single "Twist & Shout" was being released in the U.S. on Tollie (another American company their early tracks were licensed to), The Beatles began filming *A Hard Day's Night* by spending a week riding back and forth on the Paddington-to-Minehead train. They recorded with microphones tucked into their shirts, and George began a relationship with one of the young actresses, Patti Boyd, on the train.

1984 Legendary Gold Star Recording Studios in Los Angeles closed its doors. Recording home of Phil Spector and most of his classic hits, the studio was demolished to make way for a mini-mall, featuring a Del Taco stand.

1985 Sheena Easton became the first artist in history to achieve top ten hits on the U.S. pop, R&B, country, dance, and adult contemporary charts when "Sugar Walls" (written by Prince) reached #9 today.

1999 Newly elected Rock and Roll Hall of Fame member, Dusty Springfield died of breast cancer at her Henley-on-Thames home, just west of London. She was due to accept an honor from the queen of England (an OBE, Officer of the Order of the British Empire) on the day she passed away. Dusty was fifty-nine.

2003 Hank Ballard—lead singer of The Midnighters and writer of such hits as "Work with Me Annie," "Finger Poppin Time" and "The Twist"—died today at his Los Angeles home. Hank had thirteen pop charters from 1959 to 1962 and twenty-two R&B hits between 1953 and 1972. Although Chubby Checker's version (with The Dreamlovers backing vocals) was the standard, Hank's version actually made it to #6 R&B and #28 pop as a B-side more than a year before Checker's hit. Dick Clark called "The Twist," "The most important song in rock 'n' roll."

March

3

#1 Song 1990: "Escapade," Janet Jackson

Born: Junior Parker, 1927; Willie Chambers (The Chambers Brothers), 1938; Paul Kantner (Jefferson Airplane), 1941; Mike Pender (The Searchers), 1942; Jennifer Warnes, 1947

1956 Singer-actress Gale Storm assaulted the hit list with a cover of Frankie Lymon & the Teenagers #6 smash, "Why Do Fools Fall in Love." Although she reached the Top 10 (#9), it was the first time a black act had beaten a white cover artist on the pop charts.

1958 The rock 'n' roll anthem, "Rock & Roll Is Here to Stay" by Danny & the Juniors charted, eventually reaching #19.

1966 Buffalo Springfield was formed by Stephen Stills shortly after the guitarist, driving on Sunset Boulevard. in Los Angeles today, saw old Canadian friend Neil Young driving in the opposite direction at the wheel of a hearse!

1969 The *Post Card* album by Mary Hopkin was issued in America ten days after its U.K. release and with one cut the British album didn't contain, a song that would go on to be a worldwide #1 hit, "Those Were the Days."

2002 Harlan Howard, known as "Mr. Songwriter" among his constituents in the Nashville community, died today. The Detroit native wrote more than 4,000 songs and had hit recordings by Buck Owens, Johnny Cash, George Jones, Ray Price, and Patsy Cline's monumental "I Fall to Pieces." A Country Music Hall of Fame inductee, he was seventy-two when he passed away.

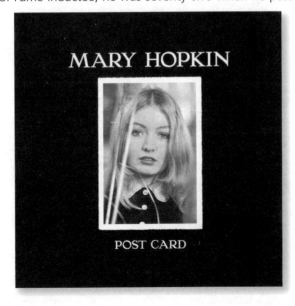

March

#1 Song 1967: "Ruby Tuesday,"
The Rolling Stones

Born: Bobby Womack, 1944;
Shakin' Stevens, 1948; Emilio Estefan
(Miami Sound Machine), 1953

1966 John Lennon made his now legendary faux pas about Jesus in the *London Evening Standard* newspaper, saying, "Christianity will go. It will vanish and shrink. I needn't argue about that. I'm right and I will be proved right. We're more popular than Jesus now. I don't know which will go first, rock 'n' roll or Christianity. Jesus was alright, but his disciples were thick and ordinary. It's them twisting it that ruins it for me." The religious right went ballistic and soon radio stations across America would be burning Beatles records.

1967 The Four Seasons thirty-third hit 45, "Beggin'," charted en route to #16.

1969 Ringo Starr, who was acting in the film *The Magic Christian*, met Britain's Princess Margaret, who was visiting the set to see her friend Peter Sellers.

1993 "I feel like a queen," Patti LaBelle exclaimed as she was honored with a star on Hollywood's Walk of Fame.

1995 Celine Dion's "Think Twice" reached U.K. #1 at the same time her *The Colour of My Love* album topped the British charts, both for five weeks, making her the first artist since The Beatles to hold the top spot on both hit lists for five weeks.

March

5

#1 Song 1983: "Billie Jean," Michael Jackson

Born: Teena Marie, 1956; Andy Gibb, 1958

1958 Youngest brother of The Bee Gees, Andy Gibb was born on this day in Manchester, England. He went on to solo success with ten American hits and four British charters, including three #1s in a row: "I Just Wanna Be Your Everything," "(Love Is) Thicker Than Water," and "Shadow Dancing."

1963 Five days after writing it, Lennon, McCartney, and company recorded "From Me to You," at Abbey Road Studio along with their song, "Thank You Girl." That day they were also photographed in the now famous balcony scene at EMI Records London office that adorned their *Please Please Me* album cover.

1964 Country music's version of "the day the music died." Patsy Cline, Cowboy Copas, and Hawkshaw Hawkins were killed in a plane crash in Camden, Tennessee. They were returning from a Kansas City benefit concert for the widow of a local disc jockey.

1999 The original Tokens performed at New York's Waldorf-Astoria Hotel in a reunion concert, the first time all four (Jay Siegel, Phil Margo, Mitch Margo, and Hank Medress) had sung together in nineteen years (1980).

Andy Gibb

March

#1 Song 1971: "One Bad Apple," The Osmonds

Born: Sylvia Vanderpool Robinson (Mickey & Sylvia), 1936; Michelle Phillips (The Mamas & the Papas), 1944; Mary Wilson (The Supremes), 1944; David Gilmour (Pink Floyd), 1944; Hugh Grundy (The Zombies), 1945; Kiki Dee, 1947

1954 Elvis Presley tried out for The Songfellows, the junior Blackwood Brothers vocal group. He was greatly disappointed when he was told that he "can't sing," although members of the group later asserted they meant he couldn't sing harmony. He also filed his first federal income tax return today. His job classification was noted as "semi-skilled."

1959 The "Ben E. King" Drifters first recording session included the timeless ballad, "There Goes My Baby" (#2 pop, #1 R&B), the first R&B hit to use strings. The group spent the previous nine months touring and originally rehearsed the song up-tempo while on the road.

1971 Paul McCartney debuted as a solo artist on the American charts with "Another Day," which went on to #5. Over the next twenty-two years he would have forty-four solo hits.

1976 Stevie Nicks sang lead on Fleetwood Mac's charter, "Rhiannon," which reached #11 and became their third of twenty-three hits between 1970 and 1990. Before her success with the band, Stevie was a hostess at a Bob's Big Boy hamburger chain restaurant.

1991 Sir Joseph Lockwood, a man who amassed a fortune gambling on horses, parlayed his organizational skills in the flour business to become the chairman of EMI Ltd., the British record empire that he would steer from the '50s through the '70s. His major accomplishments included directing his company into rock 'n' roll (being the original distributor of Elvis Presley records in England even though he much preferred classical music), buying Capitol Records as an entry into the U.S. market, and, of course, having the good fortune of having George Martin sign The Beatles. He died of natural causes in London.

March

#1 Song 1981: "I Love a Rainy Night," Eddie Rabbitt

Born: Chris White (The Zombies), 1943; Peter Wolf (J. Geils Band), 1946; Mathew Fisher (Procol Harum), 1946; Little Peggy March, 1948

1962 Due to their successful audition of February 12, The Beatles were recorded in Manchester, England, on the BBC's *Teenagers Turn-Here We Go* radio show. The songs were Roy Orbison's "Dream Baby," Chuck Berry's "Memphis, Tennessee," and The Marvelettes' "Please Mister Postman."

1965 During a Rolling Stones performance at The Palace Theatre in Manchester, England, a girl fell from the balcony.

1966 Tina Turner recorded her legendary vocal on Phil Spector's crowning achievement, "River Deep, Mountain High." Spector had already spent over $22,000 creating the backing track, and that didn't include the $20,000 he paid Tina's husband, Ike Turner, to stay *out* of the studio!

1987 Carole King and her songwriting partner–ex-husband Gerry Goffin were inducted into the Songwriters Hall of Fame at the eighteenth annual awards held at New York's Plaza Hotel.

2000 The first black woman to conduct the symphony orchestras of Chicago, Los Angeles, Detroit, and thirteen other American cities, Margaret Rosezarian Harris died of a heart attack today at age fifty-six. Originally a pianist, Harris gained her greatest acclaim as a conductor. She also worked on Broadway, most notably as music director of the landmark musical *Hair*.

March

8

#1 Song 1980: "Crazy Little Thing Called Love," Queen

Born: Micky Dolenz (The Monkees), 1945; Randy Meisner (The Eagles), 1946; Gary Numan, 1958

1957 Britain's *New Musical Express* predicted that teen idol Tommy Sands would soon eclipse the success of Elvis Presley.

1966 Lulu became the first British female singer to perform behind the Iron Curtain when she began a Polish tour with The Hollies in Warsaw.

1968 Big Brother & the Holding Company, featuring Janis Joplin, debuted at The Fillmore East in New York.

1969 The 5th Dimension's "Aquarius/Let the Sun Shine in" charted, becoming the group's first #1 and ninth hit single in two years.

1990 Bonnie Raitt won the Best Female Singer trophy in *Rolling Stone* Magazine's Critic's Awards.

Lulu

March

#1 Song 1959: "Venus," Frankie Avalon

Born: Lloyd Price, 1933; Mark Lindsey (Paul Revere & the Raiders), 1942; Robin Trower (Procul Harum), 1945; Jeffrey Osborne, 1948

1957 Fats Domino charted with "I'm Walkin'" and reached #4. The "Fat Man" went on to have sixty-six pop hits in thirteen years!

1961 The Imaginations' quintessential doo-wop songs "Hey You" and "Goodnight Baby" were recorded (Music Makers). The Brooklyn, New York, quintet included a young Bobby Bloom, who, went on to hit success as a solo act with "Montego Bay" (#8, 1970).

1967 The Beatles began recording "Getting Better," a song that Paul McCartney got the idea for from temporary touring drummer (in 1964) Jimmy Nicol, who when asked, "How's it going?" responded repeatedly, "It's getting better."

1968 The Beatles won four Grammy awards for *Sgt. Pepper's Lonely Hearts Club Band*: Album of the Year, Best Album Cover, Best Contemporary Album, and Best Engineered Recording.

1972 Barbra Streisand and Carole King performed at a benefit for presidential candidate George McGovern at the Great Western Forum, Inglewood, California.

#1 Song 1973: "Killing Me Softly (With His Song)," Roberta Flack

Born: Dexter Tisby (The Penguins), 1935; Dean Torrence (Jan & Dean), 1940

Died: Andy Gibb, 1988; LaVern Baker, 1997

1974 David Bowie recorded an in-concert album titled *David Live* at the Tower Theatre in Philadelphia. Still a year away from his first #1 and biggest hit, "Fame," Bowie would go on to chart twenty-six times through 1995 in America. David's first love was art, and before becoming a rock idol, he was an art teacher.

1977 The Sex Pistols signed with A&M Records in London. The ceremony was held in front of Buckingham Palace, to the Queen's horror!

1984 Madonna charted for the first time with "Borderline" (#10). She's since reached the Top 10 thirty-one times through 1999. Not bad for a kid who started out as a hatcheck girl, Dunkin' Donuts clerk, and nude model.

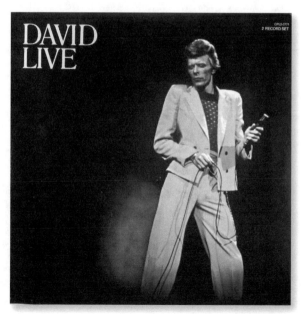

David Bowie's Live

March

11

#1 Song 1972: "Without You," Nilsson

Born: Fred Johnson (The Marcels), 1942; Mark Stein (Vanilla Fudge), 1947; Bobby McFerrin, 1950

1927 Seeburg introduced the first jukebox.

1964 The Beatles lip-synched "I Should Have Known Better" in a fake train car at Twickenham Film Studios for the film *A Hard Day's Night*, but had to reshoot when the crew kept rocking the car to the beat of the song.

1967 Dick James, The Beatles' publisher, announced that the Lennon-McCartney song "Yesterday" was the most recorded song to date, having had 446 different cover recordings.

1967 The Beatles won three Grammy Awards for records issued the previous year: Best Song for "Michelle," Best Vocal Performance for "Eleanor Rigby," and Best Cover Artwork for the album design of *Revolver* by Klaus Voormann.

1972 Dionne Warwick reached the Top 100 with "If We Only Have Love" (#84). It was her first chart single since leaving Scepter Records, where she had thirty-eight hits. She would go on to have seventeen more Top 100 outings through 1987, including #1s "Then Came You" and "That's What Friends Are for."

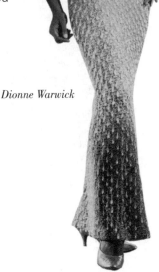

Dionne Warwick

72

March

12

#1 Song 1988: "Never Gonna Give You Up," Rick Astley

Born: Al Jarreau, 1940; Paul Kantner (Jefferson Airplane), 1942; James Taylor, 1948; Marlon Jackson (The Jackson 5), 1957

1974 John Lennon was thrown out of L.A.'s Troubadour Club for loudly berating the onstage talent, The Smothers Brothers. He reportedly assaulted a waitress and the duo's manager. The primo peacenik had been drinking heavily and, while outside, scuffled with a prying paparazzi.

1988 Gloria Estefan charted with "Anything for You," which became her first of three #1s

1961 Elvis Presley began recording his forthcoming *Something for Everyone* album at RCA's Nashville studio. Working through the night he did eleven songs, including a tune he would eventually take to #5, "I Feel So Bad."

1966 Cher's "Bang Bang" charted and would become her first solo Top 5 hit (#2).

1993 Alex Taylor was the oldest member of the Taylor siblings, which include singers Kate, Livingston, and, of course, James. He formed an R&B group, The Fabulous Corsairs, in the early '60s that brother James sang with for a while. Alex, whose style was more R&B rudimentary than his family, recorded for several labels (Capricorn, Bang, Dunhill), but only reached the R&B charts with "Don't Look at Me That Way" in 1978. Addicted on several levels, Alex died of an alcohol-related heart attack at forty-six, coincidentally on brother James's forty-sixth birthday.

March

13

#1 Song 1966: "Ballad of the Green Berets," Sgt. Barry Sadler

Born: Neil Sedaka, 1939

1961 Linda Scott debuted on the charts with her first single, "I've Told Every Little Star" (#3). She had ten more charters over the next three years.

1965 Eric Clapton left The Yardbirds for John Mayall's Bluesbreakers. He was replaced by Jeff Beck.

1966 Rod Stewart left Steampacket for a solo career.

1976 Nashville-born ex–porn star Andrea True seduced the charts today on her way to a #4 disco smash with "More, More, More."

1985 A veteran record executive and music producer, Bob Shad founded several record labels from the '40s through the '60s. His first was Sittin In With, the label for Peppermint Harris and several early R&B groups in 1948. He later started Time, which had the hit "I've Had It" by The Bell Notes, and Mainstream in the mid '60s, where he discovered Janis Joplin singing with Big Brother & the Holding Company and Ted Nugent, releasing their early recordings. Bob died of a heart attack in Beverly Hills, California, today.

Eric Clapton

March

#1 Song 1970: "Bridge over Troubled Waters" Simon & Garfunkel

Born: Lee Hays (The Weavers), 1914; Phil Phillips, 1931; Quincy Jones, 1933; David Byrne (Talking Heads), 1952

Died: Doc Pomus 1991

1964 The Who received their first piece of press when they were mentioned in Britain's *Melody Maker* magazine as an emerging new group under the banner, "Massive Swing to R&B."

1969 Super-promoter Sid Bernstein offered The Beatles $4 million for four concerts in the U.S. The band turned him down.

1972 Burglar-country music artist (now there's a combination!) Merle Haggard was granted a full pardon by California Governor Ronald Reagan twelve years after Haggard was released from San Quentin Penitentiary while serving three years.

1982 Metallica made their performance debut at Radio City in Anaheim, California.

1991 Brooklyn-born Doc Pomus (Jerome Felder) was a legendary figure among songwriters of the '50s and '60s. His first Top 10 hit was Ray Charles's "Lonely Avenue" in 1956 and was followed by a slew of chart busters, such as "A Teenager in Love" for Dion & the Belmonts, "Save the Last Dance for Me" with The Drifters, and "Turn Me Loose" for Fabian, not to mention sixteen songs for Elvis, including "Viva Las Vegas." He produced Big Joe Turner's Grammy-winning album *Blues Train* in 1983 and had a tribute album of his songs done in 1995 by such luminaries as Bob Dylan, Dion, and Lou Reed. Doc died of lung cancer in New York City at age sixty-six.

2000 Although it was billed as the Supremes Reunion Tour, Diana Ross was really the only original member when the promoters *insulted* Mary Wilson with an offer of $2 million while Diana was to get $20 million, according to TV's *Access Hollywood*. Undeterred, Diana went out with Scherrie Payne and Lynda Laurence who weren't even in the group until years after Diana left. Cindy Birdsong, original replacement for deceased Florence Ballard, wasn't even mentioned.

March

15

#1 Song 1969: "Dizzy,"
Tommy Roe"

Born: Mike Love (The Beach Boys),
1941; Sly Stone, 1944; Terence Trent
D'Arby, 1962

1929 Clarence "Pine Top" Smith is credited with starting the boogie-woogie craze when his recording of "Pine Top's Boogie Woogie" became a sensation in 1928. Unfortunately for Clarence, he did not stick around long enough to benefit from his talent as he was shot dead today in a Chicago nightclub while dancing with a young lady. The errant slug was fired by a waiter trying to break up a fight. He was only twenty-five.

1945 The first #1 pop album was by Nat "King" Cole.

1954 The Chords recorded the soon-to-be standard "Sh-Boom" (Cat, $50), which became the first pop Top 10 hit (#5 Pop, #2 R&B) by a rock 'n' roll group.

1956 Former dogcatcher and carnival huckster Tom Parker signed a youthful Elvis Presley to a management contract.

1957 Frankie Lymon & the Teenagers arrived in London for a British tour. The Harlem teen quintet was the first rock 'n' roll vocal group to have a #1 record in England when "Why Do Fools Fall in Love" topped the U.K. charts in August 1956.

1969 *Rolling Stone* magazine decimated Janis Joplin's Fillmore concerts with the cover story, "Janis: The Judy Garland of Rock?"

1986 The Bangles' chart debut in England, "Manic Monday," eventually reached #2 in both the U.K. and U.S.

#1 Song 1968: "Dock of the Bay," Otis Redding

Born: Jerry Jeff Walker, 1942; Nancy Wilson (Heart), 1954

1957 The Heartbeats' "I Won't Be the Fool" (Rama, $40), The Five Satins' "Oh, Happy Day" (Ember, $25), The Continentals' "Picture of Love" (Whirlin Disc, $75), and The Mellows' "Moon of Silver" (Candlelight, $100) were released. (Don't you wish you'd kept those old R&B 45s!)

1966 The Beatles, nominated for ten Grammy's for recordings from 1965, failed to win any of them at the awards show today.

1970 Tammi Terrell, who had ten chart-hit duets with Marvin Gaye, died of a brain tumor onstage, in Marvin's arms. She was only twenty-four.

1979 Bonnie Bramlett (Delaney & Bonnie), while singing backup for Stephen Stills in Columbus, Ohio, got into a race- and music-related argument with Elvis Costello and belted him in the face!

Marvin Gaye and Tammi Terrell

March

17

#1 Song 1958: "Tequila,"
The Champs

Born: Nat King Cole, 1917;
Vito Picone (The Elegants), 1940;
Clarence Collins (The Imperials), 1941;
John Sebastian (The Lovin' Spoonful),
1944

1958 The Coasters recorded "Yakety Yak" (#1 pop and R&B) and their great arrangement of "Zing Went the Strings of My Heart."

1969 Two singles issued today had a Beatles connection even though The Beatles weren't involved as a group. James Taylor's "Carolina in My Mind" and Cream's "Badge" were both released in the U.S. Paul McCartney had played bass on "Carolina," and George Harrison had cowritten "Badge" with Eric Clapton. "Carolina" reached #67 while "Badge" topped out at #60.

1978 The film about rock 'n' roll disc jockey Alan Freed, *American Hot Wax*, debuted.

1990 Wilson Phillips' debut single, "Hold On," charged onto the Top 100, quickly reaching #1. With seven hits in two-and-a-half years, they were truly a short-lived success story.

1996 A two-hit wonder, the Oklahoma-born, Texas-raised Terry Stafford was a Presley sound-alike who made more of the similarity than most. Taking a two-year-old tune from Elvis' *Pot Luck* album, Terry recorded "Suspicion," took it to #3 in the nation, and followed it up with "I'll Touch a Star" (#25), both in 1964. When the singing hits stopped, he went on to write Tony Orlando & Dawn's smash "Say Has Anybody Seen My Sweet Gypsy Rose," among others. He died in Amarillo, Texas, at age fifty-four today.

March

18

#1 Song 1967: "Penny Lane,"
The Beatles

Born: Wilson Pickett (The Falcons), 1941;
Helen Gathers (The Bobbettes), 1943;
John Hartman (The Doobie Brothers), 1950;
Irene Cara, 1959

1957 Bill Haley & the Comets returned to America after performing before half a million people on a world tour.

1965 Rolling Stones Mick Jagger, Bill Wyman, and Keith Richards were arrested after urinating on a gas station wall when they were refused access to the men's room.

1969 Janis Joplin appeared on *The Ed Sullivan Show*.

1982 Former Harold Melvin & the Blue Notes lead singer Teddy Pendergrass was paralyzed from the neck down after his Rolls Royce flipped over trying to avoid another car on a Philadelphia street.

2001 The Mamas & the Papas leader John Phillips passed away. Formed in New York out of The Journeymen, the group was hired to sing backup vocals for Dunhill Records artist Barry McGuire on a song John had written called "California Dreamin'." Producer Lou Adler was so impressed with their harmony that he put their background *and* lead vocals on the instrumental track. At the time of his death, Phillips was completing tracks for an album he began with the Rolling Stones Mick Jagger and Keith Richards more than twenty-five years earlier.

Bill Haley & the Comets

March

19

#1 Song 1955: "Sincerely,"
The McGuire Sisters

Born: Clarence "Frogman" Henry,
1937; Ruth Pointer (The Pointer Sisters),
1946

1957 Elvis Presley bought his now legendary mansion, Graceland.

1964 The Beatles began considering names for their film while working at Twickenham Studio in London. Ringo Starr's idea evolved from an extremely busy day when he uttered the immortal words, "Boy, this has been a hard day's night!" Before his historic remark they were considering titles like *Who Was That Little Old Man?* (a McCartney idea), *Moving On*, *Travelin' On*, *Let's Go*, and *Beatlemania*.

1974 Grace Slick's Jefferson Airplane officially became Jefferson Starship.

1981 Pioneering blues guitarist Tampa Red (Hudson Whittaker) enjoyed success with novelty hits like "Tight Like That" in the 1920s. He performed on numerous recordings with Big Bill Broonzy and Georgia Tom before retiring his bottleneck guitar style in 1960. He returned to performing during the late '60s revival. A chronic alcoholic, he nevertheless lived to be seventy-seven.

2001 Paul Simon, Aerosmith, Queen, Steely Dan, The Flamingos, Ritchie Valens, and Solomon Burke were inducted into the Rock and Roll Hall of Fame.

March 20

#1 Song 1961: "Surrender,"
Elvis Presley

Born: Jerry Reed, 1937; Carl Palmer
(Emerson, Lake & Palmer), 1951

1958 The Quarrymen (the forerunner of The Beatles) went to Liverpool's Empire Theater to see Buddy Holly & the Crickets perform.

1969 John Lennon married art exhibitionist Yoko Ono Cox in Gibraltar at the British Embassy.

1970 David Bowie married American Mary Angela Barnett at Bromley, England's registry office after both arrived half an hour late.

1989 Former bandleader Archie Bleyer founded the Cadence record label in the early '50s. He signed several acts that went on to stardom, including The Everly Brothers, Andy Williams, and The Chordettes, one of whom (Janet Ertel) he married. He closed the label in the '60s to retire. Parkinson's disease took him at age seventy-nine.

1990 Gloria Estefan was badly injured when her group's tour bus was rammed by a tractor-trailer near Scranton, Pennsylvania. Though suffering a fractured and dislocated vertebra in her spine, she was back onstage performing at the American Music Awards less than eleven months later.

Gloria Estefan

March

#1 Song 1964: "She Loves You," The Beatles

Born: Ray Dorset (Mungo Jerry), 1946; Eddie Money, 1949; Roger Hodgson (Supertramp), 1950; Russell Thompkins, Jr. (The Stylistics), 1951

1950 The Four Freshmen were discovered by bandleader Stan Kenton while playing The Esquire Lounge in Dayton, Ohio.

1952 Cleveland deejay Alan Freed held his first rock 'n' roll stage show, *The Moondog Coronation Ball*, at a theater capable of holding 10,000 occupants. When 30,000 teens showed up, the show was canceled by local officials. Though it wasn't considered at the time, the riot was the first sign of the coming rock 'n' roll era.

1961 The Beatles played The Cavern Club for the first time at an evening performance. Also on the bill were The Swinging Blue Jeans, later of "Hippy, Hippy Shake" fame.

1967 John Lennon took an accidental LSD trip while in the studio working on "Getting Better" for the *Sgt. Pepper* album. He thought he was *only* taking uppers.

1991 Leo Fender revolutionized the development of the electric guitar with the invention of the solidbody "Telecaster" in 1950 and the ultimate rock 'n' roll guitar, the "Stratocaster" in 1954. Although he studied piano and saxophone as a youth, he never played guitar. He started a radio repair shop in California, which developed into building amplifiers and, by 1947, guitars. He sold the company in 1965 to CBS for $13 million. He died at home in Fullerton, California, of Parkinson's disease at eighty-one.

March 22

#1 Song 1980: "Another Brick in the Wall," Pink Floyd

Born: George Benson, 1943;
 Keith Relf (Renaissance), 1943;
Jeremy Clyde (Chad & Jeremy), 1944;
Stephanie Mills, 1957

1956 Carl Perkins was severely injured in a car crash in Wilmington, Delaware, while he was en route to New York to perform on Perry Como's TV show.

1957 Elvis Presley's "All Shook Up"/"That's When Your Heartaches Begin" was released. "All Shook Up" would go on to #1 and stay there for eight weeks, selling about 2.5 million copies. The flip side was a fervent version of the Ink Spots song that Presley first recorded as a demo at Sun Studios in 1953.

1963 While The Beatles were on tour with Tommy Roe and Chris Montez at the Gaumont Cinema in Doncaster, England, their album *Please Please Me* was issued in Britain on Parlophone. The fourteen-song collection included "Do You Want to Know a Secret," "P.S. I Love You," "I Saw Her Standing There," "Please Please Me," "Chains" (the Cookies hit), "Love Me Do," "Boys" (a Shirelles B-side), "Ask Me Why," "Baby It's You," (The Shirelles hit), "A Taste of Honey," "There's a Place," "Twist And Shout," (The Isley Brothers hit), "Misery," and "Anna (Go to Him)."

1975 Four Seasons members Bob Gaudio and Frankie Valli bought back an unreleased recording from Motown Records and leased it to Private Stock Records. The record was sung by Valli. "My Eyes Adored You" went to #1.

1975 Janis Ian, who was discovered by classical conductor-composer Leonard Bernstein, charted with her LP *Between the Lines*. It became her only #1 of eight Top 200 albums.

March

23

#1 Song 1963: "Our Day Will Come," Ruby & the Romantics

Born: Joey d'Ambrosio (Bill Haley & the Comets), 1934; Ric Ocasek (The Cars), 1949; Chaka Khan, 1953

1985 Billy Joel married model Christie Brinkley.

1990 "Big Al" Sears was a veteran jazz saxophone player with Duke Ellington and Lionel Hampton's orchestras in the 1940s. In the '50s, he became one of the "Big 4" "honkers" (along with Red Prysock, Sam "The Man" Taylor, and Jimmy Wright), who were the most sought-after sax players for numerous R&B and rock 'n' roll acts. Al excelled at raising the excitement level in the obligatory instrumental section of each record. He also played in Alan Freed's house band and recorded several jazz albums of his own in the '60s. He died of lung cancer at his Long Island home.

1992 Janet Jackson, the youngest member of the Jackson clan, signed a $16 million contract with Virgin Records.

1996 The Beatles last American chart 45 (their seventy-second), "Real Love" debuted on the Top 100, going to #11. It was actually a demo recorded by Lennon in 1979 and had new vocals added by the other Beatles. It was released sixteen years after he died.

#1 Song 1962: "Hey Baby,"
Bruce Channel

Born: Billy Stewart (Rainbows), 1937;
Lee Oskar (War), 1948

1956 El Capris's "(Shimmy Shimmy) Ko Ko Wop" was released and became an instant collectible. Four years later, it became a hit for Little Anthony & the Imperials as "Shimmy Shimmy Ko Ko Bop."

1958 Elvis Presley enlisted in the army and went from an estimated $10,000 a month to $78 a month.

1964 The Beatles wax images went on display at Madame Tussaud museum in London. Those same figures were later a part of the cover of the *Sgt. Pepper* album.

1969 Ringo Starr announced to American reporters that The Beatles would not appear together in public again, saying, "I don't miss being a Beatle anymore. You can't get those days back. It's no good living in the past."

2000 Heartthrob hit-makers 'N Sync set a new record when their album *No Strings Attached* shipped 4.2 million copies in its first week of release. The male vocal group's nearest competitor was rival vocalists and pinup popsters The Backstreet Boys, who had a 1.13 million first week shipment of their *Millennium* album in May 1999.

March

25

#1 Song 1967: "Happy Together," The Turtles

Born: Johnny Burnette, 1934; Aretha Franklin, 1942; Elton John, 1947; Nick Lowe, 1949

1947 One of the icons of rock 'n' roll, Elton John was born today. Known for his outrageous stage costumes and oversized glasses, the prince of British rock amassed sixty-five chart singles in America, starting in 1970 with "Your Song." His four decades career produced more than twenty-five Top 10 songs, including "Philadelphia Freedom" "Crocodile Rock," and "Candle in the Wind."

1966 The Beatles did a photo session in London for the now famous "Butcher Block" cover that appeared on the *Yesterday...and Today* album until it was withdrawn due to extreme criticism for its lack of taste. John Lennon stated they did it out of boredom and rebellion against the typical covers they had previously done.

1978 Nineteen years after dying in a plane crash, Buddy Holly had his first and only British #1 album with *20 Golden Greats*.

1991 Madonna sang "Sooner or Later (I Always Get My Man)" from the film *Dick Tracy* at the 63rd annual Academy Awards. The song then won the Oscar for Best Song.

1996 Sheryl Crow performed in Baumholder, Germany, for the families of American troops stationed in Bosnia at the request of First Lady Hillary Rodham Clinton, who was visiting in support of the soldiers.

March

#1 Song 1955 "Ballad of Davy Crockett," Bill Hayes

Born: Rufus Thomas, 1917; Fred Parris (The Five Satins), 1936; Diana Ross, 1944; Steve Tyler (Aerosmith), 1948; Teddy Pendergrass (Harold Melvin & the Bluenotes), 1950

1952 Sun Records of Memphis, Tennessee, released its first single, "Selling My Whiskey" by Jackie Boy and Little Walter (Sun #174).

1955 Georgia Gibbs's "Dance with Me Henry" (a cover of Etta James' "Roll with Me Henry") charted on its trip to #1. It was her second of thirteen Top 100 singles through 1958.

1967 Peter Bergman, later of the Firesign Theatre, coined the term "Love-In" when he described the days gathering at Elysian Park in Los Angeles, California.

1969 John Lennon and Yoko Ono held their now famous "bed-in" at the Amsterdam Hilton Hotel.

1979 Bill Haley recorded his last session. Songs included "I Need the Music" and "God Bless Rock 'n' Roll."

Steven Tyler

March

27

#1 Song 1976: "December 1963 (Oh, What a Night)," The Four Seasons

Born: Sarah Vaughan, 1924; Brenda Knight (Gladys Knight & the Pips), 1941; Tony Banks (Genesis), 1951; Mariah Carey, 1970

1951 The Larks recorded their immortal ballad, "My Reverie." The record was so highly revered by R&B collectors that in the mid '60s, someone broke into Times Square Records in New York City and, faced with "The Collector's Wall" of rare and expensive records, stole only one, "My Reverie."

1954 The Spaniels' "Goodnight Sweetheart Goodnight" (Vee-Jay, $500) would go on to be a staple of oldies radio stations for the next four decades, especially as a sign-off song.

1966 A British newspaper stated that The Beatles had sold 159 million singles around the world. Considering they'd issued forty singles up to that time, they averaged an incredible almost four million sales per single release.

1971 Kiki Dee had her first American charter with "Love Makes the World Go Round" (#87). The Yorkshire, England, rocker went on to have five more through 1993, including the #1 duet with Elton John, "Don't Go Breaking My Heart."

Kiki Dee

March

#1 Song 1992: "Save the Best for Last," Vanessa Williams

Born: Johnny Burnette, 1934; Chuck Portz (The Turtles), 1945; Milan Williams (The Commodores), 1948

1956 The Five Satins legendary love song, "In the Still of the Night," was released on its original label, Standard. It was reissued soon after on the larger Ember label reaching #24 pop, #3 R&B. Even though it never made the Top 20, over the decades it has sold several million copies.

1966 Roy Orbison performed in England and was met backstage by long-time fans George Harrison and Ringo Starr.

1974 Mississippi-born Arthur "Big Boy" Crudup was an accomplished blues musician who is best known for having written and recorded "That's All Right" in the mid '40s. In 1949, RCA issued its first 45s and the first R&B single released was "That's All Right," which a young Elvis Presley heard on the radio and recorded in 1954 as his first record. The music business was not kind to Arthur, who never saw a dime from Presley's recording. Fed up, Crudup bought a farm in Virginia until the blues revival of the late '60s brought him back to perform. He died of a stroke in Virginia at sixty-eight.

1981 Kim Carnes, a former member of The New Christy Minstrels, with Kenny Rogers charted with "Bette Davis Eyes," which roared to #1 for nine weeks. It became her biggest hit of nineteen Top 100 entries.

1988 Tina Turner's "Break Every Rule" tour ended today in Osaka, Japan, after she performed 230 dates in twenty-five countries playing to over three million people. The tour broke box-office records in thirteen countries.

March

29

#1 Song 1986: "Rock Me Amadeus," Falco

Born: Frannie Beecher (Bill Haley & the Comets), 1921; Donny Conn (The Playmates), 1930; Terry Jacks, 1944

1958 W.C. Handy ran away from his Alabama home at the age of fifteen to become "The Father of the Blues." Starting with the W. A. Mahara's Minstrels as a trumpet player, he coined the term "The Blues," after hearing a singer-guitarist pouring his heart out through song at a Mississippi train station in 1903. Composing such classics as "St. Louis Blues" and "Beale Street Blues," Handy started developing the sound in Memphis's nightclubs in the teens and lived to see it spread around the country and the world. He died of bronchial pneumonia today at age eighty-four.

1962 Gene Chandler received a gold record onstage at the Regal Theater in Chicago for his #1 million-seller "Duke of Earl." The recording was originally done with Gene and his group, The Dukays, but when the record was issued, only Gene's name was on the 45, thus depriving the group of its place in history as the act on one of America's most beloved doo-wop oldies of all time.

1967 EMI Records officially announced that The Beatles new album would be called *Sgt. Peppers Lonely Hearts Club Band*. That night the group worked on recording "With a Little Help from My Friends."

1973 Twelve days after Dr. Hook & the Medicine Show hit "The Cover of Rolling Stone" peaked at #6 (March 17), the group wound up on the cover of the real *Rolling Stone* magazine.

30

#1 Song 1957: "Party Doll," Buddy Knox

Born: Graeme Edge (The Moody Blues), 1941; Eric Clapton, 1945; M.C. Hammer, 1962

1945 Eric Clapton, the rock guitar genius, was born today. Starting in 1963, he became a member of The Roosters, The Yardbirds, and John Mayall's Bluesbreakers. In 1966 he formed Cream; in 1968, Blind Faith; and by 1970, Derek and the Dominos. He's tallied twenty-seven hits in America from 1970 through 1996, including "Layla," "Change the World," and his only #1, "I Shot the Sheriff."

1953 The Crows monumental hit "Gee" was recorded at New York's Beltone Studios today. Legend has it that the record was slowly going nowhere when Los Angeles disc jockey Huggy Boy had a fight with his girlfriend. As she stormed out of the studio and went home, he frantically searched for her favorite new 45, "Gee." He played it over and over on his show and said he was going to keep playing it until she came back. By the time she relented he'd played it about twenty times and to his shock the next day, thousands of orders for the record came in. It broke out of Los Angeles and became a legendary rock 'n' roll hit (#14 pop, #2 R&B).

1967 The Beatles photo session at Michael Coopers studio in Chelsea resulted in the historic *Sgt Pepper's Lonely Hearts Club Band* LP cover.

1989 After having sung with The Pips for 37 years, Gladys Knight made her solo debut at Bally's Casino in Las Vegas.

1995 A record producer of great skill, Paul Rothchild is best known for his years at Elektra Records, where he worked with folk acts like Phil Oaks, Tom Paxton, and Fred Neil. His production of The Doors' "Light My Fire," however, made him a record industry celebrity. He went on to produce many rock acts including Janis Joplin's *Pearl* album and the film soundtrack for *The Rose*. Paul died of lung cancer at home in Los Angeles. He was fifty-nine.

March

31

#1 Song 1979: "Tragedy,"
The Bee Gees

Born: Herb Alpert, 1935; Al Goodman
(Ray, Goodman & Brown), 1947

Died: O'Kelly Isley (The Isley Brothers),
1986

1956 Brenda Lee made her professional performing debut on Red Foley's *Ozark Jubilee* ABC-TV show at the age of eleven. It led to a five-year management deal with Dub Albritton of Top Talent.

1962 The Crystals' "Uptown" charted and became their only single, featuring six members as Lala Brooks joined to replace a very pregnant Merna Girard, who held on just long enough to sing at the session.

1964 The Beatles filmed a live concert for *A Hard Day's Night*, singing "She Loves You," "And I Love Her," "I Should Have Known Better," and "Tell Me Why" at the Scala Theatre in London. Phil Collins (then thirteen) was one of 350 paid child extras in the audience.

1967 Jimi Hendrix burned his guitar on stage for the first of many times to come when he "lit up" at Finsbury Park in London.

1995 Known as the "Mexican Madonna," Selena (Selena Quintanilla Perez) was a singer on the verge of greatness. She recorded five albums in Spanish, including the Latin pop chart #1 *Amor Prohibido*, and won a Grammy for her *Live* album in 1993. She was working on her first English-language album when she was shot to death by her fan-club president (who was embezzling from Selena) in a Corpus Christi, Texas, motel room. Her posthumous English album, *Dreaming of You*, sold more than a million copies.

Selena
dreaming of you

April

#1 Song 1972: "A Horse with No Name," America

Born: Amos Milburn, 1927; Rudolph Isley (The Isley Brothers), 1939; Phil Margo (The Tokens), 1942; Danny Brooks (The Dovells), 1942; Ronnie Lane (Faces), 1946; Jeff Porcaro (Toto), 1954

1958 Elvis Presley's twenty-ninth chart single was issued today. "Wear My Ring Around Your Neck" would reach #3 nationally while its B-side, "Doncha' Think It's Time" hit #21. "Ring" became Presley's seventh #1 R&B hit—an amazing accomplishment for a white artist.

1961 The Beatles returned to Hamburg, Germany, for a thirteen-week gig at The Top Ten Club, playing seven-hour sets weekdays and eight-hour stints on weekends. Bass player Stuart Sutcliffe rejoined the group at that time for occasional performances.

1984 Marvin Gaye was one of the legendary pop and R&B artists to come on the scene in the 1960s. He originally sang with The Marquees (Okeh Records), who became The New Moonglows. When producer Harvey Fuqua disbanded the group, he took Marvin with him to Motown where the essence of his abilities were nurtured to the tune of fifty-six chart hits from 1962 through 1982. After a violent dispute, Marvin Gaye was shot by his ranting reverend father, Marvin Gaye, Sr. in their Los Angeles home. Marvin, Jr. would have been forty-five the next day.

1985 The Singing Nun (Sister Luc-Gabrielle) had one of the all-time surprise hits when "Dominique" went to #1. The Belgian nun innocently recorded an album at Philips Records studio for her friends at the Fichermont Monastery when the execs heard the work and sent out a thousand copies for sale. A European hit, the album was issued in America and "Dominique" spent two months at #1. By 1966, Sister Luc left the monastery under her real name, Jeanine Deckers, to do charity work. Making the story even more unusual was her bizarre demise in a suicide pact with her female lover when the two overdosed on drugs and alcohol. She was fifty-two.

1989 Madonna's "Like a Prayer" hit #1 in the U.K. and would soon be #1 in the U.S. The promo video caused such a religious uproar that her tour was canceled, her sponsor Pepsi dropped her, and she was banned by the Vatican.

April

2

1957 Elvis performed in one of his rare concerts outside the U.S. at the Maple Leaf Gardens, Toronto, Canada. In fact, except for Canada, Presley never performed outside of America. One reason being Colonel Parker, his manager and reported illegal alien, was concerned he might not be able to get back in the U.S. once he left. Being as controlling a factor as he was, Parker certainly wouldn't have liked Elvis traipsing around Europe without him. On that occasion in Canada, Elvis first wore his now famous gold suit.

1960 Connie Francis won the Best Selling Female Artist award at the first annual National Association of Recording Merchandisers (NARM) music industry awards. She would win again in 1961 and 1962.

1970 Janis Joplin got a tattoo over her heart, which read, "One for the boys."

1977 Kenny Nolan's follow-up ("Love's Grown Deep") to the hit "I Like Dreamin'" (#3) charted reaching #20. Previously known only as a writer, he had two #1s ("Lady Marmalade" and "My Eyes Adored You") within two months of each other in late 1974 and early 1975.

Connie Francis

94

April
3

1959 England's BBC radio banned The Coasters' "Charlie Brown" because of its inclusion of the word "spitball." Two weeks after massive listener protests, it rescinded the ban.

1960 Elvis Presley, at his energetic and prolific best, recorded twelve songs in Nashville in one night including "It's Now or Never" (based on "O Sole Mio"), Little Willie John's "Fever," and "Are You Lonesome Tonight?"

1976 The Beatles classic "Yesterday," which was a hit in America in 1965, was released as a single in Britain for the first time, rising to #8. Unlike in the U.S., past hits in the U.K. are often re-released, and the success of "Yesterday" spurred EMI to reissue other such singles as "Penny Lane" (#32) and "Hey Jude" (#12).

1998 Rob Pilatus was a member of pop music's biggest fraud, Milli Vanilli, along with his friend Fabrice Morvan. The teen runaway and dancer-model found his way to Germany from L.A., where the duo were unearthed by Boney M producer Frank Farian. Their 7-million-selling album, including four hit singles, made them instant stars until it was discovered they didn't actually sing on their recordings and had to give back the Grammy they had won. The disgraced pseudo singer died in a German hotel of a drug and alcohol overdose today. He was only thirty-two.

April

#1 Song 1987: "Nothing's Gonna Stop Us Now," Starship

Born: Muddy Waters, 1915; Margo Sylvia (The Tune Weavers), 1936; Major Lance, 1941; Mick Mars (Mötley Crüe), 1956

1964 The Beatles dominated the American charts with twelve singles on the Top 100, including the top five places with "Can't Buy Me Love" (#1), "Twist & Shout" (#2), "She Loves You" (#3), "I Want to Hold Your Hand" (#4), and "Please Please Me" (#5). The others included "I Saw Her Standing There" (#31), "From Me to You" (#41), "Do You Want to Know a Secret" (#46), "All My Loving" (#58), "You Can't Do That" (#65), "Roll Over Beethoven" (#68), and "Thank You Girl" (#79). Within a week the total was 14 with the addition of "There's a Place" (#74) and "Love Me Do" (#81).

1964 Barbra Streisand's "People" charted en route to #5. It was the first of her forty-two hit 45s over the next thirty-two years.

1967 While visiting San Francisco, Paul McCartney met Jefferson Airplane, who were rehearsing at the Fillmore Auditorium. He brought them back to his place, where he and the band jammed and listened to an acetate recording of the as yet unreleased *Sgt. Pepper* album.

1973 Elvis Presley's satellite broadcast *Aloha from Hawaii* was shown on NBC-TV. The televised performance reached 57 percent of the nation's viewers. Even Elvis watched the taped show from his home.

1970 Janis Joplin reunited with Big Brother & the Holding Company for a concert at San Francisco's Fillmore West.

April 5

#1 Song 1975: "Lovin' You," Minnie Ripperton

Born: Tony Williams (The Platters), 1928; Ronnie White (The Miracles), 1939; David LaFlame (It's a Beautiful Day), 1941; Nick Caldwell (The Whispers), 1944; Agnetha Faltskog (ABBA), 1950

Died: Danny Rapp (Danny & the Juniors), 1983

1958 Johnny Mathis's *Greatest Hits* album hit the charts. It remained there for, what was then a record, 490 weeks (almost ten years!).

1963 The Beatles received their first award—a silver disc at EMI's offices in London—for sales exceeding 250,000 copies in the U.K. of their 45 *Please, Please Me*.

1984 Cyndi Lauper's "Girls Just Want to Have Fun" won the second annual Best Female Video at the American Video Awards.

1994 As the leader of the Seattle-based grunge rock band Nirvana, Kurt Cobain spent as much time depressed and drugged out as he did rockin'. He went on to establish the grunge movement in music nationally with #1 albums like *In Utero*. When he couldn't kill himself with sixty barbiturates and a bottle of champagne in Rome, Cobain, at the height of his career, blew himself away with a twenty-gauge shotgun while sitting in a chair and looking out the window of the room above his garage. He was twenty-seven years old.

1994 Rod Stewart donated his income from a concert at the Arrowhead Pond in Anaheim, California, to the Red Cross Earthquake Relief Fund.

97

April

6

#1 Song 1963: "He's So Fine," The Chiffons

Born: Michelle Phillips (The Mamas & the Papas), 1944; Bob Marley, 1945

1963 Sixteen-year-old Lesley Gore heard her recording of "It's My Party" on New York's WINS radio while driving home from school. The Quincy Jones–produced recording had only been cut a few days earlier (and wasn't even officially released yet).

1965 One of Elvis Presley's personal favorites, "Crying in the Chapel, " was released today. The Orioles standard was an overlooked, unused recording from five years ago and its unexpected success gave Presley an international hit, reaching #3 stateside and #1 in England. The million-seller was his biggest hit since "Bossa Nova Baby" in 1963.

1996 Mariah Carey's "Always Be My Baby" charted on its way to #1. It was her nineteenth hit in six years, eleven of which were #1.

1998 "The First Lady of Country Music," Alabama-native Tammy Wynette was a superstar with seventy hits between 1966 and 1980. Originally a beautician in Birmingham, she moved to Nashville in 1966 and began a string of twenty #1s, including the anti-feminist standard, "Stand By Your Man." She died from a blood clot in her lung while taking a nap on her couch. She was fifty-five.

Tammy Wynette

April 7

#1 Song 1973: "The Night the Lights Went Out in Georgia," Vicki Lawrence

Born: Billie Holiday, 1915; Charlie Thomas (The Drifters), 1937; Bill Kreutzmann (The Grateful Dead), 1946; Patricia Bennett (The Chiffons), 1947; Carol Douglas, 1948; John Oates (Hall & Oates), 1949; Janis Ian, 1951

1915 One of the all-time great blues singers, Eleanora Fagan Gough, a.k.a. Billie Holiday, was born today in Baltimore. She took her name from her favorite actress, silent-screen star Billie Dove, but her fans dubbed her "Lady Day."

1958 Norman Fox & the Rob Roys doo-wop classic "Dance, Girl Dance" (Backbeat, $75) was released.

1962 The Rolling Stones were formed when Mick Jagger, Keith Richards, and Brian Jones met at the Ealing Blues Club in London. Before forming the group, Jagger had been an ice-cream vendor and Richards was a ball boy on a tennis court.

1967 Disc jockey Tom "Big Daddy" Donahue began programming what would become known as FM progressive rock radio on San Francisco's KMPX.

1984 Forget about the British invasion of 1964. On this date in 1984, a record forty English singles held sway on the U.S. Top 100, although only two were in the Top 10, "Against All Odds" (Phil Collins, #3) and "Here Comes the Rain Again" (Eurythmics, #4).

April

8

1960 Elvis Presley's first album since returning from the Army was released. The aptly titled *Elvis Is Back!* shipped just four days after the recording sessions finished. The LP included a gatefold of army snapshots printed in advance. The release was so rushed that the song titles had to appear on a sticker.

1963 The son of Beatle John Lennon, Julian Lennon was born today. Living in a larger-than-life shadow, Julian still managed to carve his own niche with a number of hits in the late '80s, including "Too Late for Goodbyes" and "Valotte."

1997 Mother of writer-singer Hoyt Axton, Mae Boren Axton had a varied career, especially during a period in America when a woman's place was in the home. Mae was a country music deejay and became a publicist for country star Hank Snow in the early '50s. She also was a songwriter and brought a tune to manager Tom Parker at his hotel in Nashville. Parker liked it enough to give it to his budding star, Elvis Presley, who turned it into his first #1 (for eight weeks). The song was "Heartbreak Hotel." Mae died accidentally when she drowned in her hot tub at her Henderson, Tennessee, home. She was 82.

April 9

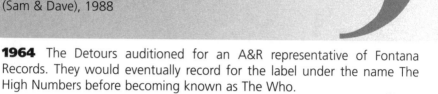

1964 The Detours auditioned for an A&R representative of Fontana Records. They would eventually record for the label under the name The High Numbers before becoming known as The Who.

1966 The Mamas & the Papas' only #1, "Monday, Monday," charted today.

1974 Janet Jackson, youngest of the nine Jackson family siblings, made her performance debut with The Jackson 5 at the MGM Grand Hotel in Las Vegas. She was seven years old.

1978 Donna Summer's "Last Dance" won an Oscar for Best Original Song at the fifty-first annual Academy Awards.

The Mamas & the Papas

April

10

#1 Song 1971: "Just My Imagination," The Temptations

Born: Nate Nelson (The Flamingos), 1932; Kenneth "Babyface" Edmonds, 1959; Brian Setzer (The Stray Cats), 1959

Died: Chuck Willis, 1958

1956 While performing for an all-white audience in Birmingham, Alabama, Nat "King" Cole was beaten senseless while onstage.

1962 Stuart Sutcliffe, The Beatles' first bass player, died of a brain hemorrhage in Hamburg, Germany, one day before John Lennon and Paul McCartney arrived to begin a seven-week engagement there. Stuart was only twenty-one. He had been with them when they were known as Johnny & the Moondogs, having joined in 1960.

1967 While in Los Angeles, Paul McCartney visited with John and Michelle Phillips of The Mamas & the Papas and later sat in on a session with The Beach Boys while they were recording "Vegetables" for their *Smiley Smile* album.

1993 Joan Baez sang from the back of a truck to refugees in Zagreb, Croatia, to benefit those of war-torn Bosnia and Croatia.

2000 *Star* magazine reported that the recently departed blues rocker Screamin' Jay Hawkins's dying wish was that his children meet each other, all fifty-seven of them! Hawkins had once boasted of having sex fourteen times a day when his career was at its peak (and apparently, so was he!).

April 11

#1 Song 1964: "Can't Buy Me Love,"
The Beatles

Born: Mark Stein (Vanilla Fudge), 1947;
Bobby McFerrin, 1950

1959 The Fleetwoods performed on Dick Clark's Saturday night show singing their #1 hit, "Come Softly To Me."

1956 Elvis Presley's "Heartbreak Hotel" single reached the one million sales mark, becoming Elvis's first gold record.

1961 The Marcels recorded their second and third singles, "Summertime" and "You Are My Sunshine," while their first single, "Blue Moon," was sitting atop the pop charts.

1961 Bob Dylan appeared at New York City's Gerde's Folk City in his first professional live gig opening for John Lee Hooker. Prior to that he lasted three weeks as a member of Bobby Vee's backing band, The Shadows, before he was fired.

1988 Jennifer Warnes and Bill Medley (of The Righteous Brothers) sang "(I've Had) The Time of My Life" at the Academy Awards. It became the third Warnes song to win an Oscar.

April

12

#1 Song 1969: "Aquarius/Let the Sun Shine In," The 5th Dimension

Born: Tiny Tim (Herbert Khaury), 1930; Herbie Hancock, 1940; John Kay (Steppenwolf), 1944; David Cassidy, 1950

1955 Billy Haley & the Comets made their first recordings for Decca, including "Rock Around the Clock." The group was previously known as Bill Haley & the Saddlemen and was mainly known for performing western swing music.

1956 The Four Lovers (formerly The Variatones) recorded their first six sides for RCA. In an unusual move, the label issued four of the six on two EP singles the same day in April, "You're the Apple of My Eye" (#62 pop) and "Honey Love." Within four years The Four Lovers would be calling themselves The Four Seasons.

1963 The Drifters recorded a sensational Leiber-Stoller song, "Only in America." Unfortunately, due to racial unrest in the country, the group's vocals were lifted from the track and replaced by Jay & the Americans, who had the hit. The Drifters recording was thought to be lost forever, but a copy found its way to Sweden and was issued as a bonus track on a Jay & the Americans CD in 1993.

1966 Jan Berry of Jan & Dean demolished his Corvette after colliding with a parked truck on Whittier Boulevard in Los Angeles. He was doing 60 mph at the time and has never fully recovered.

1975 Folk great Judy Collins's album *Judith* charted, reaching #17. It was her eleventh Top 200 hit collection since 1964 and contained "Suite: Judy Blue Eyes," written for her by Stephen Stills.

April 13

#1 Song 1957: "All Shook Up,"
Elvis Presley

Born: Jack Casady (Jefferson Airplane), 1944;
Al Green, 1946; Peabo Bryson, 1951

Died: Todd Storz, 1964

1956 While performing at the Municipal Auditorium in Amarillo, Texas, Elvis learned he was going to be booked in Las Vegas for the first time at the Frontier Hotel. His manager, Colonel Parker, suggested that he be billed as "America's Only Atomic Powered Singer."

1963 Barbra Streisand's *The Barbra Streisand Album* debuted on the pop hit list and rose to a million-selling #8. It was the first of forty-six albums she would place on the Top 200 over the next thirty-two years while winning the 1963 Grammy for Best Album of the Year.

1964 Todd Storz created the Top 40 radio style in the mid '50s at a radio station in Omaha, Nebraska, that his father had bought for him. After seeing teens play pretty much the same songs on local jukeboxes, he decided a structured format of a hit list containing forty records would be successful. He was right as his station, KOWH, went to #1 in the local ratings. He died of a cerebral hemorrhage today at thirty-nine.

1965 The Beatles recorded the title song to *Help!* at Abbey Road Studios after a day of working on the film at Britain's Twickenham Film Studios. It was originally done in a slow, acoustic arrangement, but producer George Martin felt it should be done faster, and though John Lennon had misgivings, that's the way it was done.

1967 The Rolling Stones debuted behind the Iron Curtain in Warsaw, Poland, but when a riot broke out, police dispersed the crowd with tear gas.

2000 Metallica became the first major act to file suit against Napster, Inc.—an online company whose software allows Internet users to swap digital music files for free—for copyright infringement.

April

14

#1 Song 1962: "Johnny Angel," Shelly Fabares

Born: Ritchie Blackmore (Deep Purple), 1945

1963 The Beatles attended a performance of The Rolling Stones at the Crawdaddy Club in the Station Hotel, Richmond, England. Wearing identical long leather jackets with matching hats they picked up in Hamburg, the group later elicited a comment from Stones lead, Mick Jagger, who referenced their look as that of a "four-headed monster."

1965 It was officially announced that the film called *Eight Arms to Hold You* starring The Beatles was now going to be called *Help!* Various other titles were considered and rejected, including George Harrison's suggestion, *Who's Been Sleeping in My Porridge*.

1969 Elvis Presley's comeback single in every sense of the word "In the Ghetto," with a flip side of the Chuck Jackson 1962 hit (#3), "Any Day Now," was released today. It would eventually sell over 2 million units and be his first Top 5 hit since "Crying in the Chapel," four years earlier.

1999 Anthony Newley was a prominent singer-lyricist-playwright-actor who started his quest for success as a fourteen-year-old London school dropout. Along the way he played the Artful Dodger in the 1948 film, *Oliver Twist*; had hit records in Britain with "Do You Mind" and "Why" in 1960; co-wrote the hit stage play, *Stop the World: I Want to Get Off*, which earned him a Grammy for the song, "What Kind of Fool Am I"; and co-wrote "Goldfinger" for Shirley Bassey, the worldwide hit from the James Bond film; among other notable successes. He died of cancer at his Florida home at age sixty-seven.

April 15

#1 Song 1989: "She Drives Me Crazy,"
Fine Young Cannibals

Born: Bessie Smith, 1894; Allan Clarke
(The Hollies), 1942; Dave Edmunds, 1944;
Samantha Fox, 1966

1942 Allan Clarke, lead singer of The Hollies, was born today. The group, originally called The Fourtones and then The Deltas, finally decided to name themselves after rock favorite, Buddy Holly. The band had twenty-four hits between 1964 and 1983, including "Bus Stop," "He Ain't Heavy, He's My Brother" and "Long Cool Woman (In a Black Dress)."

1970 One of the great music industry moguls of the 1950s, George Goldner started a series of record labels in New York City that would cater to teen tastes, predominantly via vocal groups that he discovered, recorded, and promoted. His first label was Rama in 1955 that included The Valentines, The Heartbeats, The Harptones, The Joytones (one of the first female rock 'n' roll vocal groups), The Pretenders (with lead Jimmy Jones later of "Handy Man" fame), The Buccaneers, The Wrens, and The Crows, whose "Gee" is considered one of the first rock 'n' roll hits. He then formed End, Gone, and Gee labels, which hosted more '50s stars like The Cleftones, The Flamingos, Frankie Lymon & the Teenagers, The Dubs, Little Anthony & the Imperials, The Chantels, and many more. Due to his gambling addiction, George wound up selling each of his labels, but was back in the '60s with the girl-group label Red Bird. He died of a heart attack at age fifty today.

1972 Roberta Flack's "The First Time Ever I Saw Your Face" reached #1 and stayed there for six weeks. It was the longest running #1 by a female solo artist since Gogi Grant's "The Wayward Wind" in 1956.

1989 Roy Orbison hit the pop Top 10 for the first time in over twenty-four years with "You Got It." Unfortunately, the Texas legend never knew of his chart rebirth. He had died four months earlier.

April

16

#1 Song 1977: "Don't Give Up on Us Baby," David Soul

Born: Roy Hamilton, 1929; Bobby Vinton, 1935; Dusty Springfield, 1939; Gerry Rafferty (Stealers Wheels), 1947; Jimmy Osmond (The Osmonds), 1963

1956 Elvis Presley performed at the Memorial Coliseum in Corpus Christi, Texas. Immediately after the show, the building manager outlawed rock 'n' roll shows at the Coliseum, when numerous fans and their parents complained that the performance was "vulgar."

1966 Bob Dylan's "Rainy Day Women #12 & 35" charted on its way to #2.

1990 Bonnie Raitt, Anita Baker, Natalie Cole, and Mica Paris sang "Blowin' in the Wind" at Nelson Mandela—An International Tribute to a Free South Africa Concert at Wembley Stadium in England.

1999 Skip Spence was a drummer and guitarist who had spent time as a member of both Jefferson Airplane and Moby Grape during the heyday of the '60s San Francisco rock era. Diagnosed as a paranoid schizophrenic, his heavy drug use didn't help. Probably his greatest contribution to music was financially helping a San Jose band named Pud, which developed into The Doobie Brothers. He died of lung cancer at age fifty-two, two days shy of his birthday.

Bob Dylan

108

April

17

#1 Song 1971: "Joy to the World," Three Dog Night

Born: Billy Fury, 1941

Died: Felix Pappalardi (bass player for Mountain and producer of Cream), 1983

1960 Legendary rockabilly artist Eddie Cochran picked up his brother's guitar in their Minnesota home and never put it down. Discovered by songwriter Jerry Capehart, the country-western singer turned to rock 'n' roll after hearing Elvis Presley records. Best known for his 1958 #8 hit, "Summertime Blues," Cochran found the British loved him even more than the Americans. Touring England with fellow rocker, Gene Vincent, the two were on their way to London's airport after their last performance when the chauffeured car they were in blew a tire and slammed into a lamppost throwing Eddie onto the pavement and killing him. Vincent and songwriter Sharon Sheeley were also badly injured but recovered. Eddie was only twenty-one. Ironically, the driver was not injured at all.

1971 Carly Simon's mesmerizing "That's the Way I've Always Heard It Should Be" charted, eventually reaching #10. It became the first of twenty-three hits through 1989 for the daughter of the Simon & Schuster publishing empire.

1976 Ann and Nancy Wilson of Heart charted, on their way to #35 and their first of thirty hits through 1993, when "Crazy on You" jumped on the Hot 100 today.

1993 Elton John's single "A Simple Life" reached #30 in America, making him the only artist with at least one Top 40 hit in twenty-four straight years, surpassing Elvis Presley who had twenty-three.

2000 Worldwide music sales hit a record $38.5 billion dollars on over 3.8 billion units. Thanks to record piracy and illegal Internet downloading, it's been downhill ever since.

April

#1 Song 1970: "Let It Be," The Beatles

Born: Michael Vickers (Manfred Mann), 1941; Skip Spence (Moby Grape), 1946

1963 The Beatles performed at the Royal Albert Hall in London along with Del Shannon, The Springfields, Rolf Harris, and Kenny Lynch, among others. The Beatles later taught Shannon (of "Runaway" fame) their song "From Me to You." Two-and-a-half months later the song, as recorded by Shannon, hit the American charts, making it the first Lennon-McCartney song to not only be recorded by a non-British act, but the first to chart by one (Shannon's version went to #77).

1966 The Lovin' Spoonful performed at The Marquee in London, where John Lennon and George Harrison attended their show.

1970 Joe Cocker charted with "The Letter," reaching #7 with a song that was a hit for The Box Tops (#1) only three years earlier.

1981 Gary "U.S." Bonds's "This Little Girl" was released reaching #11. It was written and co-produced for him by Bruce Springsteen, a longtime fan of Bonds. It was also Gary's first hit in nineteen years!

1981 Elvis Presley's "Lovin' Arms" charted country today, reaching #8. Though he was the "King of Rock 'n' Roll," Elvis still managed to chart country 84 times!

April 19

#1 Song 1975: "Philadelphia Freedom,"
The Elton John Band

Born: Alan Price (The Animals), 1941;
Mark Volman (The Turtles), 1947

1941 Alan Price, the keyboard player for The Animals, was born today. Originally called The Alan Price Combo in 1958, they became The Animals by the time their hit version of "House of the Rising Sun" reached #1 in 1964. Price left in 1965, but returned in 1976 and again in 1983 for reunions.

1960 Elvis Presley, who developed a fear of flying, boarded a train to Los Angeles from Memphis to begin shooting his new film *G.I. Blues*, a story about a young U.S. soldier in Germany.

1975 Captain & Tennille charted with "Love Will Keep Us Together" (#1). It became the first of fourteen hits—six were Top 5—over the next five years.

1980 Country charts, long dominated by males, had a Top 5 today that included Crystal Gayle, Dottie West, Debby Boone, Emmylou Harris, and Tammy Wynette.

1986 The Bangles reached #2 with "Manic Monday" (written by Prince) but could not displace his "Kiss" from the #1 spot.

Captain & Tennille

April

20

#1 Song 1959: "Come Softly to Me," The Fleetwoods

Born: Johnny Tillotson, 1939; Ronald Mundy (The Marcels), 1940; Luther Vandross, 1951

1954 Elvis Presley started working at Crown Electric, where he earned $1 an hour driving a truck, delivering supplies to building sites. He aspired to become an electrician.

1964 The Hollies' Allan Clarke was battered by a blitzkrieg of fans at Shoreham Airport, sending him into shock.

1970 Elvis Presley's "The Wonder of You," which was recorded live at his last performance in Las Vegas, was released. It would become another of Presley's ballad standards over the decades and top off at #9 on the Top 100 singles charts.

1991 Steve Marriott was a British-born guitarist who made a name for himself with the bands Humble Pie and Small Faces. He originally worked with Peter Frampton in Steve Marriot & the Moments in 1964. He then joined the pop-rock Small Faces (named because no one was over 5'6" tall) and had several hits, including "Itchycoo Park." He died today at his sixteenth-century home outside London from smoke inhalation during a fire started by a neglected cigarette. He was forty-four.

Luther Vandross

112

April 21

#1 Song 1956: "Heartbreak Hotel," Elvis Presley

Born: Clara Ward, 1924; Ernie Maresca (Sevilles), 1939; Alan Warner (The Foundations), 1947; Iggy Pop, 1947; Paul Davis, 1948

1956 Melba Records President Morty Craft announced the signing of a new group from Brooklyn called The Tokens with a young lead singer named Neil Sedaka.

1956 Eydie Gorme charted with "Too Close for Comfort" (#39), her first of seventeen Top 100 singles through 1972.

1962 Dion & the Del-Satins charted with "Lovers Who Wander" (#3 pop, #16 R&B).

1963 The Rolling Stones and The Beatles met for the first time at The Crawdaddy Club in West London, where the Stones were the regular Sunday night performers.

1978 Sandy Denny was a smooth and tender-voiced folk vocalist and member of the British group, Fairport Convention. Originally a member of the folk band, The Strawbs in 1967, Denny recorded the original version of "Who Knows Where the Time Goes" with Fairport (later made popular by Judy Collins) during her tenure between 1968 and 1970. She died by accident after falling down a flight of stairs at a friend's home at age thirty-one.

April

22

#1 Song 1967 "Something Stupid," Nancy and Frank Sinatra

Born: Glen Campbell, 1936; Mel Carter, 1939; Peter Frampton, 1950; Ace Frehley (Kiss), 1951

1969 The Carpenters signed with A&M Records. Two years earlier they were part of a group called Spectrum that recorded eleven sides for RCA, though the album was never released.

1972 Elvis Presley's album of gospel songs, *He Touched Me*, charted today, reaching #79 on the national pop 100 list, an amazing feat for a gospel album.

1990 More than 750,000 people crammed Central Park in New York City for the Earth Day festivities, including a show starring Hall & Oates, Ben E. King, and The B-52's.

1995 The Beatles landed their seventieth chart single on the U.S. Top 100 when "Baby It's You" hit today (#67). It was originally recorded on a live BBC broadcast in London for the program *Pop Goes The Beatles* on June 1, 1963, and charted twenty-six years after the group broke up.

April

#1 Song 1983: "Come On Eileen," Dexys Midnight Runners

Born: Roy Orbison, 1936; Ray Peterson, 1939; Steve Clark (Def Leppard), 1960

1960 Steve Clark, the guitarist for the hard rock foursome Def Leppard, was born in Sheffield, England, today. Weaned on classical guitar, he joined the band in 1979 and played on all their nineteen American hits, including "Love Bites" and "Pour Some Sugar on Me."

1962 The single "My Bonnie"/"The Saints" was released in the U.S. on Decca by Tony Sheridan and The Beat Brothers. By this time, John Lennon and Paul McCartney had written more than seventy original songs though neither song on their single was written by the future Beatles. Today, an original 45 RPM copy of that single is worth more than $15,000!

1976 At the low point in his career and ten years after his last Top 40 hit, Roy Orbison performed at The Van-a-Rama Auto Exposition in Cincinnati, Ohio, before a crowd of less than 100 people. Adding to the degradation, it was his birthday.

1986 A flamboyant pianist-singer Esquerita (Eskew Reeder, Jr.) made Liberace look like Axel Rose by comparison. Born in South Carolina, the gospel singer sang with The Heavenly Echoes, but his falsetto sound and frantic piano playing made him a natural for rock 'n' roll. Discovered by Gene Vincent, he recorded several poorly promoted discs on Capitol, but only began to receive recognition after Little Richard acknowledged him as a major influence. He died today of AIDS in New York at age fifty-three.

April

24

#1 Song 1961: "Runaway," Del Shannon

Born: Freddie Scott, 1933; Barbra Streisand, 1942; Doug Clifford (Creedence Clearwater Revival), 1945

1958 The Pastels ("Been So Long" #24 pop, #4 R&B) appeared on Alan Freed's *Big Beat* show at Milwaukee's Riverside Theater along with Frankie Lymon & the Teenagers, Chuck Berry, Jerry Lee Lewis, and Buddy Holly & the Crickets. Pastels lead Big Big Dee Irwin went on to solo success in the '60s with "Swingin' on a Star." The group was formed on an Air Force base in Narsarssuak, Greenland.

1961 Robert Zimmerman performed on record for the first time when he played harmonica for Harry Belafonte's *Midnight Special* album and earned $50. He soon became better known for his songs and singing as Bob Dylan.

1962 Patti LaBelle & the Bluebelles hit the Hot 100 with a song they hadn't recorded! "I Sold My Heart to the Junkman" was actually done by The Starlets (featuring Dynetta Boone) who were signed to Chicago-based Pam Records. While touring in Philadelphia they recorded "Junkman" for a used car dealer who issued the rocker as by his own unsuspecting Blue Belles. It rose to #15 as Patti and company rose to stardom, while The Starlets drifted into obscurity.

1965 Actress-singer Julie Andrews charted with her only Top 100 single, "Supercalifragilisticexpialidocious" (#66).

Harry Belafonte's Midnight Special

#1 Song 1960: "Stuck on You,"
Elvis Presley

Born: Ella Fitzgerald, 1917; Albert King, 1923; Jerry Leiber (Leiber & Stoller), 1933; Stu Cook (CCR), 1945; Bjorn Ulvaeus (ABBA), 1945; Mike Brown (Left Banke), 1949

1960 Dion & the Belmonts charted with "When You Wish Upon a Star" only months before Dion split to go solo.

1960 The Angels debut disc, *P.S. I Love You*, was released under their original name, The Starlets.

1967 Janis Ian's "Society's Child," marred in controversy over its interracial lyrics, stalled at radio until famed composer-conductor Leonard Bernstein featured the song on his CBS-TV special, *Inside Pop—The Rock Revolution*. By May it charted, topping off at #14.

1987 Madonna became the only female artist to have four #1s in England when "La Isla Bonita" topped its hit list.

April

26

#1 Song 1969: "Aquarius/Let the Sun Shine in," The 5th Dimension

Born: Ma Rainey, 1886; Duane Eddy, 1938; Maurice Williams (The Zodiacs), 1938; Bobby Rydell, 1942; Gary Wright (Spooky Tooth), 1943; Roger Taylor (Duran Duran), 1960

1957 Harry Belafonte signed for the then unheard of sum of $1 million with RCA Records. Known as the "King of Calypso," Harry was actually from The Bronx.

1964 The Beatles performed before 10,000 fans at the New Musical Express 1963–64 Annual Awards, where Roger Moore (of James Bond fame) presented them with their awards. The concert was held at Empire Pool in Wembley, England.

1964 The Rolling Stones self-titled album was issued. It went on to #11 and began a string of more than forty albums, charting in the next five decades.

1969 Dorothy Morrison & the Edwin Hawkins Singers hit the pop charts with the pure gospel song, "Oh Happy Day," which broke all barriers on its way to #4 and million-selling status.

1982 Rod Stewart was robbed on Hollywood Boulevard in Los Angeles while standing alongside his $50,000 Porsche (well, at least they didn't pilfer the Porsche!).

April

#1 Song 1963: "I Will Follow Him,"
Little Peggy March

Born: Peter Ham (Badfinger), 1947;
Kate Pierson (The B-52's), 1948;
Sheena Easton, 1959

Died: Vickie Sue Robinson, 2000

1960 Elvis Presley began work on the soundtrack recording for *G.I. Blues* at RCA studios in Hollywood. He spent the next eleven hours recording in his full dress Army uniform. Although the film was about Army life in Germany, all of Elvis's scenes were shot on the Paramount lot.

1964 John Lennon's book, *In His Own Write*, was published in America by Simon & Schuster. The same day, the 45 "P.S. I Love You"/"Love Me Do" came out on Tollie as did Tony Sheridan and The Beatles' "Why" on MGM.

1976 David Bowie was held captive for several hours by customs officers on the Polish-Russian border while they confiscated his newly acquired treasure-trove of Nazi memorabilia.

1993 Aretha Franklin's first TV special was taped at New York's Neaderlander Theatre and featured duets of "Since You've Been Gone" and "Natural Women" with Bonnie Raitt and Gloria Estefan.

1993 Prince announced he would no longer record. Forty-one days later, he changed his name to the combined symbols of men and women. By 1994, he was being called "The Artist Formerly Known as Prince."

2000 Daughter of folk singer Jolly Robinson, Vicki Sue Robinson was an actress-singer and Philadelphia native who had one of the quintessential disco hits of the '70s with "Turn the Beat Around." She performed at the Philadelphia Folk Festival when she was six and was in the original cast of the Broadway musicals *Hair* and *Jesus Christ Superstar*. She died of cancer at age forty-five.

April

28

1958 The Drifters recorded their classic, "Drip Drop." It was the last charter (#58 pop) for the original group. The "new" Drifters would actually be a group known as The Crowns (formerly The 5 Crowns) with a young lead singer named Ben E. King.

1965 While filming *Help!* in London, The Beatles were presented with their recent Grammy Award for *A Hard Day's Night* in the category of Best Vocal Performance by a Group or Duo. The presentation was made on the set by actor Peter Sellers.

1966 The Beatles recorded "Eleanor Rigby," which was originally titled by Paul McCartney as "Miss Daisy Hawkins." He wasn't happy with the title, wanting something more realistic and came up with Eleanor after seeing a clothing shop named Rigby in Bristol, England.

1981 Paul McCartney's post-Beatles group, Wings, broke up.

1988 B.W. (Louis) Stevenson was a country-rock artist from Dallas who was best known for his hit, "My Maria." He also wrote and charted with the song "Shambala," which was a bigger hit as recorded by Three Dog Night. By the way, the B.W. stood for Buckwheat, a nickname he picked up in the Army. He died of a heart attack in Nashville on this day.

April 29

Born: April Stevens, 1936; Bob Miranda (Happenings), 1942; Klaus Voorman (Manfred Mann), 1942; Tommy James, 1947; Carnie Wilson (Wilson Phillips), 1968

1967 Cindy Birdsong (Patti LaBelle and the Bluebelles) made her stage debut as replacement for Florence Ballard in The Supremes at The Hollywood Bowl in a benefit concert for the UCLA School of Music.

1968 The musical *Hair* opened on Broadway at the Biltmore Theater in New York. It ran for over 1,750 performances.

1976 Bruce Springsteen was thrown out of Graceland after sneaking in to see Elvis.

1993 Starting as a classical musician playing piano and violin, Mick Ronson switched to guitar and rock 'n' roll to play behind David Bowie during the peak of Bowie's career in the 1970s. By the mid '70s, he was playing in Mott the Hoople and with Bob Dylan. He died today in London of liver cancer at forty-six.

The musical Hair

April
30

#1 Song 1966: "Good Lovin,"
The Rascals

Born: Johnny Horton, 1925; Willie
Nelson, 1933; Bobby Vee, 1943;
Merrill Osmond (The Osmonds), 1953

Died: Muddy Waters, 1983

1954 The McGuire Sisters' "Goodnight, Sweetheart, Goodnight" was released and became their first Top 10 hit (#7). The group would amass thirty-three Top 100 singles by 1961.

1957 Elvis worked on the soundtrack for *Jailhouse Rock* at Radio Recorders in Hollywood and met the writers of the title song (who also wrote his hit "Hound Dog") for the first time, Jerry Leiber and Mike Stoller.

1965 Herman's Hermits & the Zombies began their first U.S. tour. They went on to have greater success in America than in their native Britain.

1966 Roy Orbison hit the Top 100 for the twenty-sixth time when his single "Twinkle Toes" charted on its way to #39. He would not hit the Top 40 again for twenty-six years until his comeback single, "You Got It," charted, reaching #9 in 1989.

1983 Muddy Waters (McKinley Morganfield) was a legendary blues man from Rolling Fork, Mississippi. Influenced by the likes of Robert Johnson, he migrated to Chicago, where he recorded such classics as "Rollin' Stone," "I Got My Mojo Workin'," and "I'm Your Hoochie Coochie Man." He influenced hundreds of '50s and '60s rockers from Brits like Eric Clapton, The Rolling Stones, and Eric Burdon to Americans like Paul Butterfield and Mike Bloomfield. He went on to earn six Grammy Awards. Muddy Waters died of a heart attack at age sixty-eight in Chicago.

Muddy Waters

May 1

#1 Song 1982: "I Love Rock 'n' Roll,"
Joan Jett

Born: Judy Collins, 1939; Rita Coolidge, 1944;
Reather Dixon (The Bobbettes), 1944; Ray Parker
Jr., 1954

1961 Tony Orlando appeared on *American Bandstand* to sing his first hit,
"Half Way to Paradise" and made his TV debut with his fly open.

1965 Spike Jones (Lindley Armstrong Jones) was a 1940s bandleader who
scored eighteen chart hits between 1942 and 1943. What made Spike
unique was his zany approach to musical arrangements of popular music.
His wacky versions of standards from "The William Tell Overture" and "I
Saw Mommy Kissing Santa Claus" to the outrageous "Cocktails for Two,"
which included cowbells, whistles, and gunshots as punctuating instruments made him the king of the unconventional bandleaders. He died today
of emphysema at age fifty-four.

1966 In a show that could only have happened in the '60s, Roy Orbison
performed with numerous NME poll winners at a concert in Wembly,
England, including The Beatles, The Spencer Davis Group, The Fortunes,
Herman's Hermits, Cliff Richard, The Rolling Stones, The Seekers, The Small
Faces, Dusty Springfield, The Walker Brothers, The Who, and The Yardbirds.
The Beatles played a fifteen-minute set. It was their last live performance in
Great Britain.

1974 The Carpenters performed at a White House state dinner at the
request of President Nixon in honor of West German Chancellor Willy Brandt.

1998 The Vocal Group Hall of Fame and Museum opened in Sharon,
Pennsylvania. The hall was the brainchild of Tony Butala, lead singer of The
Lettermen.

May

2

#1 Song 1970: "ABC," The Jackson 5

Born: Link Wray, 1935; Engelbert Humperdinck, 1936; Randy Cain III (The Delfonics), 1945; Goldy McJohn (Steppenwolf), 1945; Lesley Gore, 1946; Lou Gramm (Foreigner), 1950

1957 Elvis Presley recorded his immortal hit, "Jailhouse Rock." The multi-million selling single spent seven weeks at #1 and was a worldwide smash as the featured recording in the film of the same name.

1960 Jeannie Black's answer record to Jim Reeves's "He'll Have to Go," "He'll Have to Stay," charted climbing to #4.

1964 Keith Moon made his first appearance as drummer for The Who (then calling themselves The Detours) at a twenty-first birthday party at a British pub. Fifteen years to the day he was replaced by Kenney Jones (Small Faces) after his death.

1964 The Beatles' "Can't Buy Me Love" single spent its last of five weeks at #1 in America. It was beaten out for a sixth week by Louis Armstrong's "Hello Dolly."

Keith Moon

May 3

#1 Song 1980: "Call Me," Blondie

Born: Pete Seeger (The Weavers), 1919; James Brown, 1933; Frankie Valli (The Four Seasons), 1937; Mary Hopkin, 1950; Christopher Cross, 1951

1960 Cathy Jean & the Roommates recorded "Please Love Me Forever" (#12) though the lead singer hadn't ever met the group! Cathy did her vocals and left the studio before the group arrived to do the backgrounds.

1962 The Platters, America's first ambassadors of rock 'n' roll, began a ten-day tour of Spain. Afterward, they would become the first American rock 'n' roll act to perform behind the Iron Curtain when they appeared in Poland.

1965 The Beatles did some location shooting for the film *Help!* on the Salisbury Plain in England with the support of the British Army's Third Tank Division. (No, it wasn't to protect them from screaming fans. They actually participated in a scene.)

1984 After breaking up in 1976, Deep Purple regrouped. Rumor has it they (Ritchie Blackmore, Roger Glover, Jon Lord, Ian Gillan, and Ian Paice) were each offered $12 million to reunite.

1988 Madonna began her run on Broadway at the Royal Theater in *Speed the Plow* with Ron Silver and Joe Mantegna.

May

#1 Song 1974: "The Locomotion," Grand Funk Railroad

Born: Dick Dale, 1937; Tyrone Davis, 1938; Nickolas Ashford (Ashford & Simpson), 1943; Peggy Santiglia (The Angels), 1944; Jackie Jackson (Jacksons), 1951

1956 A story in the Memphis Press Scimitar quoted Elvis Presley about acts he respected: "I like Crosby, Como, Sinatra, all the big ones. They had to be good to get there. I've always been kind of partial to Dean Martin. I also like The Four Lads."

1968 Jefferson Airplane performed at The Fillmore East in New York. They went on to headline there eighteen times over the next three years.

1969 Tommy James & the Shondells' agent turned down an offer for the act to perform at Woodstock, calling it "a stupid gig on a pig farm in upstate New York."

1969 Actor Peter Sellers and Ringo Starr hosted a party at a swank London club to mark the completion of filming of *The Magic Christian*. John Lennon, Paul McCartney, and their wives attended, along with celebrities, including Sean Connery, George Peppard, Richard Harris, Christopher Lee, and Roger Moore.

1987 The white, Jewish, classically trained flutist Paul Butterfield became the unlikely exponent of blues to white America in the mid '60s. His deep reverence for the blues developed when he fell in with the likes of Muddy Waters and Little Walter. He formed The Paul Butterfield Blues Band in 1963, backed Bob Dylan when the folk legend turned electric and performed at Woodstock in 1969. He recorded numerous albums, before intestinal degradation from drugs and drink took him at age forty-four in his Los Angeles home.

May 5

#1 Song 1956: "Heartbreak Hotel," Elvis Presley

Born: Johnnie Taylor, 1938

Died: Clarence Quick (Dell Vikings), 1983

1958 Well before her first hit as a songwriter and recording artist, Carole King had her first 45, "The Right Girl," released today.

1958 The Coasters' "Yakety Yak" (Atco) was issued. Though they had six Top 10 hits, this turned out to be their only #1.

1963 Lesley Gore's debut single, "It's My Party," was rush released when producer Quincy Jones found out that Phil Spector was planning on recording the song with The Crystals. In a story that could only happen in the '60s, the record was recorded on a Monday, manufactured on Tuesday, and on the air by Wednesday!

1968 Buffalo Springfield disbanded after playing their last concert in Long Beach, California.

1968 Mary Hopkin's success with "Those Were the Days" (#1 U.S. & U.K.) occurred thanks to famed model Twiggy, who saw the pert songstress perform on Britain's TV talent show *Opportunity Knocks*, called friend Paul McCartney, and insisted he sign her. He did and she went on to have one of the biggest hits of the year.

Buffalo Springfield

May 6

#1 Song 1972: "The First Time," Roberta Flack

Born: Herb Cox (The Cleftones), 1939; Colin Earl (Mungo Jerry), 1942; Bob Seger, 1945

Died: Paul Wilson (The Flamingos), 1988

1957 Rick Nelson charted for the first time with a cover of Fats Domino's "I'm Walking." The song rose to #4 while its B-side, "A Teenager's Romance," reached #2. It was the beginning of the teen idol's recording career that would encompass 54 chart singles through 1973.

1967 Hit songwriter and former lead of The Raindrops ("The Kind of Boy You Can't Forget"), Ellie Greenwich made her only solo chart appearance with "I Want You to Be My Baby" (#83).

1969 The Beatles recorded "You Never Give Me Your Money" at Olympic Sound Studios on one of the rare occasions they recorded anywhere but at Abbey Road Studios, which their new album would be named after.

1973 After eighteen singles and seven smash albums with partner and high school friend Art Garfunkel, Paul Simon played his first solo gig at the Music Hall in Boston.

1992 Whitney Houston performed on her first network TV special, *Whitney Houston—This Is My Life* on ABC-TV.

The Beatles' Abbey Road

May 7

#1 Song 1966: "Monday, Monday,"
The Mamas & the Papas

Born: Johnny Maestro (The Crests), 1939;
Jimmy Ruffin, 1939

1953 Clyde McPhatter signed with Atlantic Records as lead of The Drifters. When Atlantic President Ahmet Ertegun heard that McPhatter had left The Dominoes, he chased the young vocalist down and went about building The Drifters around him. Contrary to public opinion, the group was not named after vagabond travelers but after a bird called a "drifter."

1966 Soul superstar James Brown appeared at the Memphis Coliseum and, after getting Elvis Presley's number from one of his friends, tried to call him during the day. Every time he called, however, he was told that Elvis was asleep. Very likely the truth as Presley, as with most entertainers, was a night owl.

1968 The Move's use of explosives caused a riot at the Rome Pop Festival.

1980 Bill Haley, suffering from a brain tumor, nevertheless set off on a performance tour of South Africa.

1998 Eddie Rabbitt was a hit country-pop artist from East Orange, New Jersey. Starting as a Nashville songwriter, his big break came when Elvis Presley recorded Eddie's "Kentucky Rain." He had forty-three country hits, including seventeen #1s. Among them were "Every Which Way but Loose," "On Second Thought," and a cover of Dion's "The Wanderer." He died of lung cancer at fifty-six.

May

#1 Song 1971: "Joy to the World," Three Dog Night

Born: Rick Nelson, 1940; Gary Glitter, 1940; Toni Tennille (Captain & Tennille), 1943; Paul Samwell-Smith (The Yardbirds), 1943; Alex Van Halen, 1953

1940 From radio to TV to teen idol, Rick Nelson—the youngest son of bandleader Ozzie Nelson and singer-wife Harriet—turned his TV exposure into fifty-four chart records between 1957 and 1973. Born today, Rick is best known for "Poor Little Fool" and "Travelin' Man," He also starred in such films as *Rio Bravo* and *Love and Kisses*. The teen idol was inducted into the Rock and Roll Hall of Fame in 1987. He died in a plane crash in Texas at age forty-five. His daughter, Tracy, is a well-known actress and his twin sons have recorded under the name Nelson.

1961 Darlene Love and The Blossoms, who were the premier vocal backup singers for everyone from Elvis to Dionne Warwick, finally earned some attention with a single of their own when "Son-in-Law" charted, reaching #79. It was their only Top 100 single and the answer record to Ernie K-Doe's "Mother-in-Law."

1964 Little Richard appeared on Britain's *Ready, Steady Go* TV show with Carl Perkins and The Swingin' Blue Jeans.

1965 Nine of the Top 10 hits in America were from British or Australian acts led by #1, "Mrs. Brown You've Got a Lovely Daughter" (Herman's Hermits). The only domestic charter was #2, "Count Me In" by Gary Lewis & the Playboys.

1971 Ronnie Spector breached the Hot 100 with "Try Some, Buy Some" (#77), produced by George Harrison and Phil Spector. It was her only chart 45 without the Ronettes.

May 9

#1 Song 1964: "Hello Dolly,"
Louis Armstrong

Born: Sonny Curtis (The Crickets), 1937;
David Prater (Sam & Dave), 1937; Tommy Roe,
1942; Richie Furay (Poco), 1944; Billy Joel, 1949

1960 Connie Francis charted with "Everybody's Somebody's Fool" (#1). Of her fifty-six Hot 100 hits, it turned out to be her biggest.

1962 To add insult to injury, the same tapes that convinced Dick Rowe of Decca Records in London to turn down The Beatles were given to George Martin of Parlophone/EMI by Brian Epstein at Abbey Road Studios. Martin offered the band a tentative recording contract based on the tapes without having seen them play.

1973 Mick Jagger donated $350,000 to help victims of the Nicaraguan earthquake.

1974 Melanie performed with Bob Dylan and Pete Seeger at New York's Felt Forum in the Friends of Chile benefit concert to aid Chilean refugees.

1999 Shel Silverstein was a cartoonist and writer for *Playboy* in 1953 who became a revered musical humorist with many hit songs such as "Cover of Rolling Stone," "Sylvia's Mother" (both hits for Dr. Hook & the Medicine Show), and Johnny Cash's "A Boy Named Sue." The Chicago resident also scored the acclaimed *Postcard from the Edge* film and received an Oscar nomination for his song "I'm Checkin' Out." He passed away at age sixty-six from heart problems at his Key West, Florida, home.

Shel Silverstein

May 10

#1 Song 1986: "West End Girls," Pet Shop Boys

Born: Fats Domino, 1929; Larry Williams, 1935; Danny Rapp (Danny & the Juniors), 1941; Donovan, 1946; Dave Mason, 1946; Bono (U2), 1960

1960 London promoter Larry Parnes came to Liverpool looking for an inexpensive band to back English rocker Billy Fury. Calling themselves The Silver Beatles, the future Beatles auditioned at the Wyvern Social Club in Liverpool and were offered the job.

1963 The Rolling Stones recorded their first single, the obscure Chuck Berry tune "Come On."

1964 Dusty Springfield performed her hit "I Only Want to Be with You" on The Ed Sullivan Show.

1969 The Turtles performed at the White House and leader Mark Volman celebrated by falling off the stage…four times! Then they spent the night in the Lincoln Bedroom smoking pot.

1985 After seven successful singles, including "We Got the Beat" and three hit albums, The Go-Go's announced they were breaking up.

Fats Domino

132

May 11

#1 Song 1959: "Happy Organ,"
Dave "Baby" Cortez

Born: Eric Burdon, 1941; Arnie Silver
(The Dovells), 1943; Tom Giuliano
(Happenings), 1943

1941 Eric Burdon, the lead singer of The Alan Price Combo, was born today. The group would go on to become The Animals with nineteen chart hits including their career making, "House of the Rising Sun." Burdon joined War in 1970 and had the hit "Spill the Wine." The Animals were inducted into the Rock and Roll Hall of Fame in 1994.

1970 The soundtrack to the August 15–17, 1969, Woodstock Festival was issued. It was a three-disc set.

1981 The name most synonymous with reggae music, Bob Marley was a Jamaican-born activist promoting marijuana use as much as he promoted his music. His best known recordings included "Get Up, Stand Up" and "I Shot the Sheriff," the latter a huge hit for Eric Clapton. His rebellious attitude garnered enemies, and on two occasions, he barely escaped murder attempts. Still, he managed to find time to father eleven children with seven women. He died at age thirty-six of lung cancer and was given a state funeral in Jamaica, where he was buried with a Bible in one hand and a guitar in the other.

1989 Anita Baker co-hosted the twentieth annual Songwriters Hall of Fame Awards ceremony at Radio City Music Hall in New York with Dick Clark.

May

12

#1 Song 1958: "All I Have to Do Is Dream," The Everly Brothers

Born: Jay Otis Washington (The Persuasions), 1941; Ian Dury (The Blockheads), 1942; Ian McLagan (The Small Faces), 1945; Steve Winwood, 1948; Billy Squier, 1950

1948 Steve Winwood, the lead singer of The Spencer Davis Group, was born today. He joined the band in 1963, garnering hits such as "Gimme Some Lovin'" and "I'm a Man." He left in 1967 to form the band Traffic.

1960 Elvis made his first TV appearance since his Army discharge on a *Welcome Back* special. The host was an old rock 'n' roller named Frank Sinatra.

1963 Bob Dylan walked off *The Ed Sullivan Show* when he was refused permission to perform "Talking John Birch Society Blues."

1983 Although his 1977 *Bat Out of Hell* album earned him millions, Meat Loaf (Marvin Lee Aday) filed for bankruptcy today.

2001 Perry Como was the most relaxed vocalist ever to sing, and when he sat on a stool on his popular '50s TV show and crooned, girls swooned. He charted an amazing 132 times (between 1943 and 1974) with songs like "Catch a Falling Star" (the first gold record ever awarded by the RIAA) and "Round and Round" (co-written by Brooklyn's Tilden High School principal Joe Shapiro). He died after a lengthy illness at eighty-eight.

Perry Como

May 13

#1 Song 1967: "The Happening," The Supremes

Born: Fred Hellerman (The Weavers), 1927; Harold Winley (The Clovers), 1933; Ritchie Valens, 1941; Mary Wells, 1943; Stevie Wonder, 1950; Peter Gabriel (Genesis), 1950

1950 Peter Gabriel, a founding member and lead singer of Genesis, was born today. The group formed in 1966 and Gabriel left in 1975 before they really came into their own with his replacement, Phil Collins. Still, Gabriel managed his own string of solo successes with "Sledgehammer" and "Big Time" among eleven U.S. charters from 1977 through 1992. Before his tenure with Genesis, Gabriel was a travel agent.

1955 After his performance at a baseball park in Jacksonville, Florida, Elvis jokingly told the audience of 14,000 girls, "I'll see you backstage." The response was a full-blown riot, with fans pursuing Presley into the dressing room and tearing off his clothes. It was at that point Colonel Tom Parker, who was in the audience, was totally sold on the potential impact of Elvis Presley.

1960 The Moondogs (later known as The Beatles) asked Jacaranda Coffee Bar owner, Allan Williams, to manage them. Though not overly excited, he agreed. Williams once stated, "There seems to be something about my personality that attracts the losers and fringe people of the world, and The Beatles just seemed to be part of the crowd."

1966 Karen Carpenter signed to musician Joe Osborn's micro label, Magic Lamp Records. Five hundred copies of the single "Looking for Love" were issued by Karen although brother Richard and Wes Jacobs were also on the recording. They went on to be signed by RCA as The Richard Carpenter Trio four years before their first success with "Ticket to Ride" in 1970.

1975 Bob Wills was a country music legend of the Western swing variety who recorded twenty-six hits between 1944 and 1976. Best known for his "New San Antonio Rose" and "New Spanish Two Step" (which were essentially the same song), he was inducted into both the Rock and Roll and the Country Music Halls of Fame. The Texan died at the age of seventy, having had four previous heart attacks.

May

14

#1 Song 1955: "Unchained Melody," Les Baxter

Born: Bobby Darin, 1936; Jack Bruce (Cream), 1943; Gene Cornish (The Rascals), 1945; David Byrne (Talking Heads), 1952

1956 Reports of Elvis Presley's performance at the Mary B. Sawyer Auditorium in LaCrosse, Wisconsin, caused the editor of a local newspaper to complain to FBI Director J. Edgar Hoover that from what he's *heard* Elvis's act consists of "sexual self-gratification onstage." With both *Newsweek* and *Time* running stories describing Elvis's spectacular rise, it became his first exposure in the national spotlight.

1968 "We made a mistake. He's human like the rest of us," John Lennon scowled, referring to his displeasure with the Maharishi Yogi while in New York on *The Johnny Carson Show*. He and Paul McCartney also announced that they were starting a record label called Apple Records. Earlier that day, Paul met Linda Eastman, who gave him her phone number on the back of a check.

1983 The Eurythmics charted with "Sweet Dreams." The duo's debut on the American charts reached #1, followed by fourteen more hits through 1989.

1991 Olivia Newton-John and Cliff Richard co-hosted the third annual World Music Awards in Monte Carlo.

1998 The first teen idol, Frank Sinatra, a.k.a "The Chairman of the Board" was a legendary crooner for almost sixty years. He started with a vocal group called The Hoboken Four and had more than 100 hit records through 1980 including "Learnin' the Blues," "Strangers in the Night," and "Something Stupid" with his daughter Nancy. He is considered by many to be the most popular male vocalist of the twentieth century. He died at Cedars-Sinai Medical Center in Los Angeles at age eighty-two.

Frank Sinatra

May

15

#1 Song 1976: "Boogie Fever,"
The Sylvers

Born: Corinthian "Kripp" Johnson
(Dell Vikings), 1933; Lenny Welch, 1938;
Brian Eno, 1948; Mike Oldfield, 1953;
K.T. Oslin, 1942; Graham Goble (The Little
River Band), 1947

1945 The first album chart was introduced in America. Albums then were collections of 78 RPM singles, usually boxed or in a sleeved binder.

1953 Classic rock musician-composer Mike Oldfield was born today. Best known for his lone American hit, "Tubular Bells," from the film *The Exorcist*, Oldfeld had seventeen chart singles in his native Britain from 1974 through 1994, including Top 10 hits "Portsmouth" and "Moonlight Shadow."

1954 Elvis Presley and his then current-girlfriend, Dixie, went to the Hi-Hat in Memphis for Presley to audition. Elvis, wearing a bolero jacket with a pink shirt, played guitar and sang two songs. The audition failed, and years later, Elvis recalled someone there told him to go back to driving a truck.

1961 Gladys Knight & the Pips became the first act in history to have two different versions of the same song on the charts at the same time when "Every Beat of My Heart" hit the Top 100. First recorded for Huntom and licensed to VeeJay (#6), they rerecorded it for Fury (#45) and both raced up the hit list starting today.

1961 The Bronx, New York doo-wop quintet, The Regents' (originally called The Montereys) "Barbara Ann" charted (#13) three years after they recorded it! The group had already disbanded and had to regroup in order to cut a quick album and get out on the road.

May
16

#1 Song 1964: "My Guy," Mary Wells

Born: Ted Kowalski (The Diamonds), 1931; Robert Fripp (King Crimson), 1946; Barbara Lee (The Chiffons), 1947; Janet Jackson, 1966

1963 The Beatles performed "From Me to You," with Lenny the Lion, a puppet at Television Theatre in London, for their second appearance on British national TV.

1964 Lulu & the Lovers debuted on Britain's ITV show *Thank Your Lucky Stars*. Sixteen-year-old lead singer Lulu (Marie Lawrie) would go on to have ten hits in America and twenty-four in the U.K., including the #1 "To Sir with Love."

1969 Pete Townshend of The Who, having mistaken a policeman for an overzealous fan, was arrested for kicking him offstage at a New York concert. He was fined $75.

1983 The Supremes (Diana Ross, Mary Wilson, and Cindy Birdsong) reunited for Motown's twenty-fifth anniversary, which was televised on NBC-TV.

1992 Bonnie Raitt performed with her father, Broadway actor-singer John Raitt, and the Boston Pops Orchestra at Symphony Hall in Boston. They sang "I'm Blowin' Away."

Bonnie Raitt

May 17

#1 Song 1975: "He Don't Love You (Like I Love You)," Tony Orlando & Dawn

Born: Taj Mahal (Henry Fredericks), 1942

1963 Joan Baez performed at the first Monterey Folk Festival with her protégé, Bob Dylan.

1967 John Lennon borrowed a lyric idea from the front cover advertisement of the London phone book that said, "You know their name, look up the number." It became the song "You Know My Name, Look Up the Number," which The Beatles began recording today.

1971 Although Christmas recording was supposed to be the order of the day, after Elvis Presley put down "Lead Me, Guide Me" the session went askew when the rock legend, practicing a karate kick, knocked one of his buddy-guards' guns through the guitar of a justifiably distraught session musician.

1978 Donna Summer's film, *Thank God It's Friday*, premiered in Los Angeles.

1986 Former Go-Go's member, Belinda Carlisle charted for the first of her nine Top 100 singles with "Mad About You." Before her tenure with the all-girl band, Belinda earned her living as a gas station attendant.

May

#1 Song 1959: "Kansas City," Wilbert Harrison

Born: Big Joe Turner, 1911; Glen D. Hardin (The Crickets), 1939; Feliciano "Butch" Tavares (Tavares), 1953; Rick Wakeman (Yes), 1949

1959 Connie Francis reached the Hot 100 with "Lipstick on Your Collar," one of seven hits she would have that year.

1960 The Silver Beatles, who were offered the job as backing band for Billy Fury, actually wound up doing a nine-day tour of Scotland with the unknown Liverpool pop singer Johnny Gentle. To hide their disdain, some of the members decided to use assumed names for the tour: George became Carl Harrison (after Carl Perkins), Paul changed his to Paul Ramon, and Stu Sutcliffe changed his last name to deStael.

1963 Jackie DeShannon charted with a Phil Spector–styled production entitled "Needles and Pins," which was arranged, written, and produced by Spector protégés Sonny Bono and Jack Nitzsche. Though it only reached #84, the British band The Searchers heard her version and less than a year later had a #13 hit with it.

1963 The Beatles performed with Roy Orbison and Gerry & the Pacemakers among other lesser-known British artists at Adelphi Cinema at Slough while on a British tour. Among the songs they performed on the tour were "Do You Want to Know a Secret," "Money (That's What I Want)," "From Me to You," and "Love Me Do."

1990 Elton John played the inaugural performance at Donald Trump's Taj Mahal Casino in Atlantic City, New Jersey.

May

#1 Song 1962: "Soldier Boy," The Shirelles

Born: Peter Townshend (The Who), 1945; Grace Jones, 1952; Joey Ramone (The Ramones), 1952; Danny Elfman (Oingo Boingo), 1953

1958 Alan Freed took his R&B records with him when he joined New York's WABC radio one week after quitting his position at WINS. The same day, The Clovers signed with Poplar Records after seven years with Atlantic, The Drifters classic "Drip Drop" (#58 pop) was released, and Jerry Butler & the Impressions' debut disc, "For Your Precious Love" (#11 pop), came out. Many historians consider it the first soul hit.

1960 Ben E. King recorded his last sides with The Drifters before going solo. They included "I Count the Tears" (#17 pop, #6 R&B) and the epic "Save the Last Dance for Me" (#1 pop & R&B).

1968 John Lennon made a *home* tape with Yoko Ono today that was later issued as the *Two Virgins* album, featuring the infamous cover of their badly proportioned personages naked. A bigger problem than the tasteless cover, however, was the return of John's wife, Cynthia, to their home that same day to find Yoko in her bed wearing Cynthia's nightshirt.

1973 The Joan Baez album *Where Are You Now My Son* placed on the Top 200 reaching #138. Her eighteenth chart LP, it contained actual war sounds taped in Vietnam.

1979 Three Beatles (Paul McCartney, Ringo Starr, and George Harrison) and a Rolling Stone (Mick Jagger) performed at Eric Clapton and Patti Boyd's wedding reception. Boyd was Harrison's ex! It was the first time since their 1969 breakup that the three Beatles played together.

Ben E. King

May
20

#1 Song 1967: "Groovin'," The Young Rascals

Born: Jill "Paula" Jackson (Paul & Paula), 1942; Joe Cocker, 1944; Cher, 1946; Susan Cowsill (The Cowsills), 1960

1944 Famous gravelly-voiced vocalist Joe Cocker was born on this day. Starting with a skiffle band called The Cavaliers in the late '50s, Cocker moved on to The Grease Band in the '60s and solo success after performing at Woodstock in 1969. He's best known for the hits "The Letter," "You Are So Beautiful," and the Jennifer Warnes duet, "Up Where We Belong."

1955 Ruth Brown's hit, "Mama, He Treats Your Daughter Mean," was banned in Britain. The BBC felt it might encourage wife beating.

1957 The Channels "I Really Love You" and The Mello-Kings classic "Tonite, Tonite" (#77 pop) were issued.

1970 The Beatles film *Let It Be* premiered in England.

#1 Song 1977: "Sir Duke," Stevie Wonder

Born: Ronald Isley (The Isley Brothers), 1941; Marcie Blaine, 1944; Leo Sayer, 1948

1955 Chess Records' new artist, Chuck Berry, recorded his first single, "Ida Red." During the session, producer Leonard Chess decided to rename it "Maybellene."

1979 Elton John became the first Western solo act to tour the U.S.S.R., starting with Leningrad.

1992 Singing her way into Johnny Carson's heart, Bette Midler vamped her way through "One for My Baby (And One More for the Road)" on Carson's last-ever *Tonight Show* telecast.

Johnny Carson on
The Tonight Show

May

22

#1 Song 1961: "Mother-in-Law," Ernie K-Doe

Born: Jimmy Keyes (The Chords), 1930; Bernie Taupin, 1950

1954 The El Rays' "Darling I Know" (Checker, $800) were released. Soon after, The El Rays changed their name to The Dells, who went on to have twenty-four pop hits, including "Stay in My Corner" and the doo-wop classic "Oh What a Night."

1958 Jerry Lee Lewis arrived in England for his first tour. After three performances, it was canceled when the British press discovered Lewis had just married his fourteen-year-old cousin.

1959 Freddy Cannon's initial single, "Tallahassee Lassie," charted, rising to #6. It was written by his mother!

1968 The Beatles' "Ticket to Ride" reached #1 in the U.S., staying there one week because The Beach Boys' "Help Me Rhonda" shuttled them aside the following week.

1993 Carnie and Wendy Wilson (Wilson Phillips) spent the day working behind the counter of a record store in Los Angeles to benefit LIFEbeat's CounterAID, a fund raiser for those with HIV or AIDS.

May 23

#1 Song 1960: "Cathy's Clown," The Everly Brothers

Born: Rosemary Clooney, 1928; General Norman Johnson (Chairmen of the Board), 1943; Misty Morgan, 1945; Shelly West, 1958

1956 Elvis saw Freddie Bell & the Bellboys' novelty performance of Big Mama Thornton's rhythm-and-blues hit "Hound Dog," at a Las Vegas show. It would stick in his mind as both a future recording and performance smash.

1964 Millie Small charted with her soon-to-be hit, "My Boy Lollipop" (#2 U.S. and U.K.). The harmonica part was played by a nineteen-year-old folk singer named Rod Stewart.

1981 George Harrison's "All Those Years Ago" debuted on the American Top 100 charts, eventually reaching #2. Also on the recording were Paul and Linda McCartney and Ringo Starr. The song was a tribute to John Lennon, who died a year earlier.

George Harrison

May

24

#1 Song 1975: "Shining Star," Earth, Wind & Fire

Born: Bob Dylan, 1941; Sara Dash (LaBelle), 1942; Patti LaBelle (LaBelle), 1944

1957 The Quarrymen (later known as The Beatles) made their performance debut on the back of a flatbed truck on Rose Street in Liverpool for the Empire Day celebration. John Lennon was quoted as saying, "We didn't get paid or anything."

1971 On Bob Dylan's thirtieth birthday, he visited the Wailing Wall in Jerusalem.

1991 Gene Clark was a Missouri native who co-founded the legendary folk-rock band, The Byrds. Originally a member of The New Christy Minstrels folk ensemble, he formed the Jet Set with David Crosby and Jim McGuinn, which evolved into The Byrds. Clark was the group's main writer and sang on hits from "Turn, Turn, Turn" to "Eight Miles High" before leaving for a solo career. A heavy drinker and drug user, he died of a heart attack at his California home at age forty-six.

2003 Thirty-five years after the release of "Back in the U.S.S.R." by The Beatles, Paul McCartney actually made his first performance appearance in Russia, playing before more than 50,000 fans in front of St. Basil's Cathedral in Moscow.

Paul McCartney

May 25

#1 Song 1963: "If You Wanna Be Happy," Jimmy Soul

Born: Miles Davis, 1925; Mitch Margo (The Tokens), 1947

Died: Sonny Boy Williamson, 1965

1951 The first R&B up-tempo hit to cross over to the pop Top 20 was Billy Ward & the Dominoes' "Sixty Minute Man" (#17).

1956 British bandleader Ted Heath stated upon his return from a U.S. tour: "Rock 'n' roll is mainly performed by colored artists for colored people and is therefore unlikely to ever prove popular in Britain."

1960 While hanging out at Stuart Sutcliffe's apartment, John Lennon and Sutcliffe thought of a new name for their group from a line in a Marlon Brando–Lee Marvin film, *The Wild One*. Marvin, talking to Brando, said: "We all missed you. (Points to the girls in the gang.) The beetles missed yuh, all the beetles missed..." Stuart suggested the Beetles because it reminded him of Buddy Holly's Crickets. John then varied the name by making the "e" an "a" as in rhythm or beat. Their new manager, Allan Williams, didn't like it and suggested Long John and the Silver Beatles. Before they settled on Beatles, they toyed with Beatals, The Silver Beats, and Silver Beetles.

1965 Dave Davies of The Kinks stumbled into drummer Mick Avory's cymbal, knocking himself unconscious and causing the rest of their tour to be canceled.

1973 Carole King performed a free concert in New York's Central Park for an audience of more than 100,000!

1986 Albert Grossman was a folk and rock music guru in the guise of a manager. The Chicago native began as a club manager and moved to New York in the late '50s, discovering and signing such talent as Odetta, Bob Dylan, Peter, Paul & Mary, Ian & Sylvia, Gordon Lightfoot, John Lee Hooker, and Janis Joplin. When several of his key acts left or died, Grossman moved to Woodstock, New York, and formed Bearsville Records, signing Foghat and Todd Rundgren. He died in his sleep on a plane to London from a heart attack at fifty-nine.

1990 Gary Usher was an unsuccessful singer who became a pioneering producer-writer in the development of surf music, working with Dick Dale, The Hondells, The Surfaris, and The Beach Boys in the early '60s. He co-wrote the classic, "In My Room," and went on to produce The Byrds, Laura Branigan, Roger Daltry, The Commodores, and Chicago. He died today of cancer in Los Angeles at age fifty-one.

May

26

#1 Song 1973: "Frankenstein," Edgar Winter Group

Born: Peggy Lee, 1920; Levon Helm (The Band), 1942; Stevie Nicks (Fleetwood Mac), 1948; Lenny Kravitz, 1964

1962 Miss Toni Fisher made her last of three chart appearances with "West of the Wall" (#37), a song inspired by the Berlin Wall crisis in Germany during the Cold War.

1963 Elvis Presley recorded fourteen sides in Nashville for a planned album that never materialized. Instead, the recordings were used as fillers for future albums along with a few singles. The one exception was "(You're the) Devil in Disguise" (#3), which would be released in June.

1969 John Lennon and Yoko Ono began their celebrated "bed-in for peace" in room number 1742 of the Queen Elizabeth Hotel in Montreal, Canada. It would be the first of an eight-day odyssey.

1989 Even in death, there is no escape: Roy Orbison's estate (he died in December, 1988) was sued by his music publisher because he failed to fulfill his song commitment under his 1985 contract.

1979 Elton John became the first Western pop star to tour Israel.

John Lennon and Yoko Ono

May

#1 Song 1978: "With a Little Luck,"
Wings

Born: Cilla Black, 1943; Susan Dallion
(Siouxsie & the Banshees), 1957

1943 British vocalist Cilla Black (actually Priscilla White) was born today. A coat-check girl at Liverpool's now famous Cavern Club, she was discovered by Beatles manager Brian Epstein in the early '60s. She became hugely popular in Britain, charting twenty-one times with covers of "Anyone Who Had a Heart," "You've Lost That Lovin' Feelin'," and Lennon and McCartney's "It's for You."

1965 While on vacation, Paul McCartney wrote the lyrics to "Yesterday" in a car on the way to a friend's villa in Portugal. His original working title for the song was "Scrambled Eggs."

1966 In a replay of his bad reception at the Newport Folk Festival when he went electric, Bob Dylan performed at The Royal Albert Hall in London with both John Lennon and George Harrison in attendance.

1967 Sixteen-year-old Janis Ian charted with "Society's Child," a song about interracial romance that was ahead of its time in 1967. She wrote it when she was fourteen!

1990 Wilson Phillips performed at the nineteenth Tokyo Song Festival and then won the coveted Grand Prize with "Hold On," their first of three #1s over the next year. Members Carnie and Wendy Wilson are daughters of Beach Boys legend Brian Wilson, and member Chynna Phillips is the daughter of Mamas & Papas members John and Michelle Phillips.

May

28

#1 Song 1966: "When a Man Loves a Woman," Percy Sledge

Born: T. Bone Walker, 1910; Gladys Knight, 1944; Billy Vera, 1944; John Fogerty, 1945; Kylie Minogue, 1968

1960 Jimmy Jones performed his #3 hit "Good Timin'" on Dick Clark's show. Also appearing on the nighttime version of *American Bandstand* were Johnny Tillotson, LaVern Baker, and Harold Dorman singing his hit "Mountain of Love."

1962 The Star-Club in Hamburg, Germany, held its Rockin' Twist Festival '62, featuring Gene Vincent, Gerry & the Pacemakers, The Bachelors, Davy Jones (years before his involvement with The Monkees), Tony Sheridan, and The Beatles, among others. The festival ran for fifteen days.

1976 The Allman Brothers Band broke up.

1977 Heart, with Ann and Nancy Wilson, rocked the Oakland-Alameda County Stadium to the delight of an audience 100,000 strong. Also on the bill were The Eagles, Foreigner, and Steve Miller.

1998 Elton John received an Ivor Novello Award in London for "Candle in the Wind" as both the International Hit of the Year and Top Selling Single. The song, rewritten for Princess Diana after her untimely death, was a sad success for Elton, who said he wished the recording never had to be made.

The Allman Brothers Band

May

#1 Song 1961: "Travelin' Man," Rick Nelson

Born: Gary Brooker (Procol Harum), 1945; Rebbie Jackson, 1950; Marie Fredriksson (Roxette), 1958; Melissa Etheridge, 1961

1945 Gary Brooker was the keyboard player and lead vocalist of Procol Harum. Born on this day, Brooker led the band through two of rocks classic recordings, "A Whiter Shade of Pale" (based on a Bach cantata) in 1967 and "Conquistador" in 1972.

1954 Frankie Valli's first recording, "Somebody Else Took Her Home," was released but not with The Four Seasons. He was then a soloist going under the name Frankie Valley.

1958 Little Anthony & the Imperials recorded their immortal "Tears on My Pillow" (#4 pop, #2 R&B), their first million-seller. They started the session as The Chesters and left the studio as The Imperials. When disc jockey Alan Freed began playing the single, he christened the group Little Anthony & the Imperials and within a month all new copies of the 45 read "Little Anthony & the Imperials."

1989 John Cipollina was the founding member of the San Francisco band Quicksilver Messenger Service, a group in the forefront of the "Acid Rock" movement of late '60s. The guitarist-pianist played on five of the band's albums and, due to ill health, often performed in a wheelchair or on crutches. He died from asthma at age forty-five.

1990 Madonna performed at the Sky Dome in Toronto, Canada, while local police scrutinized her concert very carefully due to a complaint about "lewdness."

May

30

#1 Song 1964: "Love Me Do," The Beatles

Born: Lenny Davidson (Dave Clark Five), 1944; Wynonna Judd, 1964

1960 Brenda Lee's first #1, "I'm Sorry," charted. She went on to amass fifty-five Top 100 singles in sixteen years. The country and pop icon began recording in 1956 at the age of eleven.

1963 A writer for the British paper *Daily Express*, Derek Taylor reviewed The Beatles show at the Odeon Cinema in Manchester by saying in part, "I suppose there is not yet a first-class musician among them… Their stage manner has little polish but limitless energy, and they have in abundance the fundamental rough good humour of their native city." He would later go on to become their press agent.

1966 Dolly Parton married Carl Dean in Catoosa County, Georgia. They met at the Wishy Washy Laundromat on the first day she came to Nashville as an eighteen-year-old singing hopeful.

Wynonna Judd

May 31

#1 Song 1969: "Get Back," The Beatles

Born: Peter Yarrow (Peter, Paul & Mary), 1938; John Bonham (Led Zeppelin), 1948

1948 John Bonham, original drummer for the hard rock super-group Led Zeppelin, was born today. The band formed in 1968 and went on to have numerous hits, including "Whole Lotta Love." Ironically, their most famous song, "Stairway to Heaven," was never issued as a commercial single to the public. The band was inducted into the Rock and Roll Hall of Fame in 1995.

1958 The era of surf music began three years ahead of The Beach Boys when Dick Dale performed his "Let's Go Trippin'" at The Rendezvous Ballroom in Balboa, California.

1961 Chuck Berry opened his own amusement park outside St. Louis called "Berry Park."

1966 Lulu began filming *To Sir with Love* with Sidney Poitier at England's Pinewood Studios.

2000 Tito Puente (Ernest Puente, Jr.) was known as "The King of the Mambo." A percussionist, vibraphonist, and bandleader, he was greatly responsible for the Latin music movement in America in the '50s. Born in New York, the Latin jazz musician wrote Santana's hit "Oye Como Va." He died of a heart condition at age seventy-seven today.

June

1

#1 Song 1963: "It's My Party," Lesley Gore

Born: Marie Knight, 1925; Pat Boone, 1934; Linda Scott, 1945; Ron Wood (The Jeff Beck Group, Faces, The Rolling Stones), 1947; Graham Russell (Air Supply), 1950; Alanis Morissette, 1974

1955 Patsy Cline recorded "A Church, a Courtroom and Then Goodbye" at her first recording session in Nashville at Owen Bradley's Barn. It became her debut single.

1964 The Rolling Stones arrived in New York for their first U.S. tour.

1966 An album titled *Best of The Beatles* came out in America, but it wasn't what you might expect. It was actually by former Beatle Pete Best and his new group, cleverly taking advantage of the wording.

1969 Like peasants visiting royalty, celebrities and entertainment figures flocked to the Montreal bedroom where John Lennon and Yoko Ono continued the second day of their bed-in. The list included producer Phil Spector, songwriter Paul Williams, comedian Tommy Smothers, poet Allen Ginsberg, and anti-war activist Abbie Hoffman. It was on this occasion that John recorded "Give Peace a Chance."

Alanis Morrisette

June

#1 Song 1962: "I Can't Stop Loving You,"
Ray Charles

Born: Johnny Carter (The Flamingos), 1933;
Otis Williams (The Charms), 1936; William
Guest (The Pips), 1941; Charlie Watts
(The Rolling Stones), 1941

1941 Charlie Watts, the drummer of what many consider the world's greatest rock 'n' roll band, The Rolling Stones, was born today. The band formed in 1963 and forty-one years later Charlie is still beating the skins for the foursome.

1956 Elvis Presley's "I Want You, I Need You, I Love You" charted R&B today, eventually reaching #3 and selling over a million copies. It was his second of thirty-five R&B hits. His first was "Heartbreak Hotel."

1967 One day after being issued in the U.K., The Beatles album *Sgt. Pepper's Lonely Hearts Club Band* was released in America. It included "Sgt. Pepper's Lonely Hearts Club Band," "A Day in the Life," "Lucy in the Sky with Diamonds," "When I'm Sixty-Four," "Getting Better," "She's Leaving Home," "Lovely Rita," "With a Little Help from My Friends," "Being for the Benefit of Mr. Kite," "Fixing a Hole," "Good Morning, Good Morning," "Within You, Without You," and "Sgt. Pepper's Lonely Heart's Club Band (reprise)." Unlike most of the band's previous albums that had somewhat different tracks in Britain versus the U.S. version, *Sgt. Pepper* had the same songs on both releases.

1972 Dion & the Belmonts reunited at a Madison Square Garden concert. It was their first performance together in thirteen years.

1990 Mariah Carey assaulted the Hot 100 with "Vision of Love," her first of five straight #1s.

June

3

#1 Song 1957: "Love Letters in the Sand," Pat Boone

Born: Memphis Minnie, 1897; Curtis Mayfield (The Impressions), 1942; Mike Freda (The Dovells), 1943; Michael Clarke (The Byrds), 1944; John Paul Jones (Led Zeppelin), 1946; Suzi Quatro, 1950

1940 Bass guitarist and vocalist Suzi Quatro was born today. Though born in Detroit, she moved to London in 1970 and ran a string of sixteen hits in the British Isles, including #1s "Can the Can" and "Devil Gate Drive," starting in 1972. In America, her biggest hit was "Stumblin' In" with Chris Norman in 1979. She became an actress and had an ongoing part on TV's hit *Happy Days* as Fonzie's friend Leather Tuscadero.

1955 Elvis Presley performed at the Fair Park Coliseum, Lubbock, Texas. A fourteen-year-old future singer-songwriter saw the performance and was forever inspired. He went on to have numerous hits, and even Elvis recorded several of his songs, including "In the Ghetto." The youth was Mac Davis.

1957 The Isley Brothers first single, the doo-wop styled "The Angels Cried" was released. It would be two years before they would have their first hit, "Shout."

1967 Aretha Franklin's "Respect" topped the pop charts for two weeks and the R&B list for six, giving Aretha her second million-seller.

1989 The Shangri-La's reunited for the first time since the early '70s for Cousin Brucie's "First Palisades Amusement Park Reunion" at the Meadowlands in East Rutherford, New Jersey. Also appearing were Lesley Gore, The Tokens, Bobby Rydell, and Freddy Cannon.

June 4

#1 Song 1988: "One More Try,"
George Michael

Born: Gordon Waller (Peter & Gordon), 1945;
El DeBarge (DeBarge), 1961

1942 Capitol Records was formed.

1964 The Beatles (minus a hospitalized Ringo, who was replaced by drummer Jimmy Nicol) started a world tour in Denmark. More than 6,000 fans greeted them at Copenhagen airport and 10,000 loyalists brought the city to a halt when they attacked the group's hotel. Crowd control was handled by Danish police with the help of a contingent of members of the British Royal Fusiliers. Thanks to their bodyguard Mal Evans, the group found a new way to remember the order of performance: Mal taped the song list to their guitars.

1967 The Monkees' TV show won an Emmy for Outstanding Comedy Series.

1967 Paul McCartney and George Harrison saw The Jimi Hendrix Experience at the Saville Theatre in London. Also on the bill were The Chiffons and Procol Harum. Hendrix, in tribute to The Beatles, began his performance with the title track from the *Sgt. Pepper* album.

1987 The Eurythmics, featuring Annie Lennox, performed in Berlin as more than 1,000 East Berlin fans gathered at the wall and chanted, "The wall must go."

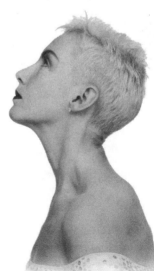

The Eurythmics

June

5

#1 Song 1961: "Running Scared," Roy Orbison

Born: Floyd Butler (Friends of Distinction), 1941

1962 The Beatles auditioned for producer George Martin.

1964 The Chiffons began a tour starting in San Bernadino, California, as the opening act for The Rolling Stones on their debut American tour.

1974 Sly Stone (Sylvester Stewart) married Kathy Silva onstage at Madison Square Garden prior to a concert by his group, Sly & the Family Stone. The marriage lasted five months.

1993 Mariah Carey married Sony Music president, Tommy Mottola, at St. Thomas Episcopal Church in New York. Among the guests were Barbra Streisand, Bruce Springsteen, and Billy Joel.

1993 Conway Twitty (Harold Lloyd Jenkins) was a monumental country-pop artist who garnered ninety-seven country chart singles, including an astounding thirty-five #1s and an additional five in duet with Loretta Lynn. He started as a pop singer charting twenty times including, "It's Only Make Believe." The Arkansas native was offered a contract to play baseball with the Philadelphia Phillies when he was drafted into the Army. He changed his name in 1957 after Conway (Arkansas) and Twitty (Texas). He died of an abdominal aneurysm at fifty-nine.

Conway Twitty

June

#1 Song 1970: "Everything Is Beautiful," Ray Stevens

Born: Levi Stubbs (The Four Tops), 1936; Gary "U.S." Bond, 1939; Howie Kirshenbaum (Jay & the Americans), 1942

1962 The Beatles entered Abbey Road Studios for the first time and recorded four songs, "Love Me Do," "P. S. I Love You," "Ask Me Why," and "Besame Mucho." Although George Martin was supposed to produce, he did not show up until later and the session was actually done by Ron Richards. Martin did not fancy Peter Best's drumming and recommended a session drummer for the actual versions. The group was now officially an EMI act.

1963 Little Miss & the Muffets (originally called The Meltones) topped the Hot 100 with "Chapel of Love." But, thanks to a last minute name change, they became known to the world as The Dixie Cups.

1971 Gladys Knight & the Pips were the last pop act to appear on *The Ed Sullivan Show.*

1986 Decca Records A&R head Dick Rowe died today of diabetes at sixty-one. Often maligned for passing on The Beatles, he more than made amends by signing Tom Jones, The Moody Blues, and The Rolling Stones—the latter mainly on the strong recommendation of George Harrison.

June

7

#1 Song 1980: "Funkytown," Lipps, Inc.

Born: Tom Jones, 1940; Prince, 1958

1954 Bill Haley & the Comets recorded "See You Later Alligator" and "Shake, Rattle & Roll."

1958 Prince Rogers Nelson was born today. Named after his father's jazz group, The Prince Rogers Trio, he would be world-famous simply as Prince. During his controversial career, where he recorded under no less than three names, the pop titan had forty-six chart singles between 1978 and 1995, including #1s "Kiss," "Bat Dance," "Cream," "When Doves Cry," and "Let's Go Crazy." He is probably best known for his #2 hit "Purple Rain," which he performed as the opening number of the 2004 Grammy Awards almost twenty years after its initial release.

1970 The Who performed their rock-opera, *Tommy*, at New York's Metropolitan Opera House.

1964 While The Beatles' plane refueled in Beirut, Lebanon, on its way to Australia, police fought off fanatic fans with fire-fighting foam as the mindless teens charged the runway.

1975 Olivia Newton-John's "Please Mr. Please" charted (#3) and becomes her fifth Top 10 hit in a row.

1979 Chuck Berry performed at the White House by the special request of President Carter. A month later (July 10) he was sentenced to four months in jail for income tax evasion.

Prince

June 8

#1 Song 1974: "Band on the Run," Wings

Born: Sherman Garnes (The Teenagers), 1940; Chuck Negron (Three Dog Night), 1942; Nancy Sinatra, 1940; Boz Scaggs, 1944; Bonnie Tyler, 1953

1967 Brian Jones of The Rolling Stones played alto sax on The Beatles' "You Know My Name, Look Up the Number." Expected to bring his guitar, he showed up with the sax instead, an instrument he played with The Ramrods, his pre-Stones band.

1968 At the height of the bubble-gum era, The Ohio Express, The Lemon Pipers, and The 1910 Fruit Gum Company headlined a concert at New York's Carnegie Hall backed by the forty-six–piece Kasenetz-Katz Singing Orchestral Circus.

1974 Dolly Parton's "I Will Always Love You" hit #1 on the country charts. Eighteen years later, it would top the pop charts as sung by Whitney Houston.

1982 Simon & Garfunkel reunited (temporarily) beginning with a tour of Europe, starting in Paris.

1991 The Chordettes, who reformed in 1988 after twenty-seven years, debuted as special guests at Radio City Music Hall for "The Royal New York Doo-Wop Show."

June

9

#1 Song 1958: "Purple People Eater," Sheb Wooley

Born: Les Paul, 1915; Johnny Ace, 1929; Jackie Wilson (The Dominoes), 1934

1957 John Lennon and The Quarrymen entered a star search talent contest at the Empire Theatre, Liverpool, but lost out to The Sunnyside Skiffle group led by a midget!

1962 The Orlons leaped onto the Hot 100 with "The Wah Watusi," rising to #2 and becoming their third straight Top 5 hit.

1962 Carole King's baby sitter, Little Eva, had her first single released. It became the rock 'n' roll standard "Locomotion," a worldwide #1.

1990 Wilson Phillips reached #1 with their debut single, "Hold On." Twenty-five years earlier to the day the Wilson sisters' (Carnie and Wendy) dad, Brian, and his Beach Boys hit #1 with "Help Me Rhonda."

Wilson Phillips

June

#1 Song 1967: "Respect,"
Aretha Franklin

Born: Hattie McDaniel, 1895; Howlin'
Wolf, 1910; Judy Garland, 1922; Gerald
Gregory (The Spaniels), 1934; Shirley Alston
(The Shirelles), 1941; Kim Deal (Pixies), 1961

1957 The Bobbettes immortal "Mr. Lee" (#6) was released today along with R&B standards "Happy Happy Birthday Baby" by The Tune Weavers, "To The Aisle" by The Five Satins, and "Desiree" by The Charts.

1961 German orchestra leader and record label executive Bert Kaempfert signed The Beatles (John, Paul, George, and Pete Best on drums) to a one-year deal to record for his production company after seeing them perform at the Top Ten Club in Hamburg. His main interest in the group was as a backup band for British rocker, Tony Sheridan. A German rock 'n' roll act, Tommy Kent, put Kaempfert onto the foursome.

1970 Janis Joplin performed with Big Brother & the Holding Company for the first time at The Avalon Ballroom.

1991 Stevie Wonder and Aretha Franklin sang at the burial of Temptations' lead singer, David Ruffin, and Michael Jackson paid for the funeral.

June

#1 Song 1966: "Paint It Black,"
The Rolling Stones

Born: James "Pookie" Hudson
(The Spaniels), 1934; Joey Dee, 1940

1964 The Beatles arrived in Sydney, Australia, during a pouring cold rain. For some odd reason, they were driven around the airport in a roofless milk truck to the delight of some 2,000 fans when a woman, obviously in a state of delusion, literally threw her six-year-old mentally challenged child into the truck bed. Paul caught him and handed the boy back to the mother, who kissed the child and cried, "He's better. Oh, he's better," as if the hands of a god had touched him.

1965 The Beatles were awarded the Member of the Order of the British Empire (MBE). John Lennon was heard to say in astonishment, "I thought you had to drive tanks and win wars to win the MBE." George was more to the point when he said, "I didn't think you got this sort of thing for playing rock 'n' roll."

1969 To coincide with the first lunar landing, David Bowie's "Space Oddity" was issued. It didn't reach the Top 100, but four years later, a reissue of it gave Bowie his first Top 20 hit (#15) in America.

June
12

#1 Song 1961: "Travelin' Man,"
Rick Nelson

Born: Len Barry (The Dovells), 1942;
Reg Presley (Troggs), 1943

1957 Jerry Lee Lewis's first single, "Whole Lot of Shakin' Going On," charted. It went on to sell 6 million copies and consequently Lewis reportedly upped his performance price from $50 to $10,000 a night!

1964 On the trip in from the Adelaide, Australia, airport, more than 200,000 Beatles fans converged on the route to the group's hotel while another 30,000 congested the downtown section waiting for the Mop Tops. The Beatles did four concerts at a venue that held 3,000 people. More than 50,000 fans requested tickets.

1968 Elvis Presley's picture *Speedway* hit theaters nationwide and reached #40 for the year in film popularity.

Jerry Lee Lewis and his wife

June

13

#1 Song 1960: "Cathy's Clown,"
The Everly Brothers

Born: Bobby Freeman, 1940;
Dennis Locorriere (Dr. Hook & the
Medicine Show), 1949

1953 "Ain't That Good News" by The Tempo Toppers was released. The group's lead singer was a new vocalist named Little Richard. It would be another three years before the start of what would become a legendary solo artist career.

1970 Bread charted with "Make It with You," their first hit and only #1 of thirteen Top 60 hits through 1977. All the hits of the group, formerly known as Pleasure Faire, were written and produced by Bread's lead singer, David Gates.

1972 The Drifters' original lead singer, Clyde McPhatter was considered by many to be one of rock 'n' roll's greatest voices. Clyde also sang lead for Billy Ward & the Dominoes before joining The Drifters. Elvis Presley frequently stated that he wished his voice were the equal of Clyde's. McPhatter died of a heart attack today in a Bronx, N.Y., hotel room, broke and despondent over a mismanaged career that made him a legend but hardly a success. He was thirty-nine.

1987 Richard Marx, a former background singer for Lionel Richie, hit the Top 100 with "Don't Mean Nothing," an eventual #3 and the first of his career nineteen chart hits, including #1s "Hold on to the Nights," "Satisfied," and "Right Here Waiting."

Bread

June 14

#1 Song 1975: "Sister Golden Hair," America

Born: Renaldo "Obie" Benson (The Four Tops), 1936; Rod Argent (The Zombies), 1945; Muff Winwood (Spencer Davis Group), 1943; Boy George, 1961

1961 Flamboyant pop vocalist Boy George (George O'Dowd), lead singer of Culture Club, was born today. In the early '80s, the group had six consecutive Top 10 hits in America, including "Karma Chameleon" and "Do You Really Want to Hurt Me," both of which were #1s in England.

1963 Dion headlined a night at Pittsburgh's Civic Center along with Dionne Warwick, The Chiffons, The Impressions, The Shirelles, Freddy Cannon, and Little Peggy March.

1964 Ringo Starr, who had been hospitalized in London for tonsillitis, arrived in Melbourne to meet the other Beatles and continue their world tour. Facing a huge and demonstrative crowd in front of the hotel, a police inspector tried to charge the fans, carrying Ringo over his shoulder like a sack. It might have worked if he hadn't tripped over The Beatles' PR person and launched Ringo into the crowd. They barely managed to escape and as the mob grew, Army and Navy units were called in as girls by the hundreds fainted, cars were demolished, and injuries mounted. By the time George Harrison, John Lennon, and Paul McCartney arrived, more than 400 police and military were mixing it up with the out-of-control fans. In hopes of containing the crowd, The Beatles were asked to wave to the frenzied fans from their balcony. In a typical, though inappropriate bit of Lennon humor, John, feeling the power of the moment, gave a Nazi salute and shouted, "Sieg Heil."

1979 Stephen Stills and Bruce Springsteen (among others) performed at The Hollywood Bowl in what was billed as the "No Nukes" benefit concert.

1986 Patti LaBelle, in a duet with Michael McDonald, topped the pop charts with "On My Own." The song was recorded by each singer in separate studios 3,000 miles apart. In fact, the two did not meet until they performed the song together on Johnny Carson's *Tonight Show*.

1994 Henry Mancini was one of America's most popular film and TV composers, amassing twenty Grammys and four Oscars. Mancini managed fifteen chart singles between 1960 and 1977, including "Love Theme from *Romeo and Juliet*," a #1 record in the middle of the psychedelic era (1969). Henry died of cancer at age seventy today.

June

15

#1 Song 1985: "Everybody Wants to Rule the World," Tears for Fears

Born: Nigel Pickering (Spanky & Our Gang), 1929, Waylon Jennings, 1937, Harry Nilsson, 1941, Russell Hitchcock (Air Supply), 1949

1955 In order to perform at the Belden High School Gym in Belden, Mississippi, without being mobbed, Elvis Presley crawled through a back window, ripping the seat of his pants as he went. All that was between Elvis and great embarrassment for the length of his performance was a small, strategically placed safety pin.

1963 Randy & the Rainbows "Denise" (#10) charted. It became the last doo-wop Top 10 hit before the beginning of The Beatles era.

1963 Kyu Sakamoto's "Sukiyaki" became the first Japanese record to reach #1 in America. For that matter, it was the first Japanese record to chart at all! His song "Ue O Muito Aruto" (which translated means "Let's Walk with Our Faces Up") became a hit in Japan and was released in England under the title "Sukiyaki." Kyu was already a Japanese recording star and actor by the time "Sukiyaki" became a hit.

1966 The Beatles album *Yesterday...And Today* was issued in America and included "Drive My Car," "Nowhere Man," "Yesterday," "Act Naturally," "We Can Work It Out," and "Day Tripper" as featured cuts.

1973 The film *American Graffiti* with its classic rock 'n' roll soundtrack opened in New York.

June

#1 Song 1956: "The Wayward Wind," Gogi Grant

Born: Lamont Dozier (Holland, Dozier & Holland), 1941; Eddie Levert (The O'Jays), 1942; Ian Matthews (Matthews' Southern Comfort), 1946; James Smith (The Stylistics), 1950

1967 The Mamas & the Papas, Simon & Garfunkel, Janis Joplin, The Grateful Dead, Otis Redding, The Association, Canned Heat, Laura Nyro, and Buffalo Springfield were among the acts who performed at the Monterey International Pop Festival, the first legendary pop and rock festival.

1990 The Rolling Stones' "Paint It Black" reached #1 in The Netherlands for the second time. The first was twenty-four years earlier (1966).

1992 The first "Madonna Appreciation Convention" (the Madonnathon) was held at the Holiday Inn, Southfield, Michigan, on the singer's thirty-fourth birthday.

Otis Redding

June

17

#1 Song 1978: "Shadow Dancing," Andy Gibb

Born: Barry Manilow, 1946

1965 The Kinks arrived in New York for their first U.S. tour.

1967 Janis Joplin performed at the Monterey Pop Festival with The Steve Miller Band, Paul Butterfield Blues Band, Canned Heat, and Al Kooper, among others. Grace Slick and Jefferson Airplane were the sixth act to perform on the festival's second night.

1968 Lulu performed with an eye patch at Issy's Club in Vancouver, Canada, because of a boating accident that morning.

1978 Kim Carnes rolled onto the charts with "You're a Part of Me" (#36), her first of nineteen hits over the next twelve years.

1986 American singer Dean Reed barely charted once (#96) in 1959 with "The Search" and then "defected" to the U.S.S.R. to become a pop superstar behind the Iron Curtain. He also appeared in eighteen films, including a number of spaghetti Westerns in Italy. He died in a supposed swimming accident in an East German lake. Perhaps the KGB thought he was a spy.

June 18

#1 Song 1983: "Flashdance," Irene Cara

Born: Jeanette MacDonald, 1901; Paul McCartney, 1942; Sandy Posey, 1944; Alison Moyet, 1961

Died: Peter Allen, 1992

1956 Paul McCartney's father bought a trumpet for him on his fourteenth birthday, which the lad promptly traded in for a Zenith acoustic guitar, worth about £15 (about $22).

1966 The Grassroots' debut 45, "Where Were You When I Needed You," charted, going to #28. The San Francisco band, originally called The Bedouins, went on to have twenty-one hits through 1975.

1967 D.A. Pennebaker filmed the legendary Monterey Pop Festival on its last of three nights. Artists included Janis Joplin, The Byrds, The Who, The Blues Project, and Jimi Hendrix. The Mamas & the Papas were the closing act. Unbeknownst to them at the time, it would be the last live performance by the original quartet.

1988 Choreographer Paula Abdul punched her way onto the charts with "Knocked Out" (#41), her first of fourteen hits through 1995.

Paula Abdul

June

19

#1 Song 1976: "Silly Love Songs," Wings

Born: Shirley Goodman (Shirley & Lee), 1936; Elaine "Spanky" McFarlane (Spanky & Our Gang), 1942; Ann Wilson (Heart), 1950; Paula Abdul, 1962

1971 Rock guru Don Kirshner, a power behind The Monkees' success, formed a new group called Tomorrow, which immediately failed and disbanded. One of the members was a winsome twenty-three-year-old Australian named Olivia Newton-John.

1980 Donna Summer became the first act signed to former William Morris Agency mailroom boy David Geffen and his Geffen Records.

1997 Bobby Helms was a country and pop singer who was best known for the hits "My Special Angel" in 1957 and the Christmas perennial "Jingle Bell Rock," which originally charted in 1957 (#6) and then charted four more times in 1958, 1960, 1961, and 1962. Bobby died from emphysema at age sixty.

Donna Summer

172

June

#1 Song 1964: "Chapel of Love,"
The Dixie Cups

Born: Billy Guy (The Coasters), 1936;
Brian Wilson (The Beach Boys), 1942;
Anne Murray, 1945; Lionel Ritchie,
1949; Cyndi Lauper, 1953

1968 Elvis Presley began working on his first TV special with record producer Bones Howe in Hollywood and with vocal backups by The Blossoms, led by Darlene Love. The Blossoms were the actual uncredited voices on The Crystals '60s hits "He's a Rebel" and "He's Sure the Boy I Love."

1969 The year 1969 was the pinnacle of the rock-pop festival with no less than seven major events, starting with Newport '69 in Northridge, California. Acts included The Rascals, Creedence Clearwater Revival, Jethro Tull, Ike & Tina Turner, Johnny Winter, Jimi Hendrix, The Byrds, Eric Burdon, Joe Cocker, and Booker T. & the MG's.

1970 *Andy Williams Presents Ray Stevens* NBC-TV show premiered with regular guests Mama Cass Elliot and Lulu.

1979 *The Blues Brothers* film opened throughout America. One of the movies highlights was Aretha Franklin's portrayal of a crusty waitress singing her 1968 hit "Think."

1987 A concert at Radio City Music Hall honoring the return of Dion to New York after fifteen years included The Del-Satins and Carlo of The Belmonts backing Dion as well as The Brooklyn Bridge and The Five Satins.

June

21

#1 Song 1975: "Love Will Keep Us Together," Captain & Tennille

Born: Mitty Collier, 1941; Ray Davies (The Kinks), 1944; Brenda Holloway, 1946; Kathy Mattea, 1959

1962 The Beatles performed at the Tower Ballroom, New Brighton, Wallesey, England, with American artists Bruce Channel and Delbert McClinton. McClinton played harmonica on Channel's hit "Hey Baby," and gave John Lennon some valuable tips on improving his technique. Subsequently, John began including harmonica parts into most of the group's original compositions for the next few years.

1964 A kid from Liverpool climbed a drainpipe to the eighth floor of The Beatles hotel in Sydney, Australia, to meet the group. John Lennon was so impressed, he brought the teen into their suite, gave him a drink, and introduced him to the others.

1969 The pop-rock trio The City had its first single released ("Why Are You Leaving"). The lead singer was Carole King.

1989 Commenting in an interview on the upcoming Jefferson Airplane reunion album, Grace Slick said, "We're your parents' worst nightmare because now we are your parents."

2001 Blues legend John Lee Hooker, one of the few remaining links to the classic R&B and blues style that developed into the foundation of rock 'n' roll, died of natural causes at his home in Los Altos, California. He had performed on more than 100 albums in a career that covered over half a century. The artists he influenced range from Eric Clapton and The Rolling Stones to ZZ Top, Bonnie Raitt, and Jimi Hendrix. John Lee was eighty-three.

John Lee Hooker

June

#1 Song 1959: "The Battle of New Orleans," Johnny Horton

Born: Ella Johnson, 1923; Kris Kristofferson, 1936; Howard Kaylan (The Turtles), 1947; Todd Rundgren, 1948; Alan Osmond (The Osmonds), 1949

Died: Judy Garland, 1969

1961 Bobby Rydell began a twelve-day stay at New York's famed Copacabana night club following two other teen idols, Paul Anka and Connie Francis. Unlike the latter, however, when Rydell finished his engagement, he so impressed the management that they offered him a twenty-year contract!

1962 Hank Ballard & the Midnighters were scheduled to perform Hank's original recording of "The Twist" on Dick Clark's *American Bandstand* today, but instead Chubby Checker showed up to sing his version. This same week, both versions were released and Checker's won the sweepstakes, reaching #1 pop and #2 R&B and starting the dance craze of the decade. Ballard's version also made #2 R&B and even peaked at #28 pop, although few people remember his historic original.

1963 Little Stevie Wonder's "Fingertips, Pt. 2" became the thirteen-year-old's first of sixty-one chart records through 1988.

1964 Former student at St. Joseph's Convent School in England and the daughter of an Austrian baroness and a British university lecturer, eighteen-year-old Marianne Faithfull met Rolling Stones manager, Andrew Loog Oldham, at a London party. He was so impressed with her looks that he offered her a recording contract. Within three months she was on the charts with a cover of The Stones' "As Tears Go By" (#9 U.K., #22 U.S.).

June

23

#1 Song 1979: "Hot Stuff," Donna Summer

Born: Helen Humes, 1913; June Carter Cash, 1929; Adam Faith, 1940; Diana Trask, 1940; Stuart Sutcliffe (The Beatles), 1940

1956 Shirley & Lee's immortal "Let the Good Times Roll" was issued (#20). The same day, doo-wop standards "Can't We Be Sweethearts" by The Cleftones ($25) and "Your Way" by The Heartbeats ($150) were released.

1958 Bobby Darin's "Splish Splash" entered the Top 100, the first of his forty-one chart hits over thirteen years (1958–73).

1958 A trio from Lyndhurst, Ohio, The Poni-Tails had their first single, "Born Too Late," released (#7). It became their first and biggest hit 45.

1959 Elvis Presley's "A Big Hunk o' Love" was released. It would go on to be another million-seller and his twelfth #1 hit in four years. The B-side, "My Wish Came True," reached #12 and became his last 45 RCA would issue before the return of the King from the Army, even though he was still more than nine months from being discharged. They must have run out of songs!

1995 Tony Romeo was a singer-producer who came into his own as a staff writer for Wes Farrell's Pocket Full O Tunes publishing company. While there, he wrote The Partridge Family's "I Think I Love You," Lou Christie's "I'm Gonna Make You Mine," and The Cowsills' "Indian Lake." He died of a heart attack at his Pleasant Valley, N.Y., home.

June

24

#1 Song 1989: "Satisfied,"
Richard Marx

Born: Arthur Brown, 1942; Mick
Fleetwood (Fleetwood Mac), 1942;
Jeff Beck, 1944; Colin Blunstone
(The Zombies), 1945; Curt Smith
(Tears For Fears), 1961

1942 A founding member of Fleetwood Mac, drummer Mick Fleetwood was born today. The band formed in 1967 and went on to stellar success with hits like "Dreams" and "Go Your Own Way."

1957 Elvis Presley's "Teddy Bear," and its B-side, "Loving You," each charted today. "Teddy" would eventually reach #1, sell a million copies, and have teen girls going back to their teddy bears in droves while "Loving" made it to #20. They were the twenty-third and twenty-fourth hits for Elvis in just sixteen months.

1957 Dion's first single was not with The Belmonts, but a group he never met called The Timberlanes. Their 45 "The Chosen Few" was issued today.

1967 Grace Slick and Jefferson Airplane hopped on the Top 100 with their classic, "White Rabbit" (#8).

1987 Jackie Gleason (Herbert John Gleason) was known as "The Great One" for his size and TV success, but he was also the "King of Mood Music" of the '50s with a series of *For Lovers Only* instrumental albums that set the stage for followers like Ray Conniff, Montovani, and Percy Faith and their orchestras. Ironically, "Ralph Cramden" couldn't read music, but composed some beautiful pieces, including "Melancholy Serenade." He died at age seventy-one.

June

25

#1 Song 1966: "Paperback Writer," The Beatles

Born: Eddie Floyd (The Falcons), 1935; Bobby Nunn (The Coasters), 1936; Harold Melvin (The Blue Notes), 1939; Carly Simon, 1945; George Michael, 1963

1961 Elvis Presley recorded "(Marie's the Name) His Latest Flame" and "Little Sister" at RCA's studio in Nashville. The two would be coupled as Presley's next single in a month. Both songs were written by Doc Pomus and Mort Shuman, who wrote many teen hits of the '50s and '60s such as "A Teenager in Love" for Dion & the Belmonts and "Hushabye" for The Mystics.

1961 The Shirelles headlined one of Alan Freed's tours of Los Angeles at The Hollywood Bowl along with Brenda Lee, Jerry Lee Lewis, and Bobby Vee, among others.

1967 The Beatles introduced their yet-to-be-released new single "All You Need Is Love" to 400 million people via satellite in twenty-six countries with a chorus including Eric Clapton, Keith Moon, Mick Jagger, and Keith Richards.

1987 Boudleaux Bryant was a tremendously talented country and pop songwriter who created over 1,500 compositions, many with his wife, Felice. He's best known for a slew of tunes he wrote for The Everly Brothers, including "Bye, Bye Love," "Bird Dog," and "All I Have to Do Is Dream." He died of cancer in Knoxville, Tennessee, today at sixty-seven.

1988 Debbie Gibson's "Foolish Beat" topped the American charts, making her the youngest vocalist to ever perform, write, and produce a #1 hit. She was seventeen at the time.

June 26

#1 Song 1961: "Quarter to Three," Gary U.S. Bonds

Born: Billy Davis, Jr. (The 5th Dimension), 1940; Georgie Fame, 1943; Patty Smyth, 1957; Terri Nunn (Berlin), 1959

1948 Patti Page's "Confess" ran up the charts to #12. It was her first of an amazing eighty-one hits from 1948 through 1968.

1965 Sonny & Cher's first chart record and only #1 together, "I Got You Babe," was released.

1966 The Beatles returned to the city where they began their recording career in 1961—Hamburg, Germany. They performed at the Ernst Merch Hall. John stated during the show, "Don't listen to our music. We're terrible these days."

1971 Country artist Jody Miller slid onto the pop charts with her version of The Chiffons hit "He's So Fine" (#53). Her arrangement of the song was similar to George Harrison's "My Sweet Lord," which was a plagiarized version of "He's So Fine."

1977 Elvis Presley made his last performance at The Market Square in Indianapolis, Indiana. The last song he sang was "Can't Help Falling in Love."

1988 Debbie Gibson graduated with honors from Calhoun High School, Merrick, Long Island. The seventeen-year-old had already amassed four Top 5 hits before leaving school.

Sonny & Cher

June

27

#1 Song 1964: "A World Without Love," Peter & Gordon

Born: Doc Pomus, 1925; Bruce Johnston (The Beach Boys), 1944

1960 Connie Francis's "Everybody's Somebody's Fool" arrived at #1, giving the songstress her sixth million-seller. The B-side, "Jealous of You," rose to #19.

1965 The Beatles performed at the Teatro Adraino in Rome, Italy. Playwright Noel Coward was told he could visit with the group at their hotel after the show by Brian Epstein; the foursome, however, refused to see him when he arrived. Finally, Paul McCartney came out to talk with him. Coward later stated, "I sent messages of congratulation to his colleagues, although the message I would have liked to have sent them was that they were bad-mannered little shits."

1971 The legendary New York rock performance venue Fillmore East closed.

1987 Whitney Houston's "I Wanna Dance with Somebody" hit #1 while her album, *Whitney*, became the first album by a female singer to debut on Billboard's chart at #1.

2002 John Entwistle was the rapid-fire bassist for the legendary British rockers, The Who. They scored twenty-six hits in America and were known for maniacal stage presence that included destroying their instruments. John died of a heart attack in his hotel room at the Hard Rock Café in Las Vegas today at age fifty-seven.

Whitney Houston's
Whitney

June

#1 Song 1986: "On My Own,"
Patti LaBelle and Michael McDonald

Born: Cathy Carr, 1936; Bobby
Harrison (Procol Harum), 1943;
Dave Knights (Procol Harum), 1945

1965 The Ronettes and Dionne Warwick appeared on the CBS-TV special *It's What's Happening Baby.*

1968 Three and a half years after they formed The Mamas & the Papas, members John Phillips, Cass Elliot, and Denny Doherty wrote a letter to Michelle Phillips (John's wife), firing her for the second time in three years.

1973 The "British Invasion" briefly returned to New York when Herman's Hermits, The Searchers, Gerry & the Pacemakers, and Wayne Fontana & the Mindbenders played a revival concert at Madison Square Garden.

1986 Sting performed at an anti-Apartheid concert in London. Also appearing were Boy George, Elvis Costello, Sade, Peter Gabriel, and Hugh Masekela, among others.

Sting

June
29

#1 Song 1974: "Sundown," Gordon Lightfoot

Born: Leonard Lee (Shirley & Lee), 1936; Little Eva, 1943; Ian Paice (Deep Purple), 1948; Evelyn "Champagne" King, 1960

1940 The historic pairing of Frank Sinatra and The Pied Pipers in a recording studio resulted in one of the biggest hits of the pre–World War II era, "I'll Never Smile Again" (#1 for twelve weeks).

1968 Mama Cass Elliot's "Dream a Little Dream of Me" was released rising to #12. It was credited as her first solo on the label even though she was backed by the rest of The Mamas & the Papas.

1968 Jethro Tull, Pink Floyd, and T. Rex played at London's Hyde Park. It was the park's first free rock festival.

1971 Highway 51 South in Memphis became Elvis Presley Boulevard, thanks to the Memphis City Council. In January 1972, when it became official, Elvis's home, Graceland, was at 3764 Elvis Presley Boulevard.

2002 Rosemary Clooney was one of the best loved pop singers of the '50s and by the '70s was popular as a jazz artist. She charted twenty-five times between 1951 and 1960 with songs like "Hey There," "This Ole House," and "Come On-A My House." She died today at the age of seventy-four.

Rosemary Clooney

June

#1 Song 1986: "On My Own"
Patti LaBelle & Michael McDonald

Born: Lena Horne, 1917; June Valli, 1930; Florence Ballard (The Supremes), 1943; Billy Brown (Ray, Goodman & Brown), 1946

1958 Elvis Presley's "Hard-Headed Woman" charted today. It would go on to be his eleventh #1 in a little over two years.

1966 The Beatles performed at Nippon Budokan Hall, Tokyo, where over 30,000 Japanese police were called out to protect them on the route from the airport to the Tokyo Hilton. More than 10,000 fans crammed the hall to see them.

1975 Cher and The Allman Brothers' Greg Allman were married four days after she and Sonny Bono were divorced. The Cher-and-Greg combine lasted ten days.

1983 The Everly Brothers reunited after a ten-year breakup.

2001 Chet Atkins was a powerful force in country music for almost half a century. The guitarist, singer, producer hit as an artist with "Yakety Axe" (#4) in 1965 and produced artists from Eddy Arnold and The Everly Brothers to Hank Williams and Elvis Presley. He was inducted into both the Country and Rock and Roll Halls of Fame. He died of lung cancer at age seventy-seven.

July

#1 Song 1967: "Windy,"
The Association

Born: Bobby Day (Hollywood Flames),
1930; Delaney Bramlett (Delaney &
Bonnie), 1939; Debbie Harry (Blondie),
1945; June Montiero (Toys), 1946; Dan
Aykroyd (The Blues Brothers), 1952

1956 Elvis Presley wore a tuxedo (given to him by Steve Allen) to perform on *The Steve Allen Show* in New York City. He performed "I Want You, I Need You, I Love You," backed by The Jordanaires, followed by "Hound Dog," singing to a basset hound who was propped up on a pedestal. His appearance earned him a lofty (for the time) $5,000. During the day Elvis listened to some demos, including a song he eventually took to #1 called "Too Much."

1957 A Philadelphia radio station with only 250 watts of power began repeat plays of The Tune Weavers' new release, "Happy, Happy Birthday Baby." By October it was #1.

1978 Martha & the Vandellas reunited for the first time in ten years for a benefit concert for actor Will Geer in Santa Cruz, California. Before Martha became a fabled Motown diva, she worked as a clerk at a Detroit dry cleaner's.

1992 Barbra Streisand, Judy Collins, Vanessa Williams, and Dinah Washington's goddaughter, Patti Austin, performed at a fundraiser for the Hollywood Women's Political Committee.

1997 Wolfman Jack (Robert Smith) was a fabled rock 'n' roll deejay. The Brooklyn teen, influenced by Alan Freed, wound up at a black radio station in Virginia and an illegal 250,000-watt Mexican border station that beamed into two-thirds of the U.S. Most listeners thought he was black, and his mystique carried him to New York and then L.A. radio. He played himself in the film *American Graffiti*. He died of a heart attack after hugging his wife in his driveway. He was fifty-seven.

July 2

#1 Song 1977: "Gonna Fly Now (Theme from *Rocky*)," Bill Conti

Born: Paul Williams (The Temptations), 1939

1956 Elvis Presley recorded three songs, "Hound Dog," "Don't Be Cruel," and "Any Way You Want Me." This was the first time that Presley took personal control over a recording session and his meticulous attention to detail resulted in "Don't Be Cruel" having twenty-eight takes and "Hound Dog" taking thirty-one.

1969 Beatles manager, Brian Epstein, presented The Jeff Beck Group, Cream, and John Mayall's Bluesbreakers at London's Saville Theatre.

1974 The man who brought bass singing into prominence in the '40s and '50s, Jimmy Ricks of The Ravens died.

1983 Elton John's "I Guess That's Why They Call It the Blues" with Stevie Wonder on harmonica peaked at #5 in Britain. It would eventually reach #4 in America.

Beatles' manager Brian Epstein

July 3

#1 Song 1971: "It's Too Late," Carole King

Born: Fontella Bass, 1940; Laura Branigan, 1957

1964 The High Numbers' first single, "I'm the Face," was issued in England. Within six months, their next record would have them known as The Who.

1965 Cher "technically" had her first Hot 100 entry today when "All I Really Want to Do" started its climb to #15. It was the beginning of her thirty-one hit singles streak between 1965 and 1999. It was "technically" because her soon-to-be ex-partner Sonny Bono sang backup on the single.

1966 The Beatles arrived in Manila, Philippines, and were met by two Army battalions fully regaled in combat gear. They were summarily strong-armed out of the plane and taken to Naval headquarters past 50,000 screaming fans.

1967 The Beatles (minus Ringo, who was out of town) attended a party for The Monkees at The Speakeasy in London. Among the guests were Eric Clapton, Lulu, Dusty Springfield, The Who, Procol Harum, Manfred Mann, and Monkees Micky Dolenz, Mike Nesmith, and Peter Tork (Davy Jones was also absent).

1969 Although it was called The Newport Jazz Festival, no less than six rock and R&B acts appeared during the three-day event in Newport, Rhode Island. Included were Led Zeppelin, Jethro Tull, Blood, Sweat & Tears, Jeff Beck, James Brown, and Ten Years After.

1971 Jim Morrison was the idiosyncratic leader of The Doors. The rebellious rocker's mystical vocals were heard on hits like "Touch Me," "People Are Strange," and the rock standard "Light My Fire." Haunted by the deaths of Jimi Hendrix and Janis Joplin, who both died at 27, Morrison died in his bathtub in Paris of a heart attack. He was twenty-seven.

July 4

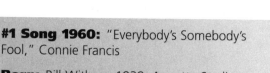

#1 Song 1960: "Everybody's Somebody's Fool," Connie Francis

Born: Bill Withers, 1938; Annette Sterling (The Vandellas), 1943; John Waite, 1955; Jesse Lee Daniels (Force M.D.'s), 1963

1960 The Demensions' magnificent cover of "Over the Rainbow" hit the Top 100 (#16). Their version was the first since Judy Garland's 1939 recording to chart even though sixty different versions had been issued during that twenty-one-year span.

1964 Independence Day may have been the result of the Americans defeating the British, but on the charts the battle was a draw! On the first July 4th since the *musical* British Invasion, both sides had five records in the Top 10. The Brits best was "My Boy Lollipop" (#2) by Millie Small while the Yanks' topper was "I Get Around" by The Beach Boys.

1966 The Beatles performed at Rizal Memorial Football Stadium in Manila, Philippines, doing two shows before a combined audience of more than 80,000 people. Due to their missing a lunch with Imelda Marcos, wife of the dictator, their security was withdrawn and the group had to fight their way to the plane. George Harrison rather seriously stated, "The only way I'd ever return to the Philippines would be to drop an atom bomb on it."

1974 *The Tony Orlando & Dawn* TV variety series debuted on CBS. It ran through December 1976.

1987 Bonnie Raitt sang at The July 4th Disarmament Festival in the Soviet Union along with Santana, The Doobie Brothers, and James Taylor.

Santana

July

#1 Song 1986: "There'll Be Sad Songs," Billy Ocean

Born: Jaime "Robbie" Robertson (The Band), 1944; Huey Lewis, 1950

1954 During Elvis Presley's "song audition" for Sam Phillips at Sun Studios, Presley ran through the gamut of his repertoire without piquing Sam's interest. Elvis then ripped into blues singer Arthur "Big Boy" Crudup's "That's All Right" and Sam Phillips came to life. Phillips now knew he had Elvis Presley's first single.

1965 The Four Seasons were invited to perform at the White House by President Johnson.

1969 The Rolling Stones performed a concert at Hyde Park in London.

1986 Janet Jackson's *Control* album soared to #1, making the twenty-year-old the youngest artist since thirteen-year-old Little Stevie Wonder to top the album Top 200.

July 6

#1 Song 1963: "Easier Said Than Done"
The Essex

Born: Bill Haley, 1925; Della Reese, 1931;
Gene Chandler (Dukays), 1937; Jeannie Seely,
1940; Jan Bradley, 1943; Nancy Griffith, 1953;
Kenny "G" Gorelick, 1956

1957 John Lennon and Paul McCartney met for the first time at the Woolton Parish Church Garden show held at St. Peter's Church in Liverpool. The Quarrymen Skiffle Group performed that afternoon and Lennon sang Gene Vincent's "Be-Bop-A-Lula" for the first time onstage. Between sets, the City of Liverpool Police Dogs performed. Paul later stated that when he met twelve-year-old Lennon, John was drunk: "He didn't know the words for anything, he'd obviously only heard the records and not bought them, but I was pretty impressed." The band also performed Elvis Presley's "Baby Let's Play House," and The Del-Vikings' "Come Go with Me," among others.

1963 Lesley Gore's follow-up to her monster hit, "It's My Party," "Judy's Turn to Cry" hit the singles survey (#2), becoming her second of nineteen eventual hits in only four years.

1963 The Four Seasons' "Candy Girl" (#3) charted. It was their eighth of forty-eight Top 100 hits between 1962 and 1994.

1964 The film *A Hard Day's Night* premiered at the London Pavillion in Piccadilly Circus. Attending the event were The Rolling Stones, Princess Margaret, Lord Snowdon, and, of course, The Beatles, as more than 12,000 fans looked on.

1971 When people think of legendary trumpet players, they think of Louis Armstrong. "Satchmo" had eighty pop hits from 1926 through 1988, including the renowned "Hello Dolly." He influenced hundreds of singers and musicians and was inducted into the Rock and Roll Hall of Fame as a forefather of rock music. He died of a heart attack at sixty-nine today.

July

7

#1 Song 1973: "Will It Go Round in Circles," Billy Preston

Born: Richard Starkey (Ringo Starr), 1940; John Salvato (The Duprees), 1940; Warren Entner (The Grass Roots), 1944

1951 One of the '50s most popular singers, Rosemary Clooney charted with "Come On-A My House." The 45 spent eight weeks at #1 and became the first of six #1s in her future. (P.S. Actor George Clooney is her nephew.)

1954 Sam Phillips journeyed to local radio station WHBQ and played an acetate of "That's All Right" by Elvis Presley for Memphis deejay Dewey Phillips, who was so excited by the recording, he promised to play it on his show the next night, even though the recording had not been pressed or released for distribution.

1961 The Tokens recorded "The Lion Sleeps Tonight" (#1). It would become the first folk rock hit, predating The Byrds, who were considered by many to be the pioneers of folk rock.

1967 The Beatles 45 "All You Need Is Love"/"Baby You're a Rich Man" was issued in Britain. "Baby You're a Rich Man" was originally titled "One of the Beautiful People."

1989 For the first time, compact discs began outselling vinyl LPs.

The Tokens

July

8

#1 Song 1957: "Teddy Bear," Elvis Presley

Born: Louis Jordan, 1908; Billy Eckstine, 1914; Steve Lawrence, 1935

1908 Born today, Louis Jordan was considered by many to be the "Father of Rhythm and Blues." He amassed fifty-seven chart hits, including eighteen #1s between 1942 and 1951. An accomplished sax and clarinet player, Louis and his Tympany 5 originated the shuffle and boogie beat style that was a forerunner of rock 'n' roll. His hits included "Caledonia," "Ain't Nobody Here but Us Chickens," "Saturday Night Fish Fry," and "Choo Choo Ch' Boogie," which spent an incredible eighteen weeks at #1. In fact, his nineteen #1 records combined for a total of 113 weeks at the top spot.

1966 Michelle Gilliam Phillips was fired from The Mamas & the Papas by her husband John Phillips and replaced by Jill Gibson, girlfriend of Jan & Dean's Jan Berry. Michelle returned within a month.

1966 The Beatles returned to London after their Far East tour. George Harrison, obviously worn out, was quoted as saying, "We're going to have a couple of weeks to recuperate before we go and get beaten up by the Americans."

1968 The Yardbirds broke up after a New York concert. Soon after, a new Yardbirds was formed. They became known as Led Zeppelin.

1969 In Australia to work on the film *Ned Kelly* with Mick Jagger, Marianne Faithfull wound up, instead, in a hospital for a drug overdose and was subsequently written out of the script.

July

9

#1 Song 1955: "Rock Around the Clock," Bill Haley & the Comets

Born: Lee Hazlewood, 1929; Phil Leavitt (The Diamonds), 1935; Debbie Sledge (Sister Sledge), 1954; Marc Almond (Soft Cell), 1959; Courtney Love, 1965

1954 With all the hoopla "That's All Right" caused on Dewey Phillips's radio show the night before, Elvis Presley was summoned back to Sun Studio's to cut a B-side, but none of the ballads Presley loved to sing stimulated producer Sam Phillips's interest. Finally he ran down Bill Monroe's hillbilly classic "Blue Moon of Kentucky," in an uptempo fashion, and Phillips had the flip side he wanted.

1955 Bill Haley & the Comets' "Rock Around the Clock" became the first rock 'n' roll record to reach #1 on the national pop charts.

1956 Dick Clark became the host of *American Bandstand* today. It had been previously hosted by local Philadelphia celebrity Bob Horn for several years and was called *Bob Horn's Bandstand*.

1977 Fleetwood Mac's "Don't Stop" charted en route to #3. The hit was later used without permission of the owners by the Dole for President campaign in 1996.

1978 The #1 record in England was Olivia Newton-John's duet with John Travolta, "You're the One That I Want" from the film *Grease*.

American Bandstand's
Dick Clark

July 10

#1 Song 1961: "Tossin' & Turnin'," Bobby Lewis

Born: Arlo Guthrie, 1947; Neil Tennant (Pet Shop Boys), 1954

1976 Captain & Tennille's remake of The Miracles' "Shop Around" peaked at #4, becoming their fourth Top 5 hit in a year.

1976 Rod Stewart's Los Angeles recording of "A Night on the Town" reached #1 in England. Despite its success, it was never issued in America.

1979 Arthur Fiedler was a Boston-bred violinist who joined the legendary Boston Pops Orchestra in 1915 and became its conductor in 1930, carrying the baton for almost fifty years. He even led the orchestra to its only chart record with an instrumental cover of The Beatles' "I Want to Hold Your Hand" in 1964. He died today at age eighty-four.

1982 Former Leonard Cohen backup vocalist Laura Branigan hit the Hot 100 with "Gloria" (#2), her second of thirteen charters between 1982 through 1990. "Gloria" was originally a hit in Italy for its singer-composer, Umberto Tozzi.

1989 Gene Pitney, B.J. Thomas, and The Shirelles appeared in Nashville, but not to perform. They were in Federal Court to sue local Gusto Records over improper payments of royalties on reissued hits. They won ten months later. Pitney for one was awarded $187,000.

July

11

#1 Song 1960: "Alley Oop,"
Hollywood Argyles

Born: Jeff Hanna (The Nitty Gritty Dirt Band), 1947; Bonnie Pointer (The Pointer Sisters), 1951; Benny Defranco (Defranco Family), 1954

1951 Alan Freed aired his first R&B radio show on WJW in Cleveland.

1955 Almost a year to the date of Elvis Presley's first recording session at Sun for "That's All Right, "Elvis recorded "I Forgot to Remember to Forget" and Little Junior Parker's "Mystery Train," which Sam Phillips originally produced on Parker in 1953 and a number by the R&B group The Eagles, "Trying to Get to You." The first two songs would soon become Presley's next single.

1966 John Lennon and Paul McCartney received two prestigious British honors when they won the Ivor Novello Awards for "We Can Work It Out" as the Top British Sales Single of 1965 and Outstanding Song of 1965 for "Yesterday."

1967 Kenny Rogers formed the First Edition. The country rock band charted ten times through 1972 before Rogers went off on his spectacular solo career. Ten years earlier, almost to the day (July 8, 1957), The Scholars' pop record "Beloved" (Imperial) was released. The quartet included nineteen-year-old tenor, Kenny Rogers.

1988 Gloria Estefan and Linda Ronstadt performed at the first International Festival of Arts in New York's Central Park.

July 12

#1 Song 1980: "Coming Up," Paul McCartney and Wings

Born: Jay "Jaybird" Uzzell (Corsairs), 1942; Jerry Williams, Jr., 1942; Christine McVie (Fleetwood Mac), 1943

1956 Shirley & Lee sang at the Carrs Beach Amphitheater in Maryland along with The Teenagers, Carl Perkins, The Cleftones, and The Spaniels. More than 8,000 lucky fans got in to see them while an unlucky 10,000 were turned away!

1962 The Rolling Stones made their debut performance at The Marquee Club in London.

Christine McVie

195

July 13

#1 Song 1959: "Lonely Boy," Paul Anka

Born: Roger McGuinn (The Byrds), 1942

1956 Elvis Presley's third RCA single, "Don't Be Cruel," with a B-side of "Hound Dog" was released. In a matter of weeks, "Hound Dog" vaulted to #2 and sold more than one million copies before being overrun by the chart-topping performance of "Don't Be Cruel." By year's end, the double-sided smash had sold more than four million singles.

1963 Neil Diamond's very first single, "Clown Town" on Columbia, was released and quickly vanished. Nine years later, he signed with Columbia again, this time for the then unheard of guarantee of $5 million!

1985 In the most ambitious rock and pop festival ever held, more than fifty legendary acts performed in two simultaneous events broadcast live from both Philadelphia, Pennsylvania, and London, England. Known as the Live Aid (to raise money for starving Africans), the concert included Paul McCartney; Bob Dylan; Mick Jagger; The Beach Boys; Madonna, Elton John; David Bowie; The Who; Queen, Santana; The Little River Band; Tina Turner; The Four Tops; Ozzy Osbourne; Joan Baez; Patti LaBelle; David Ruffin & Eddie Kendricks; The Pretenders; Tom Petty & the Heartbreakers; B.B. King; Men at Work; Black Sabbath; Jimmy Page; Robert Plant; Crosby, Stills, Nash & Young; and Duran Duran.

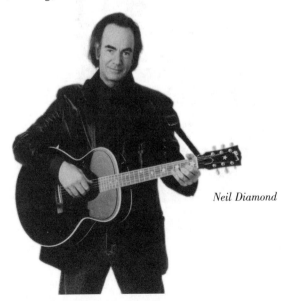

Neil Diamond

July 14

#1 Song 1962: "Roses Are Red," Bobby Vinton

Born: Woody Guthrie, 1912; Bob Scholl (Mello-Kings), 1938

1958 Sultry jazz singer Norma Jean Egstrom, better known as Peggy Lee, heated up the hit list with "Fever," her eventual signature song and a #8 winner.

1958 The Drinkard Singers' (RCA) spiritual 45 "Rise, Shine" was issued. The group consisted of Dionne Warwick, Cissy Houston (Whitney's mother), Dee Dee Warwick (Dionne's sister), and Judy Clay.

1962 One of the most powerful vocalists of the '60s, Timi Yuro rocked onto the Hot 100 with "What's a Matter Baby" (#12). Unfortunately for her fans, the petite powerhouse lost her voice in 1980 and underwent several throat operations.

1964 A new duo, Caesar & Cleo, debuted with the release of their first single, "The Letter." Although it received little attention, they would soon become known worldwide when they changed their name to Sonny & Cher.

1973 The Everly Brothers announced their breakup, or at least Don did after Phil slammed his guitar down and walked offstage in the middle of a song at the John Wayne Theatre in Buena Park, California.

July

#1 Song 1989: "If You Don't Know Me by Now," Simply Red

Born: Millie Jackson, 1944; Linda Ronstadt, 1946; Alicia Bridges, 1953

Died: Bobby Day (Hollywood Flames), 1990

1952 An eight-year-old girl won $2,000 and a gold cup for her rendition of "Too Young" on Ted Mack's *Amateur Hour*. The child was Gladys Knight.

1973 During a concert, the leader of The Kinks, Ray Davies, announced his retirement and then immediately checked into Whittington Hospital after swallowing a bottle of uppers.

1989 Madonna's single "Express Yourself" peaked at #2. It made her #2 in all-time Top 5 hits consecutively, surpassing The Beatles, who had fifteen but leaving her sixteen far removed from Elvis Presley's record of twenty-four.

1990 Bobby Day (Robert Byrd) was a terrific R&B vocalist of the '50s who recorded as lead for several Los Angeles groups (The Flames, The Hollywood Flames, The Satellites, etc.) and had hits like "Little Bitty Pretty One," "Buzz, Buzz, Buzz," and "Rockin' Robin." Bobby died of cancer at age fifty-nine today.

July 16

#1 Song 1977: "Da Doo Ron Ron," Shaun Cassidy

Born: Sollie McElroy (The Flamingos), 1933; Desmond Dekker, 1941; Stewart Copeland (The Police), 1952

1966 Elvis Presley's album *Paradise, Hawaiian Style* charted on its way to #15 on the national album chart. It was Presley's thirty-third straight hit album.

1972 Smokey Robinson left The Miracles for a solo career. He had been with them for eighteen years.

1981 One of America's great musical storytellers, Harry Chapin was a folk-rock singer who originally recorded an album with his father and brothers called *Chapin Music*. Best known for the hits "Taxi" and "Cats in the Cradle," Chapin also wrote and appeared in the Tony-nominated Broadway musical *The Night That Made America Famous*. He died today when a tractor ran into his car on the Long Island Expressway, New York, at age thirty-eight.

1983 The female version of Rod Stewart, Bonnie Tyler charted with "Total Eclipse of the Heart" (#1). Her distinctive, raspy sound was caused by a throat operation to remove nodules in 1976.

1985 Madonna's "Crazy for You" was certified gold. It was her fifth Top 10 hit and second #1 in a year.

Smokey Robinson & the Miracles

July

17

#1 Song 1982: "Don't You Want Me," The Human League

Born: Stan Bronstein (Elephant's Memory), 1938; Spencer Davis, 1942; Gale Garnett, 1942; Mick Tucker (Sweet), 1948; Nicolette Larson, 1952; Phoebe Snow, 1952

1942 Spencer Davis, the founder and leader of the Spencer Davis Group, was born today. With Steve Winwood on lead vocals, the band—formed in Birmingham, England, in 1963—went on to have numerous hits in the U.S. and U.K., including "Gimme Some Lovin'" and "I'm a Man."

1948 Margaret Whiting hit the best-seller's lists with "A Tree in the Meadow," a #1 smash for five weeks and the biggest of her career thirty-six hits. She was the daughter of composer Richard Whiting ("Till We Meet Again").

1954 Elvis Presley appeared at the Bon Air Club in Memphis, with his two musicians, Scotty and Bill, and performed the two songs ("That's All Right" and "Blue Moon of Kentucky") that would shortly become their new single. Their performance that night was limited to the two tunes because they were the only songs they knew well enough to play in front of an audience.

1967 In one of the most bizarre performance pairings in history, The Monkees appeared at Forest Hills Stadium, New York, with show opener Jimi Hendrix!

1971 Agnetha Faltskog married Bjørn Ulvaeus in Verum, Sweden. Less than three years later they would have their first hit, "Waterloo," as half of the international success ABBA.

ABBA

July 18

#1 Song 1964: "Rag Doll," The Four Seasons

Born: Screamin' Jay Hawkins, 1929; Dion DiMucci (Dion & the Belmonts), 1939; Martha Reeves, 1941; Linda Gail Lewis, 1947; Cindy Herron (En Vogue), 1965.

1960 Elvis Presley's "It's Now or Never" hit the charts on its way to #1 for five weeks. One of his biggest hits, the song was based on the 1899 Italian ballad "O Sole Mio."

1963 The Beatles began working on their second album at Abbey Road Studios. Some of the tunes included The Miracles "You Really Got a Hold on Me," Barrett Strong's "Money (That's What I Want)," and The Everly Brothers' "Till There Was You."

1966 Bobby Fuller was a Texas rocker who made his way to Los Angeles with his group, The Bobby Fuller Four. Phil Spector tried to sign them, but they wound up with Bob Keene's Mustang label having hits with the classic anti-hero anthem "I Fought the Law" and the Buddy Holly song "Love's Made a Fool of You." Fuller died of asphyxiation in his car. Some say he was beaten to death because he was dating a mobster's wife, but the coroner disputed that. He was only twenty-two.

1970 Outrageous rocker Arthur Brown of "Fire" fame was arrested in Palermo, Sicily, for stripping onstage.

1970 Canadian songbird Anne Murray charted with "Snowbird" (#8). It was her first of twenty-eight U.S. hits through 1986 along with fifty-four country winners.

1989 The Jefferson Airplane reformed with original members (Grace Slick, Marty Balin, Paul Kantner, Jorma Kaukonen, and Jack Casady). The group then became Starship.

July

#1 Song 1980: "It's Still Rock 'n' Roll to Me," Billy Joel

Born: Sue Thompson, 1926; Vikki Carr, 1941; Bernie Leadon (The Eagles), 1947; Brian May (Queen), 1947

1958 George Treadwell, The Drifters' manager, walked backstage at the Apollo Theater, fired his group, walked across to the dressing room of the group's opening act, The Crowns, hired them, and then christened them The Drifters. The Crowns' lead singer was a youngster named Ben E. Nelson, but soon he would be known as Ben E. King.

1960 Duane Eddy performed his hit "Rebel Rouser" on Dick Clark's prime time TV show. Also performed was a new Eddy work-in-progress called "Ramrod." By Monday, there were orders for 150,000 copies of "Ramrod," but no recording because the tracks were unfinished. Producer Lee Hazelwood rushed into the studio, added a sax part and vocal overdubs, and issued the single, only to later find that Eddy was most likely not even on the remixed recording as the lead guitar work was by studio veteran Al Casey. Little of the intrigue mattered to the public, which took "Ramrod" to #27, selling over 600,000 copies!

1969 The Brooklyn Bridge's fourth of seven Top 100 entries, "Your Husband, My Wife" (#46), charted. The vocal members consisted of former Crests leader Johnny Maestro and three of The Del Satins.

July 20

#1 Song 1963: "Surf City,"
Jan & Dean

Born: Buddy Knox, 1933; Jo Ann
Campbell, 1938; Kim Carnes, 1945;
John Lodge (The Moody Blues), 1945;
Carlos Santana (Santana), 1947; Merlin
DeFranco (DeFranco Family), 1957

1945 John Lodge, vocalist and bass for The Moody Blues, entered the world on this day. He joined the group two years after their formation and just in time for their renaissance, in the mid and late '60s with such epics as "Tuesday Afternoon," "Question," and "Nights in White Satin," which charted three times in England (1967, 1972, and 1979).

1954 Elvis Presley gave his first public performance outside a Memphis drug store, on a flatbed truck.

1963 The Essex's "Easier Said Than Done" hit #1 R&B (and eventually pop). Led by Anita Humes, the quintet were all active Marines and needed Marine Corps approval to tour.

1964 Seven days after releasing the single "A Hard Day's Night" in the U.S., Capitol Records issued two more 45s, "I'll Cry Instead"/"I'm Happy Just to Dance with You" and "And I Love Her"/"If I Fell," as well as the album *Something New*, which, along with the above four recordings, also included their German version of "I Want to Hold Your Hand."

July

#1 Song 1958: "Yakety Yak," The Coasters

Born: Kay Starr, 1922; Kim Fowley, 1944; Cat Stevens, 1947

1958 The Elegants' "Little Star" (#1) charted. It was based on Mozart's variations of "Twinkle, Twinkle Little Star" written by the eight-year-old in 1764!

1959 Fifteen-year-old Bobby Vee—who replaced Buddy Holly at a Fargo, North Dakota, concert when Holly died the night before—had his first single issued titled "Suzy Baby" (#77). Vee went on to have thirty-eight chart hits.

1977 Linda Ronstadt did a duet with Mick Jagger on "Tumbling Dice" at a Rolling Stones concert in Tucson, Arizona.

1990 Joni Mitchell took part in the performance of "The Wall" at the Berlin Wall in Berlin, Germany. The event was staged to raise money for the Memorial Fund For Disaster Relief and was broadcast live around the world.

July 22

#1 Song 1972: "Lean on Me," Bill Withers

Born: Margaret Whiting, 1924; Thomas Wayne (Delons), 1940; Bobby Sherman, 1943; Estelle Bennett (The Ronettes), 1944; Rick Davies (Supertramp), 1944; Don Henley (The Eagles), 1947

1960 When Las Vegas entertainer Gary Crosby became ill, Bobby Darin, himself in the middle of a Vegas stand, filled in for Crosby's four-week early show stint at The Flamingo while continuing to do his own nightly late show at The Sahara.

1962 Ray Charles performed at the Dallas Memorial Auditorium before 10,000 adoring and integrated fans. The concert was a peaceful affair, unlike his previous show in Atlanta, where he was fined for refusing to play for a segregated audience.

1967 The Beatles charted in America with "All You Need Is Love," which eventually reached #1. It was their fourteenth #1 in the U. S. in just three-and-a-half years.

1977 Tony Orlando announced during a show with his act, Dawn, that he was retiring from performing, which shocked the group, since he never told them.

1991 Twenty-five years after its release, Simon & Garfunkel's *Sounds of Silence* album was certified by the RIAA as a two-million-seller.

July

#1 Song 1977: "Looks Like We Made It," Barry Manilow

Born: Cleve Duncan (The Penguins), 1935; Tony Joe White, 1943; Dino Danelli (The Rascals), 1945; David Essex, 1947; Martin Gore (Depeche Mode), 1961

1965 Four days after its American release, The Beatles' "Help!" was released in England. John later stated that he was going through great depression when he wrote the tune, which was really a cry on his behalf for help. He said, "It was my fat Elvis period."

1977 Rod Stewart's "The Killing of Georgie" peaked at #30 in the U.S. The story of a gay friend's death in New York reached #2 in the U.K.

1977 Foreigner's "Cold as Ice" charted on its way to #6. It was their second of twenty-one chart singles.

1977 Carly Simon ascended the Hot 100 with "Nobody Does It Better" (#2) from the James Bond film *The Spy Who Loved Me.*

1988 Former Polish vocalist for the British group Matt Bianco, Basia charted in the U.S. with "Time and Tide" (#26).

July 24

#1 Song 1971: "Indian Reservation," The Raiders

Born: Barbara Love (Friends of Distinction), 1941; Pam Tillis, 1957

1961 Timi Yuro reached the best-seller's list with the scorching ballad "Hurt" (#4). It was the first of eleven hits through 1965 for the Chicago native.

1964 The Who performed at The Refectory in North West London, but were told not to return when they maxed out the volume after pleas to turn it down.

1965 The California folk quintet The We Five, with Beverly Bivens singing lead, charged onto the pop survey with "You Were on My Mind" (#3).

1965 The Lovin' Spoonful performed in a Greenwich Village club for an audience that included Bob Dylan and Phil Spector.

1971 Carole King's landmark album *Tapestry* hit the British charts en route to #4. It was already #1 for five weeks in the U.S., along with the hit single "It's Too Late." The album stayed at #1 for fifteen weeks while staying on the charts for an amazing 302 weeks and selling more than 15 million albums.

July 25

#1 Song 1960: "I'm Sorry," Brenda Lee

Born: Rudy West (The Five Keys), 1932; Verdine White (Earth, Wind & Fire), 1951

1936 Ella Fitzgerald bounced onto the singles survey with "Sing Me a Swing Song" (#18). It became the first of fifty-three pop hits through 1963 for the all-time jazz great, who was discovered after a winning performance on the Harlem Amateur Hour in 1934.

1965 Bob Dylan's folk era changed to rock when he performed at The Newport Folk Festival with an electric back-up group, The Paul Butterfield Blues Band. He was roundly booed.

1970 Dawn's "Candida" charted (#3), becoming their first of twenty-five Top 100 hits.

1981 Stevie Nicks, formerly of Fritz and Fleetwood Mac, leaped onto the Hot 100 with "Stop Draggin' My Heart Around" (#3). It was her debut solo success of fourteen hits she would have through 1994.

1984 Willie Mae "Big Mama" Thornton was a powerful blues singer who also played drums and harmonica. It must have been a sight to see a 350-pound woman pounding out drumbeats in the '40s. She's best known for her original growling version of "Hound Dog" (later recorded by Elvis Presley) and "Ball and Chain" (later cut by Janis Joplin). She died of alcohol dependency in Los Angeles at age fifty-seven today.

July 26

1954 Elvis Presley signed a formal contract with Sun Records. It was for a minimum of eight sides over a period of two years, with the contract renewable at the record company's option for a second period of two years. Elvis's royalty rate was three percent of the wholesale price.

1963 The Beatles American album debut, *Introducing The Beatles*, was released in the U.S. on Vee Jay. The original issue in order was, Side A: "I Saw Her Standing There," Misery," "Anna (Go to Him)," "Chains," "Boys," "Love Me Do." Side B: "P.S. I Love You," "Baby It's You," "Do You Want to Know a Secret," "A Taste of Honey," "There's a Place," and "Twist & Shout."

1969 Dionne Warwick charted two albums (*Odds and Ends*, #43 in 1969; and *No Night So Long*, #23 in 1980) the same day, eleven years apart.

1986 The Eurythmics reached the Hot 100 with "Missionary Man" (#15), their eleventh hit in less than three years.

1992 Mary Wells was Motown's first million-selling singer when she hit with "My Guy." She came to Motown as an aspiring songwriter with a tune intended for Jackie Wilson, but Berry Gordy heard her and recorded the seventeen-year-old on her song, "Bye Bye Baby" (#45 pop, #8 R&B). She went on to have twenty-three hits through 1968. She died of cancer today at forty-nine.

Mick Jagger

July

27

#1 Song 1959: "Lonely Boy," Paul Anka

Born: Harvey Fuqua (The Moonglows), 1928; Nick Reynolds (The Kingston Trio), 1933; Bobbie Gentry, 1944

1974 Bo Donaldson & the Heywoods' hit (#15) "Who Do You Think You Are" charted, in part thanks to a young New York music publisher who heard the song from England and sent it to producer Steve Barri in Los Angeles. Barri was quick to respond since the same publishing company had supplied him with another English song months earlier for Bo & the Heywoods, the #1 million-seller "Billy Don't Be a Hero."

1974 Dionne Warwick teamed with The Spinners on "Then Came You," which charted today. It would go on to become the first #1 single for both acts, even though Dionne had thirty-nine previous pop charters over twelve years, and The Spinners had broached the Top 100 thirteen times since 1961.

1976 John Lennon finally received his U.S. green card, three years and four months after U.S. Immigration had ordered him to leave.

1991 When Natalie Cole brought the idea of singing a duet album with her father Nat "King" Cole's old recordings to her label, EMI refused, so she signed with Electra Records, recorded the album titled *Unforgettable...With Love*, and today it topped the album charts.

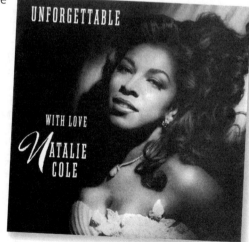

210

July 28

#1 Song 1956: "I Want You, I Need You, I Love You," Elvis Presley

Born: Michael Bloomfield (Electric Flag), 1944; Richard Wright (Pink Floyd), 1945

1945 Richard Wright, the keyboard player for the rock superband Pink Floyd, was born today. A founding member of the group that formed in 1965, Wright performed on such hits as "Another Brick in the Wall" and "Money." The band took its name from two blues artists, Pink Anderson and Floyd Council.

1954 Publicity over Elvis's first performance at Overton Park Shell in Memphis included one ad that had him listed as "*Ellis* Presley." Another stated, "Elvis *Pesley* new Memphis star who sings 'Blue Moon of Kentucky' and 'That's All Right Mama.'"

1966 Janis Joplin and Big Brother & the Holding Company were discovered playing at California Hall by Mainstream Records president Bob Shad. He offered them a recording contract, but they turned him down.

1973 The largest rock concert to date happened at a Watkins Glen race-track in Upstate New York when The Band, The Allman Brothers, and The Grateful Dead performed for more than 600,000 people.

1996 Margie Ganser was a member of the "Queens of Musical Melodrama," The Shangri-Las. She and her twin sister, Mary Ann, joined sisters Mary and Betty Weiss to form the group in high school. Discovered by svengali George "Shadow" Morton, they turned out teen angst classics like "Remember," "Leader of the Pack," and "Give Us Your Blessings." Blending sensuality with innocence, they rode the charts eleven times from 1964 through 1966. Margie died of breast cancer at age forty-nine.

July

29

#1 Song 1972: "Alone Again, Naturally," Gilbert O'Sullivan

Born: Neal Doughty (REO Speedwagon), 1946; Geddy Lee (Rush), 1953

1969 Elvis Presley performed his opening night show at the International Hotel in Las Vegas (later known as the Hilton Hotel), with The Sweet Inspirations backing him vocally. The packed house of celebrities included Fats Domino, folksinger Phil Ochs, Cary Grant, Sam Phillips, and Pat Boone. Elvis started with "Blue Suede Shoes" and, by the time he was done, Colonel Parker had negotiated a new deal with the hotel for Elvis to receive $1 million a year for eight weeks on the job, covering the next five years. The deal was written out on a tablecloth in the hotel's coffee shop!

1965 The Beatles film *Help!* was premiered at the London Pavilion in Piccadilly Circus. John Lennon's opinion: "The best stuff is on the cutting room floor, with us breaking up and falling about all over the place." True or not, more than ten thousand fans congregated in Piccadilly Circus outside the Pavilion for a glimpse of their heroes, and the film would go on to be a landmark success.

1966 Bob Dylan suffered severe injuries during a motorcycle accident near his Woodstock, New York, home.

1974 Cass Elliot (Ellen Naomi Cohen) was a great vocalist with the '60s trendsetters, The Mamas & the Papas. She had sixteen hits with the quartet, including "California Dreamin'" and "Monday, Monday." She also had seven solo charters, including "Dream a Little Dream of Me." She died in singer Harry Nilsson's London flat from a heart attack brought on by choking on a ham sandwich. She was only thirty-two. It was the same apartment where The Who's Keith Moon died four years later.

1978 Barbra Streisand charted with "Prisoner (Captured by Your Eyes)" (#21), the theme song from the film *Eyes of Laura Mars*. The song was originally recorded by Karen Lawrence & the L.A. Jets and brought to Streisand's attention by music publisher Jay Warner.

July

30

#1 Song 1966: "Wild Thing,"
The Troggs

Born: Paul Anka, 1941;
Kate Bush, 1958

1954 Elvis Presley's first professional live performance was held at the Overton Park Shell, Memphis, Tennessee.

1963 The Beatles recorded "It Won't Be Long," "Please Mister Postman," "All My Loving," "Roll Over Beethoven," and "Till There Was You."

1989 Pete Seeger performed at the thirtieth Newport Folk Festival in Newport, Rhode Island, along with a cross section of artists from John Lee Hooker to Emmylou Harris.

1991 Arsenio Hall's entire TV program was devoted to Patti LaBelle.

Pete Seeger

July

31

#1 Song 1971: "You've Got a Friend," James Taylor

Born: John West (Gary Lewis & the Playboys), 1939; Gary Lewis (The Playboys), 1945; Bob Welch, 1946

1960 The Silver Beatles, without a regular drummer, were relegated to playing at an illegal strip club as the backing band for a stripper named Janice. They earned 50 pence a night. Paul McCartney played drums and once noted, "At the end of the act she would turn round and...well, we were all young lads, we'd never seen anything like it before, and all blushed...four blushing, red-faced lads."

1961 The group that sang backup for most of Chubby Checker's hits finally scored with one of their own when The Dreamlovers "When We Get Married," charted eventually reaching #10.

1964 In one of their early performances, The Who performed at the Goldhawk Social club, Sheperd's Bush, England, alongside Gerry & the Pacemakers and The Nashville Teens. In order to get their ten-minute performance they grudgingly agreed to back unknown female vocalist Valerie McCullam.

1967 Janis Joplin played a benefit for The Free Clinic with Blue Cheer and The Charlatans (with Bill Cosby playing drums).

1968 The Beatles' "Hey Jude" was released.

The Who

214

August

#1 Song 1964: "A Hard Day's Night,"
The Beatles

Born: Jerry Garcia (The Grateful Dead), 1942;
Rick Coonce (Grassroots), 1947; Robert Cray,
1953; Joe Elliot (Def Leppard), 1959

Died: Johnny Burnette, 1964

1958 The Teddy Bears' ballad, "To Know Him Is to Love Him" with Carol Connors singing lead, was released. It reached #1 while launching the production career of group member Phil Spector.

1960 When the originally scheduled vocalist didn't show, producer Ike Turner took his twenty-two-year-old wife, Tina, and recorded her on "A Fool in Love," which was released today. It rose to #27 and became the first of twenty Hot 100 hits for the volatile couple.

1964 Boxer-turned-rockabilly singer Johnny Burnette formed the Memphis area rock 'n' roll trio with his brother Dorsey and friend Paul Burlison in 1952. They recorded the rockabilly classic, "Train Kept a-Rollin'," and appeared in Alan Freed's film *Rock, Rock, Rock*. Johnny moved to L.A. as a writer and had hits as a solo act with 1960s "Dreamin" and "You're Sixteen," in which he took on an Elvis persona. He died today in a boating accident when a larger craft hit his while he was fishing at dusk. He was thirty.

1971 *The Sonny & Cher Comedy Hour* began its run on CBS-TV today. It would run for sixty-one episodes through May 1974.

1981 Pat Benatar's video of "You Better Run," a cover of The Rascals 1966 hit, became the second video broadcast on the fledgling MTV cable network, the first being The Buggles' "Video Killed the Radio Star."

August

2

#1 Song 1975: "One of These Nights," The Eagles

Born: Edward Patten (Gladys Knight & the Pips), 1939; Doris Kenner (The Shirelles), 1941; Andrew Gold, 1951; Apollonia, 1961

Died: Brian Cole (The Association), 1972

1964 The Kinks performed at the Gaumont Cinema in Bournemouth England with The Beatles. The band had formed in 1963 and were still a month away from their first American hit, "You Really Got Me."

1965 Elvis Presley began working on the motion picture *Paradise, Hawaiian Style*.

1970 Janis Joplin played a concert in Forest Hills, New York.

1973 The Mamas & the Papas leader, John Phillips, sued the group's old label, Dunhill Records, for $9 million claiming "systematic theft" of royalties.

2001 Ron Townson of the Grammy-winning pop group The 5th Dimension died at his home in Las Vegas. Townson and his childhood friend LaMonte McLemore formed a doo-wop singing group in 1965 that they called The Versatiles. Soon after they were renamed The Fifth Dimension at the suggestion of Townson's wife.

August
3

#1 Song 1963: "So Much in Love," The Tymes

Born: Gordon Stoker (The Jordanaires), 1935; Beverly Lee (The Shirelles), 1941

1963 The Beatles' made their last performance at Liverpool's Cavern Club, reportedly their 292nd, although the number has often been questioned.

1963 The Beach Boys' "Surfer Girl" charted on its way to #7 nationally. The Brian Wilson composition was inspired by "When You Wish upon a Star," the first song Brian ever sang.

1969 Janis Joplin sung a duet with Little Richard at the Atlantic City Pop Festival.

1974 Anne Murray headlined a Schaefer Festival concert in New York. The opening act was Bruce Springsteen's E Street Band.

Anne Murray

August

#1 Song 1956: "My Prayer," The Platters

Born: Louis Armstrong, 1901; Elsbeary Hobbs (The Drifters), 1936; Big Dee Irwin (The Pastels), 1939; Frankie Ford, 1939; Timi Yuro, 1941

1937 The legendary Golden Gate Quartet recorded an amazing fourteen songs in two hours at the Charlotte Hotel in Charlotte, North Carolina.

1958 *Billboard*'s "Hot 100" singles chart was born.

1963 In what would become one of the many unique ways The Beatles would get to their performances in future years, they entered the Queen's Theatre in Blackpool through a trapdoor on the roof, reached via scaffolding from the next building's yard, because the regular entrances were blocked by fans.

1968 The Newport Pop Festival, the second major rock festival, was held and included such acts as The Byrds, Steppenwolf, Iron Butterfly, The Chambers Brothers, and two acts from the previous year's Monterey International Pop Festival—The Paul Butterfield Blues Band and Quicksilver Messenger Service.

1979 Nicolette Larson, Bonnie Raitt, Emmylou Harris, and Linda Ronstadt were among the performers at a benefit concert to aid the widow of Lowell George at the Great Western Forum in Inglewood, California.

August
5

#1 Song 1967: "Light My Fire," The Doors

Born: Rick Derringer (The McCoys), 1947

Died: Jeff Porcaro (Toto), 1992

1952 The "5" Royales recorded "You Know, I Know" (Apollo), their second of a career fifty-one secular singles. Moving across town, they passed themselves off as a gospel group, The Royal Sons Quartet, and recorded two songs the same day, for the same label!

1957 The Chordettes were the first guests on Dick Clark's *American Bandstand* after it began airing on ABC-TV nationally. The show would go on to be a national institution for more than thirty years and, as always hosted, by Dick Clark.

1966 The Beatles' "Eleanor Rigby"/"Yellow Submarine" was issued in England, along with the *Revolver* album, which included "Eleanor Rigby," "Here There and Everywhere," "Got to Get You into My Life," "Yellow Submarine," "She Said She Said," "Good Day Sunshine," "And Your Bird Can Sing," and "Taxman." Three days later the album and single would be released in America.

1972 Bill Haley & the Comets headlined the first U.K. rock 'n' roll revival concert, featuring Chuck Berry, Little Richard, Jerry Lee Lewis, and Bo Diddley.

1981 Olivia Newton-John was honored with a star on Hollywood's Walk of Fame.

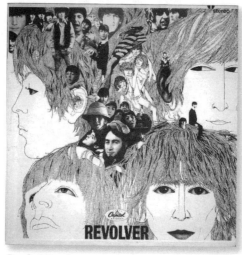

Beatles' Revolver

219

August

#1 Song 1977: "I Just Want to Be Your Everything," Andy Gibb

Born: Judy Craig (The Chiffons), 1946; Randy DeBarge (DeBarge). 1958

1956 Filming began on Alan Freed's classic flick *Rock, Rock, Rock*, featuring Chuck Berry, Frankie Lymon & the Teenagers, The Flamingos, The Moonglows, and LaVern Baker.

1960 Chubby Checker debuted "The Twist" on national TV when he performed it on *American Bandstand*.

1965 The Beatles album *Help!* was issued in England on Parlophone. Aside from the title tune, the album contained thirteen songs, including "You've Got to Hide Your Love Away," "You're Going to Lose that Girl," "Ticket to Ride," "Act Naturally," "You Like Me Too Much," "Yesterday," and "Dizzy Miss Lizzy."

1994 Former public school teacher Sheryl Crow charted on the road to immense success and frustration when "All I Wanna Do" peaked at #2 for six straight weeks! Nothing it seemed was going to dislodge Boyz II Men and their "I'll Make Love to You" single, which stayed in the top slot for fourteen weeks.

1994 Melissa Etheridge hit the singles survey with "I'm the Only One" (#8).

August 7

#1 Song 1971: "How Can You Mend a Broken Heart," The Bee Gees

Born: Herb Reed (The Platters), 1931; B.J. Thomas, 1942; Kerry Chater (Gary Puckett & the Union Gap), 1945

Died: Little Esther Phillips, 1984

1954 Willie Mays (the sensational young center fielder for the New York Giants) and The Treniers recorded "Say Hey" for Epic Records and it was issued today. Although it was heavily played in New York, obviously other baseball towns didn't appreciate it and the single never gained national attention. The record remained popular in New York until Willie and the Giants moved to San Francisco in 1958.

1957 John Lennon debuted at The Cavern Club in Liverpool with The Quarrymen Skiffle Group. The Cavern was a jazz and skiffle club at the time and when the group performed "Come Go with Me," "Hound Dog," and "Blue Suede Shoes," the owner Alan Sytner sent a note to the stage reading, "Cut out the bloody rock!"

1960 Jacquie O'Sullivan, a vocalist with the group Bananarama, was born today. The vocal trio charted eleven times in America, including "Venus" and "Cruel Summer" in the '80s.

1966 Roy Orbison began work on the soundtrack and film *The Fastest Gun Alive*, which was his only film. His role was originally intended for Elvis.

1971 Frank Zappa and The Mothers of Invention recorded a live album, *Just Another Band from L.A.*, at U.C.L.A. with Turtles members Mark Volman and Howard Kaylan.

August

8

#1 Song 1960: "Itsy Bitsy Teenie Weenie Yellow Polka Dot Bikini," Brian Hyland

Born: Joe Tex, 1933; Connie Stevens, 1938; Airrion Love (The Stylistics), 1949; The Edge (U2), 1961

1957 Elvis Presley appeared at the Mayfair Building in Tyler, Texas, with Jim Ed Brown and Maxine Brown. Drummer D. J. Fontana, who would go on to play with Presley for years to come, joined Elvis for the first time on a regular basis.

1964 Gale Garnett was on her way to her biggest hit when "We'll Sing in the Sunshine" charted, becoming a million-selling #4.

1966 Due to John Lennon's remarks about The Beatles being bigger than Jesus, their records were banned in South Africa. The ban lasted until after the group broke up and John's solo recordings remained banned until long after he died.

1969 The world-famous *Abbey Road* album cover was shot today outside the namesake studio and street. A police officer held up traffic while The Beatles' photographer, Ian Macmillan, stood atop a step ladder and marched the Mop Tops across the zebra-like street corner in order to get the historic picture.

1991 Paul Simon and Billy Joel performed at Indian Field Ranch in Montauk, Long Island, New York, for a benefit sponsored by Joel.

August

9

#1 Song 1975: "Jive Talkin'," The Bee Gees

Born: Billy Henderson (The Spinners), 1939; Kurtis Blow, 1959; Whitney Houston, 1963; Barbara Mason, 1947

Died: Jerry Garcia, 1995

1952 Former Pied Pipers member Jo Stafford reached the hit list today with "You Belong to Me." The standard spent an incredible twelve weeks at #1 and was the biggest of seventy-eight hits for the #1 female vocalist of the pre-rock era.

1963 The American Bandstand of England, *Ready, Steady, Go* debuted on BBC TV.

1965 A band from Hull, England, called The Silkie was discovered by Brian Epstein. The four-piece group fronted by Sylvia Tatler recorded "You've Got to Hide Your Love Away" today, with John Lennon overseeing. George Harrison played tambourine while Paul McCartney played guitar on a record that eventually reached #10 in America and #28 in the U.K.

1986 Billy Joel's thirtieth Top 100 hit, "A Matter of Trust," charted today, en route to #10 becoming the tenth Top 10 single of his career.

1995 Jerry Garcia was the legendary leader of the San Francisco hippie musicians, The Grateful Dead. Their break came when they performed at the Monterey Pop Festival in 1967. Always more popular in person than on record, the band had a legion of fans who followed them around the country. Ben & Jerry's Ice Cream named a flavor after the aging hippie, "Cherry Garcia." He died of a heart attack today brought on by his constant drug use at age fifty-three.

Jerry Garcia

August

10

#1 Song 1959: "A Big Hunk o' Love," Elvis Presley

Born: Bobby Hatfield (The Righteous Brothers), 1940; Ronnie Spector (The Ronettes), 1945; Ian Anderson (Jethro Tull), 1947; Michael Bivins (New Edition), 1968

1956 The Penguins rerecorded version of "Earth Angel" was released when the group signed with Mercury Records. It was almost two years after their original hit was out, and the new recording went nowhere. Interestingly, Penguins manager Buck Ram parlayed a deal with Mercury whereby the label had to take an unknown group Ram handled if they wanted The Penguins. They agreed and reluctantly signed The Platters, who went on to have thirty-five hits for the label through 1962, while becoming America's first worldwide musical ambassadors. The Penguins, whom Mercury desperately wanted, never had another hit.

1958 Elvis Presley performed at the Florida Theater in Jacksonville. A local judge hauled Presley into the judge's chambers after his first show and ordered him to tone down his act. Elvis told reporters, "I can't figure out what I'm doing wrong. I know my mother approves of what I'm doing."

1975 Manhattan Transfer began a four-week run with their own CBS-TV comedy-variety show.

1991 The 5th Dimension received a star on Hollywood's Walk of Fame, and then the original quintet began a reunion tour after being two separate entities—The 5th Dimension, Marilyn McCoo & Billy Davis—for sixteen years.

1991 Metallica embarked on the Monsters of Rock tour with Black Crowes, Mötley Crüe, and Queensrÿche in Copenhagen, Denmark.

1995 Rod Stewart's *Spanner in the Works* went gold in America even though the album only reached #35 on the national charts.

August
11

#1 Song 1958: "Poor Little Fool,"
Ricky Nelson

Born: Mike Hugg (Manfred Mann), 1942;
Eric Carmen (The Raspberries), 1949

1962 Formerly known as The Primettes, the newly named Supremes hit the Hot 100 with "Your Heart Belongs to Me," their first of forty-seven hits through 1976.

1962 Carole King's "It Might as Well Rain Until September" was issued. It became her first chart single (#22) of an eighteen-hit career.

1965 The Beatles film *Help!* premiered in New York.

1968 Apple Records issued its first releases to the press today, which included The Beatles' "Hey Jude," Mary Hopkin's "Those Were the Days," Jackie Lomax's "Sour Milk Sea," and The Black Dyke Mills Band's "Thingumybob." Mary's #2 U.S. hit was based on the melody of a traditional Russian folk song, "Darogoi Dlimmoyo," and sold four million copies. "Hey Jude" went on to sell 8 million copies, becoming their biggest hit.

1986 Monkee mania returned as their first four LPs reentered the Top 100 album charts after eighteen years.

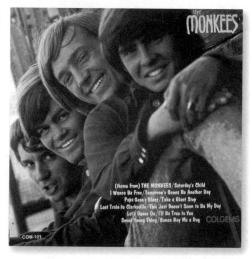

225

August

12

#1 Song 1978: "Three Times a Lady," The Commodores

Born: Mark Knopfler (Dire Straits), 1949

Died: Kyu Sakamoto, 1985

1955 A youthful Bob Luman, who would go on to be a star in his own right, saw Elvis Presley perform at Driller Park in Kilgore, Texas. After seeing Elvis's effect on the teen girls, Luman knew what he was going to do with his life.

1957 Buddy Holly & the Crickets' immortal "That'll Be the Day" charted, reaching #1. A different version was recorded in July 1956 and released in September 1957 by Buddy Holly & the Three Tunes. (What a collector's item that 45 is!)

1960 Pete Best auditioned for John Lennon, Paul McCartney, and George Harrison for their first-ever performances in Hamburg, Germany. The group had now decided to call themselves The Beatles, and Best became their new regular drummer.

1970 Janis Joplin gave her last performance at Harvard Stadium.

1994 Thirty thousand people showed up at "Yasgur's Farm" in Upstate New York to relive Woodstock's twenty-fifth anniversary. Performing as they did a quarter of a century earlier were a radiant Melanie and Richie Havens along with Arlo Guthrie, among others. Though it was on the original site they had to call it Bethel '94 (after the town near Woodstock) because a rival festival named Woodstock '94 in Saugerties, New York, with a cast of contemporary wanna-be Woodstockers, was competing nearby. Although it did have a smattering of such baby-boomer icons as Bob Dylan and Crosby, Stills & Nash, Woodstock '94 was mainly catering to the new generation with acts like Nine Inch Nails, Sheryl Crow, The Violent Femmes, Cypress Hill, Blind Melon, Melissa Etheridge, Salt-n-Pepa, and Porno for Pyros.

August
13

#1 Song 1966: "Summer in the City," The Lovin' Spoonful

Born: Tony Bennett, 1926; Dan Fogelberg, 1951

Died: Joe Tex, 1982

1952 Willie Mae "Big Mama" Thornton, an early R&B shouter, recorded Leiber & Stoller's original "Hound Dog" in Los Angeles backed by The Johnny Otis Orchestra. By mid 1953, it was a smash, holding down the #1 spot on the R&B charts for seven weeks. It was, however, only a prelude to the song's success. Three years later, Elvis Presley took the song to #1 on the pop charts for eleven weeks!

1965 Jefferson Airplane, with original lead singer Signe Anderson, made their performance debut at San Francisco's Matrix Club.

1966 The Beatles performed at the Olympic Stadium in Detroit while the uproar about Lennon's remarks regarding "Jesus" had spread to Spain and The Netherlands, where efforts were underway to have their records banned from radio. Meanwhile in the U.S., the Grand Dragon of the South Carolina Ku Klux Klan, not to be outdone by the Europeans, nailed a Beatles record to a large wooden cross that he then set on fire. Meanwhile, George Harrison took a position of defiance when he said, "They've got to buy them before they can burn them." Also on this busy Beatles day, the *Revolver* album hit #1 after one week in the U.K. and stayed there for nine weeks.

1975 Bruce Springsteen began his "Born to Run" tour.

1977 Cherie Currie quit The Runaways and was replaced on lead by Joan Jett.

Willie Mae "Big Mama" Thornton

August

14

#1 Song 1982: "Eye of the Tiger," Survivor

Born: Dash Crofts (Seals & Crofts), 1940; David Crosby, 1941; Connie Smith, 1941; Larry Graham, 1946

1965 The Beatles performed "I Feel Fine," "I'm Down," "Act Naturally," "Ticket to Ride," "Yesterday," and "Help!" on *The Ed Sullivan Show* in New York. John was so nervous he forgot some of the words to "Help!"

1966 While The Beatles performed at the Municipal Stadium in Cleveland, Ohio, with The Ronettes, Bobby Hebb, and The Cyrkle, a Texas radio station that had instigated a Beatles records burning the day before was shut down when lightning hit their transmission tower, destroying their equipment.

1971 Joan Baez stunned the pop world when the folk protest singer charted with "The Night They Drove Old Dixie Down" and ascended to #3. Her pop-chart efforts before and after, never rose higher than #35.

1992 Tony Williams was the smooth-as-silk lead singer of The Platters, the most popular pop-R&B group of the '50s. With hits like "Only You," "My Prayer," "Magic Touch," and "Smoke Gets in Your Eyes," Tony's Platters became worldwide musical ambassadors for American pop culture. The group had thirty-five hits between 1955 and 1962 with Williams on lead. A heavy smoker, he died of emphysema at age sixty-four.

Joan Baez

August

#1 Song 1960: "It's Now or Never,"
Elvis Presley

Born: Bill Pinkney (The Drifters), 1925;
Stix Hooper (The Crusaders), 1938;
Jimmy Webb, 1946

1953 The Prisonaires, five inmates from the Tennessee State Penitentiary, had their debut disc, "Just Walkin' in the Rain," issued on Sun records. It would reach #10 R&B nationally and become a #1 worldwide hit for Johnny Ray three years later. Lead singer, Johnny Bragg, was helped with his diction at that June 1 session by a young would-be vocalist who was hanging around the studio. The teen's name was Elvis Presley!

1958 Buddy Holly married Marie Elena Santiago, a Decca Records secretary.

1962 After several covert meetings between John Lennon and Rory Storm & the Hurricanes drummer, Ringo Starr, Ringo agreed to be the Beatles new drummer. The group then performed a day and a night gig at The Cavern, which would become the last two performances with Pete Best on drums.

1965 The Beatles performed at New York's Shea Stadium before 56,000 fans, a then current outdoor record. It took more than 2,000 security personnel to maintain even a semblance of order. They played for about thirty minutes and made $160,000.

1969 The Woodstock Festival began its first of three memorable days of concerts and torrential rains. Artists included Arlo Guthrie, Tim Hardin, Joan Baez, Richie Havens, Ravi Shankar, and The Incredible String Band.

1971 Thomas Wayne (Perkins) was a one-hit wonder whose claim to fame was the 1959 #5 hit "Tragedy." He went to the same high school as Elvis Presley and formed his backup group there, the female trio The Delons. He died today in a car accident near Memphis at age thirty-one.

August

16

#1 Song 1980: "Magic," Olivia Newton-John

Born: Madonna (Madonna Louise Ciccone), 1958

1964 The Beatles performed at the Opera House in Blackpool, England along with The Kinks and a group known at the time as The High Numbers, who would later go on to fame as The Who.

1969 Melanie performed at the now legendary Woodstock Festival in Bethel, New York, during a rainstorm. She was so moved by the audience appreciation, the experience inspired her to write her hit "Lay Down (Candles in the Rain)."

1969 The Dells rerecording of their hit "Oh, What a Night" (#10 pop) charted thirteen years after the original. One of the few recordings to be a hit in two different versions by the same act, the 1956 recording went to #4 R&B.

1977 The "King of Rock 'n' Roll" Elvis Presley died at his Graceland mansion in Memphis of heart failure. Among his record-breaking accomplishments: He charted country eighty-four times, AC 52 times, R&B thirty-five times, and had 151 Top 100 hits. He also starred in thirty-one films. Shortly before he passed on, he sat at the piano and one of the last songs he played was Willie Nelson's "Blue Eyes Crying in the Rain." He was only forty-two.

August 17

#1 Song 1991: "(Everything I Do) I Do It for You," Bryan Adams

Born: Georgia Gibbs, 1920, Belinda Carlisle (The Go-Go's), 1958; Donnie Wahlberg (New Kids on the Block), 1969

Died: Paul Williams (The Temptations), 1973

1960 The Beatles arrived in Hamburg, Germany. Their contract called for them to play four to six sets a night, for 30 Deutsch Marks per night! Many times they played for eight hours each evening at the Indra Club. George often referred to what they did as "Hamburg stomp and yell music... It was all that work on various club stages in Germany that built up our beat." Paul considered it "a good exercise in commercialism." They were so broke in those days that their cleaning lady used to give them a few Marks so they could eat French fries, corn flakes, and chicken soup.

1969 The Woodstock Festival ended. Performers included Crosby, Stills & Nash; Mountain; Sha Na Na; John Sebastian; Joe Cocker; Joan Baez; Jefferson Airplane; Santana; Richie Havens; Blood, Sweat & Tears; Iron Butterfly; The Band; and Creedence Clearwater Revival. More than half a million attended, three died, two were born, and there were six miscarriages. Not bad for $7!

1985 Whitney Houston stormed the Hot 100 with "Saving All My Love for You." It was her first of eleven #1s through 1999.

1974 The #1 record today was "The Night Chicago Died" by Paper Lace, an English band formed in 1969. It was #3 in the U.K. The foursome also had the original hit "Billy Don't Be a Hero," which was covered in America by Bo Donaldson & the Heywoods. In a rare occurrence, both versions of "Billy" went to #1 in their respective countries in 1974.

Woodstock Festival

August

18

#1 Song 1962: "Breaking Up Is Hard to Do," Neil Sedaka

Born: Sonny Til (The Orioles), 1928; Johnny Preston, 1939; Sarah Dash (LaBelle), 1943; Nona Hendryx (LaBelle), 1945; Barbara Harris (The Toys), 1945

1962 Ringo Starr joined The Beatles, consequently their drummer Peter Best was fired. His official performing debut with The Beatles was at the Horticulture Society Dance, Hulme Hall, Port Sunlight, Birkenhead, England.

1968 The Drifters and Bill Haley & the Comets performed at San Francisco's Avalon Ballroom.

1969 Joni Mitchell appeared on Dick Cavett's TV talk show. Because of that scheduled appearance, her agent, David Geffen, had convinced her to pull out of her planned performance at the Woodstock Festival. In tribute to the monumental event, she then wrote "Woodstock."

1969 While filming *Ned Kelly* in Australia, Mick Jagger was shot in the hand when a gun exploded.

1990 Garth Brooks's "Friends in Low Places" charted, on its way to #1 on the country Top 100. It would later receive the Country Music Association (CMA) Single of the Year Award.

Joni Mitchell

August

19

#1 Song 1957: "Tammy,"
Debbie Reynolds

Born: Peter "Ginger" Baker (Cream),
1939; Johnny Nash, 1940; Ian Gillan
(Deep Purple), 1945

1957 The Mello-Kings charted with their doo-wop classic "Tonite, Tonite" (#77 pop). The record was released as by The Mellotones (Herald Records, $400), but since there already was a Mellotones (Gee Records), they revised their moniker to Mello-Kings. The group began performing on the "chitlin circuit" (the black theatre venue scene) to the shock of their audiences, since the booking agents and audiences alike had no idea the black-sounding group was white!

1962 The realigned Beatles performed at The Cavern with The Swinging Blue Jeans and Peppy & the New York Twisters. The revised foursome, now including Ringo Starr, was attacked as they entered the club by irate Pete Best fans, and one gave George Harrison a larger-than-life black eye that stayed around long enough to show up in their first publicity photo session for EMI almost two weeks later.

1964 The Beatles started their first American tour at San Francisco's Cow Palace. Also on the bill were The Righteous Brothers, The Exciters, Jackie DeShannon, and Bill Black's Combo. They earned over $49,000 for less than thirty minutes onstage, although the screaming was such that not a note was heard. A sheriff summed it up this way, "That's 16,000 kids who aren't out stealing hubcaps."

1979 Dorsey Burnette was the older brother of Johnny Burnette and father of Billy Burnette. The Memphis country-pop vocalist is best remembered for his hits "Tall Oak Tree" and "Hey Little One" in 1960. He died of a heart attack at forty-six.

1991 Joan Baez sang "We Shall Overcome" along with a Russian protest song over a phone to Radio Free Europe, which broadcast it to the Soviet Union.

233

August

#1 Song 1977: "Best of My Love," The Emotions

Born: Isaac Hayes, 1942; Robert Plant (Led Zeppelin), 1948; Phil Lynott (Thin Lizzy), 1951

1955 A vocal trio from New Milford, New Jersey, The Fontane Sisters charted with "Seventeen," en route to #3. It was their fifth of eighteen hits between 1954 and 1958.

1964 The High Numbers (later The Who) taped their debut TV performance on BBC-2's *The Beat Room*, doing The Miracles' "I Gotta Dance to Keep from Crying." Also on the show were Brenda Lee and The Swinging Blue Jeans.

1964 The Beatles performed at the Convention Center in Las Vegas. Two thousand fans who came to the airport to see them arrive at one in the morning had to be scattered by police dogs. The ever resourceful fanatics scaled garbage shoots, commandeered fright elevators, and climbed over walls to reach the Fab Four at the Sahara Hotel. While fans at the performance shouted, "Ringo for President," a bomb scare was phoned in. Gambling during their stay was limited to having slot machines brought into their rooms.

1968 Bobby Darin sold his music publishing company for $1 million.

1969 The Beatles recorded "I Want You (She's So Heavy)." It was the last time all of The Beatles were together at Abbey Road Studios, where almost all of their recordings had been done.

August 21

#1 Song 1993: "Can't Help Falling in Love," UB40

Born: Savannah Churchill (Four Tunes), 1920; Kenny Rogers (First Edition), 1938; Jackie DeShannon, 1944; Joe Strummer (The Clash), 1955

1953 Colonel Tom Parker, more than a year from finding Elvis Presley, was fired by his only client, top-selling country vocalist Eddy Arnold.

1961 Patsy Cline recorded her all-time classic "Crazy," while on crutches. She was still recuperating from a car crash, in which she was thrown through the windshield.

1964 Continuing their American tour, The Beatles performed at the Coliseum in Seattle. More than 14,000 teen girls screamed their way through the concert. During the show, the police drafted Navy men from the audience to form a human wall from the stage exit to the dressing room. One female fan, hanging from the scaffolding, fell and landed onstage near Ringo Starr. Their escape car was destroyed by fans, and the group had to make their exit in an ambulance. A day after they left, sixteen-year-old girls were still being found in the hotel, hiding under the group's beds and in their closets.

1982 Jennifer Warnes and Joe Cocker climbed onto the singles survey with, "Up Where We Belong." The duet from the film *An Officer and a Gentlemen* spent three weeks in the top spot.

1998 Elton John's *Greatest Hits* album was certified as a fifteen-million-seller by the RIAA.

August

22

#1 Song 1970: "Make It with You," Bread

Born: John Lee Hooker, 1917; Dale Hawkins, 1938; Fred Milano (The Belmonts), 1939; Ron Dante (The Archies), 1945; Roland Orzabal (Tears for Fears), 1961; Debbi Peterson (The Bangles), 1961

1961 Roland Orzabal, of the duo Tears for Fears, was born today. Along with Curt Smith, the act had several decade-defining hits, including "Shout" and "Everybody Wants to Rule the World" in the '80s.

1963 The Shangri-Las teen angst standard "Remember" charted en route to #5. It was their first of eleven hits in less than two years.

1965 During a press conference in Minneapolis, Ringo Starr was asked by a gate-crashing teenager about how to play drums. Ringo said, "You'll never get anywhere listening to me," and John Lennon chimed in, "And he's been playing drums for thirty years." The same day their plane's engine caught fire as they arrived in Portland, Oregon. John was heard yelling as they deplaned, "Beatles, women, and children first!"

1969 The Beatles attended their last photo shoot together when they gathered at Tittenhurst Park in London. They would never again join together as a group at any Beatles-related happening.

Tears for Fears

August

23

#1 Song 1975: '"Fallin' in Love,"
Hamilton, Joe Frank & Reynolds

Born: Rudy Lewis (The Drifters),
1936; Keith Moon (The Who), 1947;
Rick Springfield, 1949

1962 Cynthia Powell married John Lennon at the Mount Pleasant Register Office in Liverpool with Paul McCartney as best man. Cynthia's brother Tony and his wife, Marjorie, George Harrison, and Brian Epstein were the only guests. Most of the ceremony was drowned out by a nearby construction worker and the sound of his pneumatic drill. John spent his wedding night onstage. The reason they decided to marry…she was pregnant.

1963 The Beatles single "She Loves You" was released in England. The anticipated demand was so great that EMI pressed over a quarter of a million copies in the four weeks prior to its release.

1966 Broke and desperate in Chicago, Janis Joplin and Big Brother & the Holding Company reconsidered and signed with Bob Shad's Mainstream Records. Their album was recorded, with Shad not allowing the group in the studio during the final mix. It was not issued until their successful performance at the Monterey Pop Festival the next year.

1969 Lou Christie's "I'm Gonna' Make You Mine" charted, becoming his last of three Top 10 hits.

1969 Ray, Goodman & Brown's cover of The Platters' "My Prayer" (#47) became their last of fourteen Top 100 entries, including eleven as The Moments.

August

24

#1 Song 1974: "(You're) Having My Baby," Paul Anka

Born: Willie Winfield (The Harptones), 1929; Ernest Wright, Jr. (The Imperials), 1941; Jim Capaldi (Traffic), 1944; Jeffrey Daniel (Shalamar), 1955

1962 Bob B. Soxx & the Blue Jeans recorded the Phil Spector–produced "Zip a Dee Doo Dah" (#8). The group was really The Blossoms with Darlene Love and studio singer Bobby Sheen on lead.

1968 Topping off his birthday party, Keith Moon (The Who) drove a Lincoln Continental into a Holiday Inn swimming pool in Flint, Michigan.

1978 Louis Prima was a popular bandleader in the '30s and '40s. He had numerous chart hits including "Bell Bottom Trousers" and "Sing, Sing, Sing," but his signature tune was his humorous rendition of "That Old Black Magic," in duet with his wife, Keely Smith. She would sing a line straight and slow, while he would do the next line to a frantic novelty tempo. Somehow it worked and audiences loved it. Louis died of a brain tumor at age sixty-six today.

1996 Brandy, with help from Gladys Knight, Chaka Khan, and Tamia, charted with "Missing You" (#25).

Brandy

August
25

#1 Song 1958: "Little Star,"
The Elegants

Born: Walter Williams (The O'Jays),
1942; Gene Simmons (Kiss), 1949;
Elvis Costello, 1954

1954 Elvis Presley attended a star-studded rhythm-and-blues concert in Memphis that included The Drifters, The Spaniels, Big Maybelle, Roy Hamilton, and LaVern Baker. The early show was for "whites only" and the late show was for "colored."

1962 The Crystals' "He's a Rebel" was issued, eventually climbing to #1 pop and #2 R&B. Unknown to the group at the time, producer Phil Spector had lifted their vocals and replaced them with Darlene Love and The Blossoms, even though The Crystals got the credit.

1970 Elton John made his American performance debut at Los Angeles's Troubadour. He was the opening act for David Ackles.

2000 Arranger, composer, and pianist Bernard Alfred "Jack" Nitzsche—who helped create the "Wall of Sound" recordings with Phil Spector for such acts as The Ronettes, The Crystals, The Righteous Brothers, Ike & Tina Turner, as well as arranging for acts like The Rolling Stones, Neil Young, and Ringo Starr—died today at the age of sixty-three. Nitzsche co-wrote such hits as "Up Where We Belong" and "Needles and Pins."

August

26

#1 Song 1972: "Brandy (You're a Fine Girl)," Looking Glass

Born: Valerie Simpson, 1946; Bob & Dick Cowsill (Cowsills), 1950

Died: Lee Hays (The Weavers), 1981

1964 The Supremes "Where Did Our Love Go" became their first #1 this week. Before Diana Ross left in 1969, they would have eleven more.

1970 While Elvis Presley was performing at the International Hotel in Las Vegas, the hotel received a threat to kidnap the King. Security was heavily increased and no attempt was made.

1970 Jimi Hendrix held his last performance at the Isle of Wight Pop Festival off the coast of England.

1993 Shawn Colvin, Melissa Etheridge, and Heart performed at the Voices for Choices concert in Santa Monica, California.

Jimi Hendrix

August

#1 Song 1983: "Every Breath You Take," The Police

Born: Harold Lucas (The Clovers), 1932; Daryl Dragon (Captain & Tennille), 1942; Tim Bogert (Vanilla Fudge), 1944

1955 The Four Aces' "Love Is a Many Splendid Thing" (#1) charted, becoming the quartet's twentieth of thirty-six hits between 1951 and 1959.

1965 The Beatles came to visit Elvis Presley at his Bel Air, California, home. An awkward introductory period was overcome when Elvis picked up a bass and began playing along with a tune on his jukebox called "Mohair Sam." This was the one and only meeting of the Fab Four and the King. John Lennon later confided to Elvis's friend Jerry Schilling that the evening meant a lot to him and asked Jerry to tell Elvis that, "If it hadn't been for him we would have been nothing."

1967 Brian Epstein was one of the most famous managers of all time, representing such British acts as Gerry & the Pacemakers, Billy J. Kramer, Cilla Black, and, of course, The Beatles. He discovered them in Liverpool on December 3, 1961, when he went to a lunchtime performance at the city's Cavern Club. He died in his London home of a drug overdose two months before his contract to manage The Beatles was to expire. The Beatles were in Wales at the time. Brian was only thirty-two years old.

August

28

#1 Song 1971: "How Can You Mend a Broken Heart," The Bee Gees

Born: Wayne Osmond (The Osmonds), 1951

1956 Alan Freed's second anniversary Rock 'n' Roll Show at the Brooklyn Paramount featured The Harptones, The Penguins, The Cleftones, and Frankie Lymon & the Teenagers.

1964 The Beatles flew by helicopter from Wall Street in New York City to perform at the Forest Hills Tennis Stadium, New York. The more than 16,000 fans were kept from the stage by an eight-foot-high fence with a barbed wire bouffant. Prior to the concert, John remarked at a press conference, "I don't mind not being as popular as Ringo, or George, or Paul, because if the group is popular, that's what matters." This trip featured several resourceful schoolgirls in nurses' uniforms breaching hotel security to meet them. Bob Dylan made a social call to their hotel after the concert, and promptly introduced The Beatles to marijuana for the first time.

1973 Deep Purple received a gold record for "Smoke on the Water." The song was based on a true incident. While the group was recording in Switzerland's Montreux Casino, a fire broke out during a concert by Frank Zappa in an adjoining part of the building. As the structure burned to the ground, smoke could be seen on nearby Lake Geneva, and vocalist Ian Gillan then wrote what he saw.

1986 Tina Turner was honored with a star on the Hollywood Walk of Fame in front of Capitol Records, the company for which she recorded.

Alan Freed

August

29

#1 Song 1964: "Where Did Our Love Go," The Supremes

Born: Dinah Washington, 1924; Michael Jackson (The Jackson 5), 1958; Carl Martin (Shai), 1970

1958 Alan Freed's Brooklyn Fox show featured The Elegants, The Cleftones, The Danleers, The Poni-Tails, The Royal Teens, and The Olympics. The show ran for ten days.

1965 The Beatles were transported from Capitol Records' Hollywood offices via an armored truck to the Hollywood Bowl for their concert in front of some 18,000 fans.

1966 The Beatles performed at Candlestick Park in San Francisco, home of the Giants, in what would become their last paid performance and the last Beatles concert ever. There were 25,000 fans in attendance. Their last performed song was Little Richard's "Long Tall Sally."

1966 The final broadcast of TV's "Hullabaloo" featured Paul Anka, Lesley Gore, and Peter & Gordon.

1968 Grace Slick and Jefferson Airplane made their British debut appearance at the Revolution Club in London while on their first European tour.

August

30

#1 Song 1969: "Honky Tonk Women," The Rolling Stones

Born: John Phillips (The Mamas & the Papas), 1935; John McNally (The Searchers), 1941

1964 The Beatles performed at the Convention Hall in Atlantic City, New Jersey. To get there, they had to sneak out of their motel and were conveyed to the concert in the back of a fish truck. Present at the concert were 19,000 fans and five ambulances.

1968 Janis Joplin performed at The Palace of Fine Arts Festival in San Francisco.

1969 A major pop festival Texas-style was held in Lewisville, drawing more than 120,000 people for the three-day event that encompassed fifteen acts, including Janis Joplin, Chicago, Led Zeppelin, Sam & Dave, Santana, The Nazz, Grand Funk Railroad, Rotary Connection (with Minnie Ripperton), and Delaney & Bonnie.

1975 Natalie Cole bounced onto the Hot 100 with "This Will Be" (#6), her first of seventeen hits through 1991.

1975 The British pop-rock group Jigsaw's "Sky High" (from the film *The Dragon Flies*) charted on its way to #3 in the U.S. The group's leaders Clive Scott and Des Dyer wrote Bo Donaldson's 1974 hit "Who Do You Think You Are."

Natalie Cole

244

August

31

#1 Song 1963: "My Boyfriend's Back,"
The Angels

Born: Jerry Allison (The Crickets), 1939;
Wilton Felder (The Crusaders), 1940;
Van Morrison, 1945; Tony DeFranco
(The Defranco Family), 1959;
Debbie Gibson, 1970

1956 Before the British Invasion, the Americans had their own version in England when the top nine records on the U.K. singles chart were all by Yanks. Number one was "Whatever Will Be, Will Be" by Doris Day, followed by Frankie Lymon & The Teenagers with "Why Do Fools Fall In Love."

1963 The Ronettes charted with "Be My Baby," a single The Beach Boys' Brian Wilson called, "The most perfect pop record of all time." It peaked at #2 for three weeks, becoming their first of eight hits.

1968 Big Brother & the Holding Company's "Piece of My Heart" tore onto the Hot 100, peaking at #12. It was the first chart 45 for lead Janis Joplin and company.

1976 A U.S. Judge ruled George Harrison guilty of "Subconscious Plagiarism" when he lifted The Chiffons' "He's So Fine" melody for his "My Sweet Lord." Taking advantage of the publicity, The Chiffons then recorded their own version of "My Sweet Lord."

1991 Metallica charted with their self-titled album, which would become their biggest U.S. hit, reaching #1 while selling more than 9 million copies. By 1996, they would amass 25 million sales on nine albums.

September

1

#1 Song 1962: "Sheila," Tommy Roe

Born: Conway Twitty, 1933; Tommy Evans (The Drifters), 1934; Archie Bell (Drells), 1944; Barry Gibb (The Bee Gees), 1946; Gloria Estefan, 1957

1956 Elvis began recording his second LP at Radio Recorders in Los Angeles. Both he and Jordanaires member Gordon Stoker alternated on piano for some of the album's tracks, including "Ready Teddy," "Rip It Up," and "Long Tall Sally"—all former Little Richard hits.

1961 The Marcels had their first session as an all black group, recording "Heartaches" (#7 pop, #19 R&B). Originally, the "Blue Moon" hit-makers had three black and two white members.

1961 While in Las Vegas, Elvis Presley went to see some of his favorite acts perform, including Jackie Wilson, The Dominoes (for whom Wilson previously sang lead), Fats Domino, and The Four Aces.

1970 Blondie, led by Debbie Harry, signed with Chrysalis Records, which, in an unusual move, bought their contract from Larry Uttal's Private Stock label.

1978 Gloria Fajardo married musician Emilio Estefan after a two-year romance, becoming Gloria Estefan on her twenty-first birthday.

September

#1 Song 1967: "Ode to Billie Joe," Bobbie Gentry

Born: Sam Gooden (The Impressions), 1939; Jimmy Clanton, 1940; Rosalind Ashford (The Vandellas), 1943; Steve Porcaro (Toto), 1957

1959 Los Angeles radio disc jockey Art Laboe created the first rock 'n' roll compilation album, *Oldies but Goodies*. It was inspired by his girlfriend's complaints about the stack of 45s that failed to drop properly onto her record player.

1962 With his hit "Sheila" sitting at #1, artist Tommy Roe finally agreed to leave his day job soldering wires at General Electric when ABC Records offered him $5,000.

1986 Sixteen-year-old Debbie Gibson signed with Atlantic Records, beginning a string of eleven chart singles.

1988 A worldwide charity tour to raise money for Amnesty International was begun with a concert at London's Wembley Stadium, featuring Bruce Springsteen and Sting.

1995 The Rock and Roll Hall of Fame and Museum opened its doors in Cleveland, Ohio. A concert to honor the event featured Chuck Berry, Little Richard, Aretha Franklin, Bruce Springsteen, and Martha & the Vandellas.

September

3

#1 Song 1966: "Sunshine Superman," Donovan

Born: Memphis Slim, 1915; Al Jardine (The Beach Boys), 1942; Greg Leads (The Walker Brothers), 1944; Walter and Wallace Scott (The Whispers), 1943

1955 The Four Lads' "Moments to Remember" charted, reaching #2. It was their first of eighteen Top 100 singles over the next four years.

1968 With the violence of the Democratic National Convention still looming over the city, it wasn't surprising that The Rolling Stones single "Street Fighting Man" was banned on Chicago radio today.

1977 Former member of the Boone Gospel Quartet and daughter of singer Pat Boone, Debbie Boone jumped on the charts with her soon-to-be #1, "You Light Up My Life."

1983 The Eurythmics reached #1 with "Sweet Dreams."

2000 Rebert H. Harris was a gospel music giant who took The Soul Stirrers of the mid '30s, one of gospel music's pioneers from jubilee style toward modern gospel. The innovative vocalist was the first to use a second lead singer, turned quartets into quintets, and arranged consistent four-part harmony under the alternating leads. He also created the ad-libbing of lyrics, singing in delayed time and repeating words in the background. Rebert led the group through the '50s when he turned his spot over to a youthful Sam Cooke. Harris died at age eighty-five, only days before he was to be inducted into the Vocal Group Hall of Fame with the Stirrers.

September

#1 Song 1961: "Michael," The Highwaymen

Born: Merald "Bubba" Knight (The Pips), 1942; Gary Elmore and Gary Duncan (Quicksilver Messenger Service), 1946

1948 Sonny Til & the Orioles' first single, "It's Too Soon to Know" (Jubilee, $1,200), was released. It reached #11 pop and #1 R&B. Never before had a black group singing black (not pop) music hit the pop Top 15.

1961 The Paris Sisters moved onto the singles survey with "I Love How You Love Me" (#5). The trio began recording for Decca in 1954, and it took them almost eight years to achieve their first hit.

1962 The Beatles, produced by George Martin, laid down their first tracks as EMI recording artists at Abbey Road Studios in London. Recording with them for the first time was newest member Ringo Starr. They recorded "Love Me Do" and the Mitch Murray composition "How Do You Do It." The group hated the latter song and their performance on tape showed it. It would later become a hit for a group they often shared the stage with Gerry & the Pacemakers.

1982 Choreographer Toni Basil (*American Graffiti*) hit the best-seller's list with the novelty song "Mickey," which became a #1 international smash.

1991 Country artist Dottie West (Dorothy Marie Marsh) spent more than twenty years on the charts from 1963 to 1985. The Tennessee native had two solo #1s ("A Lesson in Leavin'" and "Are You Happy Baby?"), but was even more popular in duet with Kenny Rogers, with whom she won vocal duo of the year in 1978 and 1979. All told, she had sixty-three country hits before her untimely demise in a car accident in the parking lot of the Grand Ole Opry at age fifty-eight.

Dottie West

September

#1 Song 1964: "The House of the Rising Sun," The Animals

Born: John Stewart (The Kingston Trio), 1939; Al Stewart, 1945; Freddie Mercury (Queen), 1946; Buddy Miles (Electric Flag), 1946; Terry Ellis (En Vogue), 1966

1946 Freddie Mercury (Farookh Bulsara), the in-your-face lead singer for the British rock band Queen, was born today. The raucously gay Mercury led Queen through twenty-seven hits from 1975 to 1993 (three charting after his death), including the rock opera classic "Bohemian Rhapsody," "Somebody to Love," and "Another One Bites the Dust." He died of AIDS at age forty-five in 1991.

1955 Elvis Presley headlined at the St. Francis County Fair in Forrest City, Arkansas. The show featured Johnny Cash, Floyd Cramer, and Eddie Bond. It was Bond who, a year earlier, during an audition at the Hi Hat Club on May 15, 1954, told Elvis (in reference to his singing) to go back to driving a truck.

1978 Frankie Lymon & the Teenagers member Joe Negroni died at thirty-seven. He was the third member of the group to die before the age of thirty-eight.

1987 Debbie Gibson's self-penned chart debut, "Only in My Dreams," reached #4 and went on to become the #1 twelve-inch Dance Single of the Year.

1991 Mariah Carey sang her hit "Emotions" (#1) at the eighth annual MTV Awards ceremony at the Universal Amphitheater, Universal City, California.

September

#1 Song 1980: "Upside Down,"
Diana Ross

Born: Jimmy Reed, 1925;
Roger Waters (Pink Floyd), 1944

1963 The Beatles first EP of hits was released in England and included "From Me to You," "Thank You Girl," "Please Please Me," and "Love Me Do."

1976 Fleetwood Mac's self-titled LP reached #1. It first charted in August 1975 and took thirteen months to journey to the top.

1989 Elton John performed at the first of eight Madison Square Garden concerts in New York City. The previous year his appearances at the "Garden" resulted in a record twenty-five sold-out performances at the venue, surpassing the previous record held by The Grateful Dead.

1990 Tom Fogerty was the guitarist for The Golliwogs, a swamp rock and blues band in the mid '60s, featuring lead singing and writing by his younger brother, John. Working as a clerk at Fantasy Records, he convinced them to sign the band, which was later renamed Creedence Clearwater Revival. They went on to have twenty hits, including "Proud Mary" and "Green River" between 1968 and 1976. But because of sibling rivalry, Tom left the act in 1971 and died of tuberculosis at age forty-eight today.

1997 Elton John performed his song "Candle in the Wind" at the funeral for Diana, Princess of Wales, at London's Westminster Abbey.

September

#1 Song 1985: "St. Elmo's Fire," John Parr

Born: Buddy Holly, 1936; Gloria Gaynor, 1949; Chrissie Hynde (The Pretenders), 1951

1957 While working on Elvis Presley's Christmas album, producers found they were a song short. Songwriters Jerry Leiber and Mike Stoller quickly remedied the problem by writing "Santa Claus Is Back in Town," right in the studio.

1959 The Fleetwoods' second #1, "Mr. Blue," charted.

1978 Keith Moon was the drummer for the British band The Who from their beginning as the High Numbers in 1964, through most of their hits into 1978, including "I Can See for Miles" and "Won't Get Fooled Again." He died of a drug overdose on this day at age thirty-one, after seeing the premiere of The Buddy Holly Story.

1986 Mike Nesmith joined the other three Monkees for their encore at the Greek Theater in Los Angeles during their reunion tour.

1991 Mötley Crüe signed a new recording deal for a guaranteed $20.5 million.

Vince Neil of Mötley Crüe

September

#1 Song 1979: "My Sharona," The Knack

Born: Jimmy Rodgers (rockabilly pioneer), 1897; Patsy Cline, 1932; Dante Drowty (Dante & the Evergreens), 1941; Cathy Jean, 1945

1956 Due to the success of Johnnie Ray's "Just Walking in the Rain," Sun Records reissued the three-year-old original version by The Prisonaires, a group of inmates at the Tennessee State Penitentiary, featuring Johnny Bragg. Although it originally reached #10 R&B, The Prisonaires' recording received little attention compared to the Ray recording.

1962 Thirteen days after its release, The Crystals' "He's a Rebel" charted, on its way to #1 for two weeks. The Gene Pitney song was rush released to beat out a competing version by Vikki Carr.

1965 An advertisement in *Variety* announced auditions for The Monkees. Among those who tried & failed were Stephen Stills, Danny Hutton (later of Three Dog Night), composer Paul Williams, and the future mass-murderer Charles Manson.

September

9

#1 Song 1957: "Diana," Paul Anka

Born: Jacob Carey (The Flamingos), 1926; Joe Negroni (The Teenagers), 1940; Otis Redding, 1941; Inez Foxx, 1942; Dee Dee Sharp, 1945; Billy Preston, 1946; Doug Ingle (Iron Butterfly), 1946; Dave Stewart (The Eurythmics), 1952

1952 Dave Stewart, musician, composer, and co-founder of The Eurythmics, was born today. Along with vocalist-musician Annie Lennox, The Eurythmics were consistent chart residents throughout the '80s and are best known for hits like "Sweet Dreams," "Would I Lie to You," and "Here Comes the Rain Again." They were originally in a band called The Tourists before forming The Eurythmics in 1980.

1954 Raised on their father's sugar plantation in Cuba, The DeCastro Sisters ascended the hit list with "Teach Me Tonight," an eventual #2.

1956 Elvis Presley made his first appearance on *The Ed Sullivan Show* at CBS Studios, Los Angeles. He sang "Don't Be Cruel," "Love Me Tender," "Ready Teddy," and "Hound Dog." Due to a car accident, Sullivan was not able to host the show and his replacement was actor Charles Laughton. The show garnered the largest TV audience up to that time, a viewing audience of 50 million, one third of the population.

1957 Former Dominoes lead Jackie Wilson signed with Brunswick Records as a solo artist. His first single was "Reet Petite." Jackie would go on to have fifty-four pop hits through 1972, including "Lonely Teardrops" and "Higher and Higher."

1982 Patti LaBelle opened on Broadway, co-starring with Al Green in the gospel musical *Your Arm's Too Short to Box with God.* The Alvin Theater schedule called for thirty shows, but because of rave reviews, the show ran for eighty performances.

Patti LaBelle

254

September

10

#1 Song 1966: "You Can't Hurry Love," The Supremes

Born: Danny Hutton (Three Dog Night), 1942; Jose Feliciano, 1945; Siobhan Fahey (Bananarama), 1957

1963 The Beatles were honored by a Variety Club of Great Britain luncheon at the Savoy Hotel in London as Top Vocal Group of the Year. John Lennon and Paul McCartney attended to pick up the awards. In a fatalistic aftermath, The Rolling Stones' manager, Andrew Loog Oldham, was walking down Jermyn Street when a taxi pulled alongside, with the duo inside. Andrew mentioned he was looking for songs for the Stones and John and Paul suggested a song they'd just written, called "I Wanna Be Your Man." They then proceeded to a local studio, borrowed two guitars, and ripped into the song for Oldham, which was only partially done. They disappeared into a room and reappeared a few minutes later with the finished song that would go on to be The Rolling Stones' first Top 20 hit.

1966 Consummate pop entertainer Bobby Darin turned folk rocker with the release of "If I Were a Carpenter." The style change renewed his popularity as he reached the Top 10 (#8) for the first time in three years.

1966 The Monkees' first of twenty-one hits, "Last Train to Clarksville" (#1), charted.

1977 Linda Ronstadt charted with "Blue Bayou" (#3 pop), her eighteenth hit since she first reached the pop listings with "Different Drum" as lead of The Stone Poneys ten years earlier.

September

11

#1 Song 1982: "Hard to Say I'm Sorry," Chicago

Born: Harry Connick, Jr., 1967

1960 Teen idol Tommy Sands married Nancy Sinatra. They were divorced in 1965.

1962 The Beatles again recorded at Abbey Road, doing another version of "Love Me Do" along with "Please Please Me." This time Ringo Starr was consigned to playing maracas and tambourine as studio musician Andy White played the drums. Ringo's drumming was later added and both versions wound up on early single releases, though Andy's percussion work was on the debut album.

1965 A New York female trio, The Toys hit the big time with "Lover's Concerto" (#2). The song's melody was based on a Bach minuet from *The Anna Magdalena Notebook*.

1969 John Lennon told his business manager he was leaving The Beatles. It took him another nine days to get around to telling the band.

1987 Peter Tosh was a noted proponent of 1960s reggae music who taught Bob Marley the nuances of songwriting. He also was a member of Marley's group, The Wailers, in Jamaica and recorded for Island Records and Rolling Stone Records. He was in The Wailers when they recorded their original versions of "I Shot the Sheriff" and "Get Up, Stand Up." He was shot to death in his Jamaica home during a robbery, although some say it was actually a revenge killing. He was forty-two.

Harry Connick, Jr.

September

#1 Song 1970: "War," Edwin Starr

Born: Warren Corbin (The Cleftones), 1938; Maria Muldaur, 1943; Barry White (Upfronts), 1944; Gerry Beckley (America), 1952

12

1952 Vocalist-guitarist Gerry Beckley of the group America was born today. Originally members of the band Daze in 1970, the trio formed on a U.S. Air Force base. Best known for their hits "I Need You," "Ventura Highway," and "A Horse with No Name," They charted seventeen times in the '70s and '80s.

1960 The Chiffons, locked in a cover battle with The Shirelles, charted today with "Tonight's the Night." Although the New Jersey Shirelles outpaced The Bronx, New York, quartet (#39 to #76), the recording was memorable as The Chiffons' first Hot 100 contender of a career twelve hits through 1966.

1964 The Butterflys' "Good Night Baby" charted, en route to #51. The trio was actually singer-writer Ellie Greenwich multi-tracking her voice.

1966 The Monkees' TV show debuted on NBC. It ran for fifty-eight episodes through August 1968. The group would become known as "The Pre-Fab Four."

1970 Joan Baez, among others, performed at the Woody Guthrie Memorial Concert at L.A.'s Hollywood Bowl.

1992 Garth Brooks hit the charts with "We Shall Be Free," a song that was inspired by the aftermath of the riots in Los Angeles, and the Rodney King case.

September

13

#1 Song 1975: "Rhinestone Cowboy," Glen Campbell

Born: David Clayton-Thomas (Blood Sweat & Tears), 1941; Peter Cetera (Chicago), 1944; Don Was, 1952

1964 Martha & the Vandellas, The Supremes, The Temptations, The Miracles, and Marvin Gaye performed in Murray the K's ten-day Rock' n' Roll Spectacular at the Brooklyn Fox Theater.

1964 The Beatles appeared at the Civic Center in Baltimore. Two enterprising girls had a cardboard box delivered to the center marked "Beatles Fan Mail" with the two teens packed inside. Guards foiled the smuggling attempt when they checked the deliveries.

1969 Chuck Berry, Little Richard, Jerry Lee Lewis, Bo Diddley, Alice Cooper, Gene Vincent, and The Doors appeared at the Toronto Rock 'n' Roll Revival Concert. After the concert, they met one of their most avid fans, John Lennon.

1975 Less than three months after "Love Will Keep Us Together" by Captain & Tennille hit #1, the duo rerecorded the song in Spanish as "Por Amor Viviremos" and reached #49.

September

#1 Song 1974: "I Shot the Sheriff,"
Eric Clapton

Born: John "Bowser" Baumann
(Sha Na Na), 1947

1963 The King's *Elvis' Golden Records, Volume III* charted, rising to #3 and selling over a million copies. It was his twenty-fifth chart album.

1963 Dion & the Del Satins' "Donna the Prima Donna" (#6) charted. It was The Del Satins 13th hit with Dion, all uncredited.

1968 The Beatles classic "Hey Jude" (#1 in U.S., U.K., Germany, The Netherlands, Japan, France, and Israel) was inspired by The Drifters 1960 #1 hit "Save the Last Dance for Me."

1984 Bette Midler co-hosted (with Dan Aykroyd) the first MTV Awards from Radio City Music Hall in New York.

1989 Shirley Alston Reeves of The Shirelles joined with members of The Five Satins, The Belmonts, The Silhouettes, The Jive Five, and The Falcons in a doo-wop performance outside the Berklee Performance Center in Boston to promote the formation of the Doo-Wop Hall of Fame of America.

September

#1 Song 1962: "Sherry," The Four Seasons

Born: Signe Anderson (first lead, Jefferson Airplane), 1941

1951 The Four Aces first 45, "(It's No) Sin" (Decca), charted, reaching #4. The group paid for their session with lead Al Alberts and his fiancée's wedding money and $500 from two supportive college students.

1956 Paul Anka recorded his first single, "I Confess," at Modern Records in Los Angeles with vocal backing by The Cadets of "Stranded in the Jungle" fame.

1958 Elvis Presley's *King Creole* film soundtrack album charted today, reaching #2. It was his tenth straight chart album in only two-and-a-half years.

1963 The Beatles performed at the Royal Albert Hall, London, for the annual Great Pop Prom, along with eleven other acts, including The Rolling Stones. The same day, the single "She Loves You" was released in the U.S. on Swan.

1990 Dolly Parton was fined $20,000 by the Department of Labor for making her teenage staff work longer than "9 to 5" at her amusement park, Dollywood.

September

#1 Song 1978: "Boogie Oogie Oogie," A Taste of Honey

Born: B.B. King, 1925; Joe Butler (The Lovin' Spoonful), 1943; Betty Kelly (The Vandellas), 1944; Richard Marx, 1963

1962 Dion began his first British tour with The Angels, Del Shannon, and Buzz Clifford.

1964 The *Shindig* TV show debuted on ABC with The Righteous Brothers, The Everly Brothers, and Sam Cooke.

1977 Marc Bolan was the leader of the British band T. Rex. Originally in a skiffle group and later a folk duo, he became a sensation as a glam-rocker with songs like "Bang a Gong (Get It On)" in the early '70s. Bolan died in a car crash when his inebriated wife smashed his mini GT into a tree outside London. He was twenty-nine.

1965 The Rolling Stones appeared on the TV show *Shindig* and promptly had several insignificant words bleeped from the song "(I Can't Get No) Satisfaction" by the censors who thought the term referred to a girl getting pregnant.

September

17

#1 Song 1988: "Sweet Child o' Mine," Guns N' Roses

Born: Hank Williams, 1923; Bill Black, 1926; Lamonte McLemore (The 5th Dimension), 1939; Fee Waybill (The Tubes), 1950

1954 Young Carl Perkins saw Elvis Presley play at the high school gym in Bethel Springs, Tennessee. He asked Elvis after the show if Sun Records might be interested in another artist who sang in a similar style, and it was that show that led to Perkins's first visit to Sun in October. He would go on to record his immortal single, "Blue Suede Shoes," for the Memphis company.

1955 Ella Fitzgerald and Peggy Lee's album, *Songs from Pete Kelly's Blues*, ascended the album hit list, leveling off at #7. It became Ella's biggest of eleven charters through 1969.

1964 Originally scheduled as an off-day on their U.S. tour, The Beatles were asked to come to Kansas City and play at the Municipal Stadium, thanks to Kansas City A's baseball team owner, Charles O. Finley, who convinced Brian Epstein to accept a fee of $150,000 for one show, more than any American artist had ever received to play a single concert. To celebrate their visit, the group added "Kansas City" to their repertoire for the night. The hotel where they stayed sold their bedsheets to a man who cut them up into small pieces to sell as souvenirs.

1977 *The Best of Rod Stewart* album peaked at #18 in England. Within eight months, it would go gold in America.

1991 Rob Tyner was the leader of the punk-rock group, MC5 (Motor City Five). Their anti-government rhetoric and flag burning in concerts garnered a deal with Elektra Records, where they recorded *Kick Out the Jams*, considered the first punk album by many. Tyner died of a heart attack at the wheel of his car in his driveway. He was forty-six.

September

#1 Song 1961: "Take Good Care of My Baby," Bobby Vee

Born: Frankie Avalon, 1939; Dee Dee Ramone (The Ramones), 1952; Ricky Bell (The New Edition), 1967

Died: Jimi Hendrix, 1970

1948 Dinah Shore ascended the Hot 100 with "Buttons & Bows," her biggest success of a career sixty-nine hits. The bouncy tune spent ten weeks at #1.

1954 The Diablos classic "The Wind" was released. It would become one of the singles that would inspire a young Smokey Robinson to emulate The Diablos' lead singer, Nolan Strong.

1984 Four days after Bette Midler hosted the first MTV Music Awards, Madonna performed at The MTV Video Awards at Radio City Music Hall.

1987 The Beatles, Bob Dylan, and Brian Wilson were nominated for The Rock and Roll Hall of Fame.

Brian Wilson

September

19

#1 Song 1960: "The Twist," Chubby Checker

Born: Brook Benton, 1931; Brian Epstein, 1934; Nick Massi (The Four Seasons), 1935; Bill Medley (The Righteous Brothers), 1940; Cass Elliot (The Mamas & the Papas), 1941; Freda Payne, 1945

1934 Brian Epstein—the man who discovered, nurtured, and brought the greatest phenomenon in pop music since Elvis Presley to the masses, namely The Beatles—was born today. Epstein discovered the band at Liverpool's Cavern Club in 1962 and became their manager soon after. Prior to his management career, he had been a record store owner.

1970 Diana Ross's "Ain't No Mountain High Enough" reached #1 and became her first chart topper sans The Supremes. Produced by its writers, Valerie Simpson and Nick Ashford, it was originally a hit (#19) in 1967 for Tammi Terrell and Marvin Gaye. Diana would go on to a hugely successful solo career encompassing forty-one hits through 1986.

1979 Carly Simon performed with Bonnie Raitt, who was one of the organizers, at the Musicians United for Safe Energy (MUSE) anti-nuclear concert at Madison Square Garden in New York. The event included performances by The Doobie Brothers, Bruce Springsteen, and Jackson Browne.

September

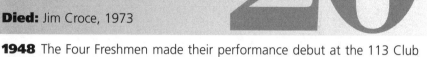

#1 Song 1969: "Sugar, Sugar," The Archies

Born: Mac Rebennack (Dr. John), 1941; John Panozzo (Styx), 1947; Matthew and Gunnar Nelson (both of Nelson), 1967

Died: Jim Croce, 1973

1948 The Four Freshmen made their performance debut at the 113 Club in Fort Wayne, Indiana.

1957 Elvis Presley, doing his public service best, appeared on WKNO-TV in Memphis to promote driver education along with traffic safety. At that point in his life, he had already had about half-a-dozen speeding tickets.

1959 The first "oldies" compilation album, *Oldies but Goodies* (original Sound Records) was issued. It included such classics as "In the Still of the Night" by The Five Satins and "Earth Angel" by The Penguins.

1977 Thirty-one-year-old Linda Ronstadt performed at the Universal Amphitheater, decked out in a cub scout uniform!

1986 Although mainly a contemporary Christian artist, Amy Grant (with Peter Cetera) charted with "Next Time I Fall." The #1 recording was the first of seven Top 20 pop hits for the Augusta, Georgia, native.

Linda Ronstadt

September

#1 Song 1959: "Sleep Walk," Santo & Johnny

Born: Leonard Cohen, 1934; Dickie Lee, 1936; Tony Moon (Dante & the Evergreens), 1941; Don Felder (Eagles), 1947

1959 The Isley Brothers charted pop with "Shout" (#47), their first of forty-one Top 100 hits during a thirty-eight-year period.

1961 Bob Dylan recorded his first album for Columbia.

1989 Formed in 1981 and after twelve Top 100 hits, The Bangles announced they were disbanding.

1991 Diana Ross performed the last of three sell-out shows at New York's Radio City Music Hall, grossing over $650,000.

Diana Ross

September

#1 Song 1956: "Don't Be Cruel,"
Elvis Presley

Born: Debby Boone, 1956;
Joan Jett, 1960

1958 The Teddy Bears, with Carol Connors on lead, had their first single released today. The song was "To Know Him Is To Love Him," written by group member Phil Spector, and went all the way to #1.

1958 Elvis Presley shipped off to Germany for his two-year military hitch. During his last press conference, he indicated his wish that his fans not forget him while he was gone. While on the troop transport, Presley was assigned to put together a talent show and weathered the crossing playing piano in the impromptu band.

1962 The Springfields became the first British vocal group to reach the American Top 20 when their single "Silver Threads & Golden Needles" hit #20. The group's lead singer was Mary O'Brien, who became Dusty Springfield. Coming full circle, the song was originally a hit in 1950 for American artist Dinah Shore.

1979 The Buggles' "Video Killed the Radio Star" charted in Britain on its way to #1. Ironically, it would become the first video to be played on America's new MTV network.

1989 Music legend Irving Berlin died. One of America's great composers, he wrote, among hundreds of others, the standard "White Christmas." He was 101.

September

23

#1 Song 1957: "That'll Be the Day," Buddy Holly

Born: Ray Charles, 1930; Ben E. King (The Drifters), 1938; Steve Boone (The Lovin' Spoonful), 1943; Jerry Corbetta (Sugarloaf), 1947; Bruce Springsteen, 1949; Lita Ford, 1959

1956 Elvis Presley, who often traveled under assumed names, flew to Memphis using the alias Clint Reno. Reno was the name of his character in his current film, *Love Me Tender.*

1967 Aretha Franklin's "A Natural Women" was released, inevitably reaching #8.

1974 Robbie McIntosh was the drummer for the British rock-soul group The Average White Band. Best known for the hit "Pick Up the Pieces," AWB had seven pop charters between 1974 and 1980. Formerly with Brian Auger's Oblivion Express, Robbie played on Chuck Berry's famous novelty hit, "My Ding-a-Ling." He died at a party in Los Angeles when he inhaled a mix of heroin and morphine, believing it was cocaine. He was exactly twenty-four, dying on his birthday.

1978 Foreigner's "Double Vision" charted. It was their fourth of nine Top 10 hits and eventually reached #2.

Ray Charles

September

#1 Song 1983: "Tell Her About It," Billy Joel

Born: Barbara Allbut (The Angels), 1940; Phyllis Allbut (The Angels), 1942; Gerry Marsden (The Pacemakers), 1942; Linda McCartney (Wings), 1941; Cedric Dent (Take 6), 1962

1957 Elvis Presley's much-anticipated single "Jailhouse Rock" from the motion picture of the same name was released. His twenty-fifth chart 45, it would go on to become the eighth #1 single of his unprecedented career.

1963 The Springfields announced they were disbanding. Lead Dusty Springfield then signed with Philips Records.

1978 One of the great torch song vocalists of Broadway, Ruth Etting became a star in *The Ziegfeld Follies* of 1927. She had sixty-two pop hits between 1926 and 1937, including "Life Is a Song" and "Love Me or Leave Me," which was the title of the movie of her life in 1955 as played by Doris Day. She died at age seventy today.

1983 Billy Joel's tribute to The Four Seasons, "Uptown Girl," charted, en route to #3. On December 5, 1990, The Four Seasons repaid the favor, singing "Uptown Girl" at the NARAS Living Legends Awards honoring Billy.

1992 Madonna performed in the AMFAR-AIDS fashion benefit at the Shrine Auditorium in Los Angeles. As if the crowd of 6,000 hadn't seen enough, Madonna found the need to expose her breasts!

September

25

#1 Song 1982: "Abracadabra," Steve Miller Band

Born: Joseph Russell (The Persuasions), 1939

Died: John Bonham (Led Zeppelin), 1980

1954 Jubilee issued a special Four Tunes *Harmonizing Quartet* LP. The album was marked with bass, tenor, alto, and baritone parts so would-be vocalists could sing along to the album's collection of standards. Fourteen years later, The Beach Boys would do the same thing with their *Stack o' Tracks* album containing fifteen tracks of their past hits.

1970 *The Partridge Family* TV show debuted on ABC. It ran for ninety-six episodes through September 1974 and was modeled on the real-life vocal group The Cowsills.

1980 John "Bonzo" Bonham was the drummer for the British blues-rock legends Led Zeppelin. Originally a member of Terry Web and the Spiders, Bonzo, the former bricklayer, was with the band throughout its historic run that included the hits "Whole Lotta Love" and "Stairway to Heaven." Bonham died of alcohol and drug abuse at band member Jimmy Page's house while reportedly trying to consume his body weight in vodka. He was only thirty-two.

1981 After escaping with thirty-six cents and a Mobil gas credit card from a brutal relationship with husband Ike Turner, Tina Turner began her comeback as the supporting act for The Rolling Stones' tenth American tour, starting at JFK Stadium, Philadelphia.

September

#1 Song 1964: "Oh Pretty Woman," Roy Orbison

Born: George Chambers (The Chambers Brothers), 1931; Bryan Ferry, 1945; Lynn Anderson, 1947; Olivia Newton-John, 1948; Carlene Carter, 1955; Cindy Herron (En Vogue), 1965

1937 A pioneering blues great, Bessie Smith influenced many stars, including Janis Joplin. Known as "The Empress of the Blues," the Tennessee orphan was tutored by Ma Rainey while in *The Rabbit Foot Minstrels Revue*, circa 1912. Most remembered for "Tain't Nobody's Business if I Do" and "Careless Love Blues," Bessie died today when her car hit a truck near Clarksdale, Mississippi. She was forty-three.

1953 In what was the beginning of the golden age of vocal groups, seven of the R&B charts' Top 10 positions were occupied by singing groups: The Orioles, The Clovers, The Five Royales, The Royals, The Spaniels, The Dominoes, and The Coronets.

1960 Connie Francis became the first female singer to ever have two consecutive #1s when her recording of "My Heart Has a Mind of Its Own" topped the singles charts. The first was "Everybody's Somebody's Fool."

1969 The Beatles' *Abbey Road* album was issued in England. The record's highlights included "Something," "Come Together," "Here Comes the Sun," "Carry that Weight," "Maxwell's Silver Hammer," "You Never Give Me Your Money," "Octopus's Garden," "Because," and "She Came in Through the Bathroom Window." Five days later it was issued in America.

Bessie Smith

September

#1 Song 1997: "Honey," Maria Carey

Born: Randy Bachman
(Bachman-Turner Overdrive), 1943;
Meat Loaf, 1947; Shaun Cassidy, 1959

1965 EMI Records, the British label for The Fab Four, stated that The Beatles would begin recording their next album in October for Christmas release. The album would eventually be titled *Rubber Soul*.

1975 Captain & Tennille's second hit, "The Way I Want to Touch You," charted, reaching #4. It had been previously released three times in 1974 on three different labels and bombed each time, but being the follow-up to their #1 hit, "Love Will Keep Us Together," gave it new attention.

1976 The Runaways were held by bobbies in London after the theft of a hair dryer from a hotel during their first British tour.

1986 The Bangles' "Walk Like an Egyptian" ran onto the Hot 100, finally stopping at #1.

1987 The ill-fated Dolly Parton ABC-TV variety show, *Dolly*, began its Sunday night run.

The Bangles

September

#1 Song 1963: "Blue Velvet," Bobby Vinton

Born: Koko Taylor, 1935

1956 Elvis Presley's long-awaited "Love Me Tender" single made record industry history when it became the first single to ever have one million orders prior to release. The 45 did not disappoint, spending five weeks at #1, while selling over two-and-a-half million copies in three months.

1959 "Sweet Nothin's," Brenda Lee's first Top 5 hit, was released today. Although it reached #4, it was actually the B-side as its flip, "I'm Sorry," spent three weeks at #1.

1963 The Angels' album *My Boyfriend's Back* (#33) became their only chart LP, despite six hit singles over a four-year period.

1966 Lucky Millinder was a rare example of a '30s and '40s bandleader who did not play an instrument. His band registered ten hits in the '40s, including his biggest, "Who Threw the Whiskey in the Well?," with Wynonie Harris on vocals. His band also contained, at various times, Dizzy Gillespie, Sam "The Man" Taylor, Rosetta Tharpe, Annisteen Allen, and, for a few gigs before firing her, Ruth Brown. He died of liver ailments in New York City at age sixty-six.

1968 Dewey Phillips' claim to fame was that of being the first deejay to play an Elvis Presley record when on July 10, 1954, he put an acetate of "That's All Right" on his WHBQ radio show in Memphis and the phone lines lit up. The personable, fast-talking platter-spinner was shocked when he found out Presley was white. The heavy drinker was fired in the '60s and drifted to several stations before finishing up in Little Rock, Arkansas. He died homeless today at the age of forty-two of a heart attack.

1991 One of the great innovators of jazz, Miles Davis influenced the likes of Chick Corea, Herbie Hancock, and John Coltrane. The trumpet-playing legend was taken under the wing of Charlie Parker at an early age and recorded trend-setting albums like *The Birth of Cool*, *Bitches Brew*, *On the Corner*, and *Kind of Blue*. He died of a stroke at the age of sixty-five.

1997 Fifty-six-year-old Bob Dylan, wearing a white cowboy hat, gave new meaning to the phrase "an audience with the Pope," when he performed at a Bologna, Italy, concert with a bored Pontiff John Paul II looking on. The Jewish legend sang "Knockin' on Heaven's Door."

September

#1 Song 1958: "It's All in the Game," Tommy Edwards

Born: Jerry Lee Lewis, 1935; Mike Pinera (Blues Image), 1948; Mark Farner (Grand Funk Railroad), 1948

1959 Little Anthony & the Imperials recorded "Shimmy, Shimmy, Ko-Ko-Bop" (#14 pop, #24 R&B), a song that would become their last hit for five years and a record Anthony was quoted as saying was "stupid!"

1963 The Rolling Stones began their first British tour as the opening act for The Everly Brothers, Little Richard, and Bo Diddley.

1976 Pistol-packin' Jerry Lee Lewis accidentally shot his bass player twice in the chest, while target shooting at soda bottles.

1979 Genya Ravan reached the album Top 200 with *And I Mean It* (#106). It was the second and last solo charter for the former Goldie Zelkowitz of Brooklyn, who had previously driven the hard-rock act Ten Wheel Drive as lead vocalist.

1984 The major exponents of thrash/speed metal music Metlallica charted in America with their scond album. Although the LP only reached #100 on the Top 200, it would eventually sell more than 3 million copies. In the U.K., it rose only to #87 yet sold half a million copies.

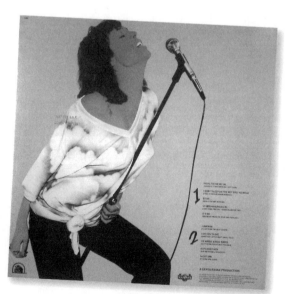

*Genya Raven's
And I Mean It*

September

30

#1 Song 1972: "Baby Don't Get Hooked on Me," Mac Davis

Born: Johnny Mathis, 1935; Frankie Lymon (The Teenagers), 1942; Marilyn McCoo (The 5th Dimension), 1943; Marc Bolan (T. Rex), 1948; Deborah Allen, 1953; Patrice Rushen, 1954

1957 The legendary girl group The Chantels' first single, "He's Gone," written by lead singer Arlene Smith, debuted on the charts, reaching #71.

1957 Four siblings from Middletown, Ohio, The Shepherd Sisters had their lone hit when "Alone" reached the best-seller's list today, rising to #18.

1967 England's BBC Radio 1 began its move to rock 'n' roll with The Move's "Flowers in the Rain."

1972 Country star Donna Fargo reached the Hot 100 with "Funny Face" (#5). It was her only Top 10 pop hit.

1977 Mary Ford was a superlative country singer who combined with Les Paul's jazz influence to create numerous pop hits in the '50s like "Vaya con Dios" and "How High the Moon." Paul's innovative electric guitar sound and double-tracking of Mary's voice made for a most identifiable hit sound. Mary died of diabetes in Los Angeles at forty-nine.

October

1

#1 Song 1966: "Cherish," The Association

Born: Barbara Parritt (The Toys), 1944; Herbert "Tubo" Rhoad (The Persuasions), 1944; Scott McKenzie, 1944; Donny Hathaway, 1945; Howard Hewett (Shalamar), 1957

1958 Little Anthony & the Imperials recorded Neil Sedaka's "The Diary," which was planned as their next single. When producer George Goldner went out of town, he left instructions with his associate Richard Barrett to release the record, but Barrett issued a song titled "So Much," which he had just happened to have written. When Sedaka heard The Imperials single was not coming out, he recorded "The Diary" himself and had the hit.

1963 Elvis Presley's newest single "Bossa Nova Baby" from the film *Fun in Acapulco* was paired with The Spiders' 1955 #5 R&B hit, "Witchcraft," and released. "Bossa Nova" would go on to reach #8, while "Witchcraft" made it to #32.

1964 The Beatles film *A Hard Day's Night* was shown in Prague, Czechoslovakia, the first time a Western pop-culture film was seen behind the Iron Curtain. The same day, Vee Jay Records issued their *Beatles vs. The Four Seasons* album.

1966 Cher, who recorded as Bonnie Jo Mason and Cherilyn in 1964, hit the Top 200 album charts with the self-titled *Cher* (#59).

1994 Actress-singer Brandy charted with "I Wanna Be Down" (#6), her first of twelve hits through 1999, including #1s "The Boy Is Mine" in a duet with Monica, and "Have You Ever."

October

#1 Song 1976: "Play that Funky Music," Wild Cherry

Born: David Somerville (The Diamonds), 1933; Don McLean, 1945; Michael Rutherford (Genesis), 1950; Sting (Gordon Sumner), 1951; Freddie Jackson, 1956; Claude McKnight (Take 6), 1962; Tiffany (Tiffany Darwish), 1971

1951 Sting (Gordon Sumner) was born today. The bass-guitarist was the lead singer of The Police. Formed in 1977, the band hit with "Don't Stand So Close to Me" and the #1 "Every Breath You Take," among twelve charters through 1986. Sting went solo in 1985, adding sixteen more Top 100 singles to his credit, including "If You Love Somebody Set Them Free" and "All for Love," with Rod Stewart and Bryan Adams.

1954 Elvis Presley performed at the Grand Ole Opry, Ryman Auditorium, Nashville, Tennessee for the first time. He sang "Blue Moon of Kentucky" and was given a courteous though not overly enthusiastic response.

1961 Phil Spector launched his successful label Philles (with partner Lester Sill) with the release of The Crystals' first single, "There's No Other." The label's name was a combination of Phil and Les.

1971 Joan Baez's "The Night They Drove Old Dixie Down" hit #3. It was a cover version of The Band's B-side of "Up On Cripple Creek" from 1969.

1981 Ann and Nancy Wilson (Heart) performed along with Joan Baez and Paul Simon at the Greek Theater in Berkeley, California, at the Bread & Roses Festival, a benefit for prisoners aid run by Baez's sister, Mimi Farina.

October

#1 Song 1970: "Ain't No Mountain High Enough," Diana Ross

Born: Eddie Cochran, 1938; Chubby Checker, 1941; Lindsey Buckingham (Fleetwood Mac), 1947; Stevie Ray Vaughan, 1954

1955 Elvis Presley made his first public performance at age ten in a dairy show talent contest. He sang "Old Shep" and won $5, finishing second.

1958 Dion began touring on The Biggest Show of Stars for 1958 tour with Buddy Holly & the Crickets, Clyde McPhatter, The Coasters, Bobby Darin, Bobby Freeman, and Frankie Avalon. The nineteen dates were done in sixteen days.

1967 Woodrow Wilson "Woody" Guthrie was the most influential and important folksinger of the century. The Okemah, Oklahoma, native influenced hundreds of artists, including Bob Dylan and Bruce Springsteen. He is best known for the recordings, "This Land Is Your Land" and "I Ain't Got No Home." He died at age fifty-five today.

1970 Janis Joplin listened to the final track to be included in her album, *Pearl*. She planned to record her vocals the next day on the song titled "Buried Alive in the Blues." It never happened. (See October 4 entry.)

1992 Sinead O'Connor sang a noxious interpretation of the song "War" to stunned audience silence on NBC-TV's *Saturday Night Live*. She then tore apart a photo of the Pope and stated, "Fight the real enemy." She was banned for life from the show.

October

1958 George Goldner, End Records President, signed The Flamingos, who would have their greatest career successes under his tutelage with hits like "I Only Have Eyes for You" and "Nobody Loves Me Like You."

1962 Bob Dylan showcased at New York's Carnegie Hall. Fifty-three people showed up.

1970 Alone in her room at the Landmark Hotel in Los Angeles at 1:40 a.m., Janis Joplin died of a drug overdose combined with alcohol. The day before, Janis had listened to the final track to be included in her album, *Pearl*. She planned to record her vocals today on the song title: "Buried Alive in the Blues." She was twenty-seven.

Janis Joplin

October

#1 Song 1959: "Mack the Knife," Bobby Darin

Born: Carlo Mastrangelo (The Belmonts), 1938; Arlene Smith (The Chantels), 1941; Richard Street (The Temptations), 1942; Steve Miller, 1943; Bob Geldof (The Boomtown Rats), 1954

1944 Dinah Shore became the first woman in history to top the American singles chart when her recording of "I'll Walk Alone" reached #1 today.

1962 The Beatles' first single, "Love Me Do"/"P.S. I Love You," was released in the U.K. on the EMI records affiliate Parlophone. Radio Luxembourg played the record for the first time that evening. The group couldn't believe it. Rumor has it that manager Brian Epstein bought 10,000 copies for sale through his NEMS record store chain, knowing that was the magic number of sales needed to make the British Top 20. He sold them all.

1963 The Four Seasons' "New Mexican Rose" was their tenth and last chart single on Vee Jay before they signed with Phillips and began a string of twenty-three hits for the Dutch label starting with "Dawn."

1968 Cream, the three-and-a-half-year-old "supergroup" led by Eric Clapton, began its farewell tour. All three of their LPs were million-sellers.

1974 Olivia Newton-John's "I Honestly Love You" became her first #1, selling more than a million copies.

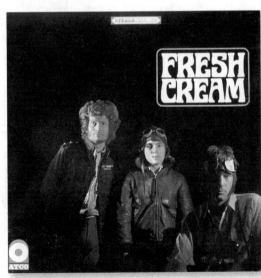

*Cream's
Fresh Cream*

October

#1 Song 1979: "Sad Eyes," Robert John

Born: Millie Small, 1946; Thomas McClary (The Commodores), 1950; Kevin Cronin (REO Speedwagon), 1951

1956 Bill Haley & the Comets had five hits on the British Top 20 led by "Rockin' Through the Rye" (#6).

1958 B. B. King sang lead with the doo-wop group The Vocal Chords on the single, "Please Accept My Love," which was released today.

1960 Two interesting records became instant flops when they were issued today, but they were portents of things to come. The first was Tommy Roe & the Satins 45 "Sheila" (Judd Records) and the second was "I'd Like to Be the Lipstick on Your Lips" by Jerry Landis (Warwick Records). A revised version of Roe's "Sheila" came out two years later on the larger ABC-Paramount label and raced to the top, starting the twenty-two–hit career of Roe. Landis would take a little longer to emerge (five years, in fact) when he went back to his real name, Paul Simon, and hit with "Sounds of Silence" as half of Simon & Garfunkel.

1963 The Angels appeared on *The Ed Sullivan Show*, performing their current #1 million-seller, "My Boyfriend's Back."

1979 Stevie Nicks and Fleetwood Mac rocked onto the charts with "Tusk" (#8), a single recorded with the University of Southern California Marching Band at Dodger Stadium in Los Angeles.

October

#1 Song 1967: "The Letter," The Box Tops

Born: Tony Silvester (The Main Ingredient), 1941; John Cougar Mellencamp, 1951; Toni Braxton, 1968

1957 Ricky Nelson hit the charts with "Be-Bop Baby" (#3), his third Top 5 hit in five months and first for his new label, Imperial Records. Rick would go on to have fifty-four hits through 1973.

1957 The Crests' first single, "My Juanita," was released. The record reached #86 pop and the five group members each earned $17.50.

1967 The Mamas & the Papas British tour and TV appearances were canceled when Mama Cass Elliot was jailed for a night, accused of stealing items from a hotel.

1995 Alanis Morissette topped the album chart with *Jagged Little Pill* and became the first Canadian female artist to reach #1 in the U.S. (Joni Mitchell only reached #2…twice.)

1995 Brian Beirne, the West Coast's answer to New York's legendary disc jockey "Cousin" Bruce Morrow, held his eighth annual Legends of Rock 'n' Roll Concert at Los Angeles's Greek Theater, featuring The Diamonds, The Drifters, The Angels, We Five, The Olympics, Gene Chandler, Bobby "Boris" Pickett, Tommy Sands, and The Velvetones. The Velvetones of "Glory of Love" fame had not performed together since the mid '50s.

October

#1 Song 1977: "*Star Wars* Theme/Cantina Band," Meco

Born: Dock Green (The Drifters), 1934; Fred Cash (The Impressions), 1940; Johnny Ramone (The Ramones), 1948; Ray Royer (Procol Harum), 1945; Robert Bell (Kool & the Gang), 1950

1957 Jerry Lee Lewis recorded the classic "Great Balls of Fire."

1962 Little Richard and Sam Cooke began a tour of Europe at the Gaumont Cinema in Doncaster, England. The ever flamboyant Richard performed in a flowing white robe. His keyboard player was sixteen-year-old Billy Preston. Gene Vincent was the reluctant M.C. since his work permit had expired and he wasn't allowed to sing.

1966 The title song from Elvis Presley's movie *Spinout* charted today. It would go on to sell more than 400,000 copies, although it reached only #40 on the national charts.

1968 Three months after The Mamas & Papas disbanded, Mama Cass opened as a solo act at Caesar's Palace in Las Vegas, but collapsed with a throat hemorrhage, necessitating a major operation, thus canceling the six-week stint. She was back recording by early 1969.

1977 The Emotions' (the three Hutchinson sisters—Wanda, Sheila, and Jeanette) "Don't Ask My Neighbors" (#44 pop, #7 R&B) charted as the follow-up to their huge hit, "Best of My Love" (#1 pop & R&B). It was the seventeenth of thirty R&B hits they would have between 1969 and 1984.

October

#1 Song 1961: "Hit the Road Jack," Ray Charles

Born: Shirley Gunter, 1934; John Lennon, 1940; John Entwistle (The Who), 1944; Jackson Browne, 1948

1958 Eddie Cochran recorded "C'mon Everybody (#35), the follow-up to his career best, "Summertime Blues (#8)." The twenty-year-old originally sang in The Cochran Brothers with Hank Cochran (no relation).

1961 While in Paris celebrating his twenty-first birthday with Paul McCartney, John Lennon ran into Jurgen Vollmer, a friend from Hamburg. Jurgen wore his hair like many French teens, brushed forward, a style he learned from Astrid Kirchnerr, who did Stuart Sutcliffe's hair in Hamburg. Deciding they liked it, they had Jurgen give them their first Beatles haircut in his hotel room on the Left Bank. Astrid copied the style from the 1959 Jean Cocteau movie *Le Testament d'Orphee* where the lead actor, Jean Marais, playing Oedipus, was first known to have worn what would become the legendary Beatles hairstyle.

1973 Elvis and Priscilla Presley were divorced.

1989 British thrushes Kylie Minogue, Sonia and Hazel Dean began a tour called The Hitman Roadshow, named after their producer, Peter "Hitman" Waterman.

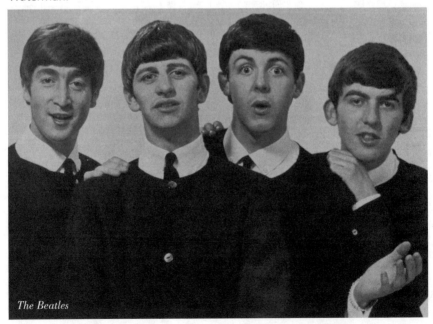

The Beatles

October

#1 Song 1960: "Mr. Custer,"
Larry Verne

Born: Ivory Joe Hunter, 1914; John
Prine, 1946; Cyril Neville (The Neville
Brothers), 1948; David Lee Roth (Van
Halen), 1955; Tanya Tucker, 1958

1960 During a visit by their original manager, Allan Williams, The Beatles—performing at the Kaiserkeller in Hamburg, Germany—were encouraged by Williams and the club manager to "Make a show, boys!" ("Much schau!") when they seemed to be dragging. This led to rowdy onstage behavior that included drinking, smoking, fighting, and insulting the audience. John Lennon took to wearing a toilet seat around his neck and parading in his underwear while the group threw microphones and instruments across the stage. They goosestepped and "Seig Heiled" their way through perform-ances, often drunk, while calling the audience Nazis! Luckily for them, the patrons loved it.

1962 In a bizarre compromise of British law, Gene Vincent, who was allowed to host but not perform on a tour of England with Little Richard and Sam Cooke because his work permit had expired, was finally allowed to sing in front of the stage but not on it!

1970 Elvis Presley, who was an avid collector of police badges, received his official deputy sheriff's badge from Shelby County, which also entitled him to carry a gun.

1978 Aerosmith members Joe Perry and Steven Tyler were injured when an overzealous fan launched a cherry bomb onto the stage in Philadelphia.

1980 The motion picture *The Rose*, starring Bette Midler, opened in America. The story of a Janis Joplin–like performer earned Midler an Academy Award nomination.

October

#1 Song 1997: "Candle in the Wind 1997," Elton John

Born: Dottie West, 1932; Gary Mallaber (The Steve Miller Band), 1946; Greg Douglas (The Steve Miller Band), 1949; Daryl Hall (Hall & Oates), 1949

1962 "Love Me Do" became the first Beatles 45 to chart when it debuted at #49 on the British hit list.

1986 Joan Jett and her new band, The Blackhearts, charted with "Good Music." Although it only reached #83 (their worst showing of their five previous releases, which all reached the Top 40), its distinction was having background vocals done by The Beach Boys, a group who hadn't backed another solo act on a single since Annette's recording of "The Monkey's Uncle" in 1965.

1986 When Janet Jackson's "When I Think of You" reached #1, she and her brother Michael became the first siblings to have solo #1s in the rock era. Michael's #1 was "Ben" in 1972.

Janet Jackson

286

October

#1 Song 1963: "Sugar Shack," Jimmy Gilmer & the Fireballs

Born: Sam Moore (Sam & Dave), 1935; Melvin Franklin (The Temptations), 1942

Died: Gene Vincent, 1971

1940 Former vocalist for Xavier Cugat's Orchestra, Dinah Shore charted with "May Be" (#17), her first of sixty-nine hits through 1957.

1962 Little Richard headlined a show in New Brighton, England, with three new bands—Billy J. Kramer & the Dakotas, Lee Curtis & the All-Stars (with Peter Best on drums), and The Beatles. Madness reigned as an usher was trampled by fans charging the stage, and police dogs were called in to restore order. Little Richard later commented, "Man, those Beatles are fabulous. If I hadn't seen them I'd never have dreamed they were white. They have a real authentic Negro sound."

1965 The Beatles began recording their new album, starting work on "Run for Your Life" and "This Bird Has Flown," later known as "Norwegian Wood." John Lennon commented, "I was trying to write about an affair without letting my wife know I was writing about an affair."

1966 The Jimi Hendrix Experience was formed in London.

1971 Gene Vincent turned his convalescence from a Navy accident into a career as a pioneer rockabilly artist when he used the time to become a proficient guitar player. He signed with Capitol Records, while still in a cast and on crutches and with a song he bought from writer Donald Graves, and achieved legendary status when he hit with "Be-Bop-a-Lula." He was a sensation in Britain, even more so than America. He almost died in the car crash that killed fellow rocker Eddie Cochran in England in 1960, and eventually succumbed to complications of an ulcer at the age of thirty-six.

October

13

#1 Song 1973: "Half-Breed," Cher

Born: Shirley Caesar, 1938; Paul Simon, 1941; Robert Lamm (Chicago), 1944; Lacy J. Dalton, 1946; Sammy Hagar, 1947; Marie Osmond (The Osmonds), 1959

1900 The Haydn Quartet's "Because" reached #1 today, becoming the first vocal group chart topper of the twentieth century.

1950 The Four Freshmen recorded "Mr. B's Blues" as their debut disc for Capitol Records.

1956 The Heartbeats evergreen, "A Thousand Miles Away" (#53 pop, #5 R&B), was released. The group's lead singer, James Sheppard, wrote the standard while lounging in his bathtub.

1963 The term "Beatlemania" was coined after a near riot at a TV show, Sunday Night at the London Palladium, where the Mop Tops appeared.

1977 Orlons member Shirley Brickley was shot to death. One of the hottest dance music groups of the early '60s, She was a member through all nine of their Top 100 hits. Shirley was only thirty-two.

October

#1 Song 1978: "Kiss You All Over," Exile

Born: Bill Justis, 1926; Cliff Richard, 1940; Justin Hayward (The Moody Blues), 1946; Thomas Dolby, 1958; Karyn White, 1965

1946 Justin Hayward, lead singer for The Moody Blues, was born today. Hayward replaced Denny Laine, who went on to join Paul McCartney's Wings. Hayward led the band through its renaissance with recordings like "Knights in White Satin," "Tuesday Afternoon," and "Question."

1955 Nineteen-year-old Buddy Holly and his friend Bob Montgomery were the opening act (as Buddy & Bob) in their hometown of Lubbock, Texas, for visiting rock stars Bill Haley & the Comets. The next day they opened for Elvis Presley.

1966 The Mamas & the Papas performed at New York's prestigious Carnegie Hall.

1980 Carly Simon collapsed onstage in Pittsburgh due to exhaustion, while in the middle of a national tour. Soon after she developed a fear of performing live.

2000 Zeke Manners (Leo Ezekiel Mannes) was a Los Angeles radio personality in the '50s who became a singer-musician. Known as "the Jewish Hillbilly" because of his penchant for Western swing music, he wrote "The Pennsylvania Polka." Zeke died of heart failure at age eighty-nine today.

Carly Simon

289

October

15

#1 Song 1983: "Total Eclipse of the Heart," Bonnie Tyler

Born: Mickey "Guitar" Baker (Mickey & Sylvia), 1925; Barry McGuire, 1935; Marv Johnson, 1938; Richard Carpenter (The Carpenters), 1946; Chris De Burgh, 1948; Tito Jackson (The Jackson 5), 1953

1957 The elegant gatefold-jacketed *Elvis' Christmas Album* was released today. Reaching #1, the Christmas collection would become a perennial fan favorite for decades at holiday time.

1960 While in Hamburg, Germany, Walter Eymond (stage name, Lou Walters), lead singer of The Hurricanes, made a demo recording of the *Porgy & Bess* standard "Summertime." Accompanying him was The Hurricanes drummer, Ringo Starr, and The Beatles George Harrison, John Lennon, and Paul McCartney—the first time the Fab Four ever recorded together! Nine copies of the 78 RPM single were made, but only one is known to have survived to this day.

1973 Patsy Cline became the first female solo performer to be inducted into the Country Music Hall of Fame. The induction finally came ten years after she died.

1991 Cher was named the "worst dressed woman of the last three decades" by fashion critic Mr. Blackwell, who said in summation, "From toes to nose, she's the tacky tattoo'd terror of the twentieth century. A Bono-fied fashion fiasco of the legendary kind."

1996 The Monkees album *Justus* was released. It was the first recording to include all four original members since the 1960s.

Patsy Cline

October

#1 Song 1976: "Disco Duck," Rick Dees

Born: Bob Weir (The Grateful Dead), 1947; Wendy Wilson (Wilson Phillips), 1969

1966 One day after Jefferson Airplane original lead singer Signe Toly Anderson left to raise her new child, Grace Slick joined the band, bringing with her two songs she had performed with her previous group, Great Society. The songs were "Somebody to Love" and "White Rabbit."

1966 Joan Baez and 123 others were arrested for blocking the entrance to the armed forces induction center in Oakland during draft demonstrations. She spent ten days in jail.

1969 Leonard Chess (Lazur Shmuel Chez) was, along with his brother Phil, a pioneer producer and label exec of late '40s and early '50s blues and rock 'n' roll. The brothers formed Aristocrat Records in 1947, having their first hit with Muddy Waters's "Going Home." By 1950, they renamed the label Chess and scored hundreds of ground breaking hits by artists like Chuck Berry, Howlin' Wolf, Bo Diddley, Muddy Waters, The Moonglows, The Flamingos, Little Walter, The Dells, Etta James, and Billy Stewart. The Jewish immigrant from Russia died of a heart attack today at age fifty-two.

1986 Chuck Berry celebrated his sixtieth birthday by participating in an all-star concert in St. Louis which was filmed as part of his biography, *Hail! Hail! Rock 'n' Roll*. Performers included Keith Richards, Julian Lennon, Linda Ronstadt, and Eric Clapton.

1999 Ella Mae Morse—who had Capitol Records first million-selling hit, "Cow, Cow Boogie," in 1942—died in Bullhead City, Arizona. The Texas-born singer combined boogie-woogie, jazz, blues, swing, and country influences during the '40s and '50s, helping to create a pioneering pop sound that would later become rock 'n' roll. Elvis Presley once praised her for teaching him how to sing. She was seventy-five.

October

17

#1 Song 1960: "Save the Last Dance for Me," The Drifters

Born: Jim Seals (Seals & Crofts), 1941; Gary Puckett (Union Gap), 1942; Ziggy Marley, 1968

1960 Dion & the Belmonts split up. Dion stayed with Laurie Records while The Belmonts formed their own Sabina Records.

1964 "Walking in the Rain," the classic Ronettes ballad, was released today, ultimately reaching #23. It gave producer Phil Spector his only Grammy…and it was for sound effects.

1981 Sheena Easton's "For Your Eyes Only," theme from the James Bond movie of the same name, reached #4 (and #8 in England). She became the only Bond-theme vocalist to be seen on screen as she sang the song during the credits.

1990 The first #1 album not available on vinyl (only CD or cassette) was *To the Extreme* by Vanilla Ice.

1999 Thomas Durden, who wrote the lyrics to Elvis Presley's "Heartbreak Hotel," died at his home in Houghton Lake, Michigan. The song—co-written with Mae Axton, mother of Hoyt Axton—was Durden's only hit and the steel guitarist went on to a career as a dishwasher repairman.

Sheena Easton

October

#1 Song 1969: "I Can't Get Next to You," The Temptations

Born: Chuck Berry, 1926; Russ Giguere (The Association), 1943; Laura Nyro, 1947; Gary Richrath (REO Speedwagon), 1949

Died: Orville "Hoppy" Jones (Ink Spots), 1944

1931 Thomas Edison, the inventor of the phonograph, died.

1944 Orville "Hoppy" Jones was the pioneering bass singer of the Legendary Ink Spots, a group that, along with The Mills Brothers, were founding fathers of pop R&B. "Hoppy" sang on such standards as "Don't Get Around Much Anymore" and "If I Didn't Care," among the forty-six singles he recorded with the group before passing away at age thirty-nine.

1957 Paul McCartney played with The Quarrymen, who later became The Beatles, for the first time at the Conservative Club, New Clubmoor Hall, Liverpool. He remembered it as a disaster, having fumbled the solo on "Guitar Boogie Shuffle." The incident made him resolve not to be a lead guitarist.

1969 At Richard Nader's legendary first Rock 'n' Roll Revival Concert in New York, Bill Haley was given an eight-minute standing ovation!

1986 Hard to believe, but for the first time in rock history, females held the top three spots on the charts: Janet Jackson ("When I Think of You"), Tina Turner ("Typical Male"), and Cyndi Lauper ("True Colors").

October

19

#1 Song 1974: "Nothing from Nothing," Billy Preston

Born: Cass Elliot (Ellen Naomi Cohen, The Mamas & the Papas), 1941; Jeannie C. Riley, 1945; Wilbert Hart (The Delfonics), 1947; Nino DeFranco (The DeFranco Family), 1956; Jennifer Holiday, 1960

1954 The Penguins' all-time favorite "Earth Angel" (#8 pop, #1 R&B) was released.

1958 Backup vocalist for Gene Vincent, Tommy Facenda charted with a most unique single, "High School U.S.A.," which was issued with twenty-eight different versions, each mentioning the names of different schools in major metropolitan areas. Collectively, the record reached #28!

1961 The Beatles and their friends Gerry & the Pacemakers joined together as one band to play at Litherland Town Hall in England. They went under the name The Beatmakers for that one and only evening.

1963 Timi Yuro and Lesley Gore began what was billed as "The Greatest Record Show of 1963" British tour along with Dion, Trini Lopez, and Brook Benton. The tour's first stop was at Finsbury Park, Astoria, in London.

1985 Gloria Estefan—responsible with her husband and bandmate Emilio Estefan, Jr., for the Latin-pop influence on music in the 1980s—charted with "Conga" (#10), her first of twenty-eight hits through 1999. She escaped to Miami from Cuba in 1960 shortly after Fidel Castro overthrew dictator Fulgencio Batista. Her father was one of Batista's bodyguards.

October

#1 Song 1962: "Monster Mash," Bobby "Boris" Pickett

Born: Jay Siegel (The Tokens), 1939; Tom Petty, 1952

1956 The two biggest names in '50s rock 'n' roll, Bill Haley & the Comets and Elvis Presley, performed on the same bill at Brooklyn High School in Cleveland.

1962 Eighteen-year-old Brooklynite Marcie Blane became a one-hit wonder when she charted with "Bobby's Girl," which ultimately peaked at #3.

1963 Dusty Springfield made her solo debut after the breakup of The Springfields. The performance was at a show for British troops stationed in what was then West Germany.

1977 Ronnie Van Zant was the leader of the country rock band Lynyrd Skynyrd, named after the group's disliked gym teacher, Leonard Skinner. The group was originally called My Backyard and was best known for their hit "Sweet Home Alabama." Van Zant died in a plane crash near Gillsburg, Mississippi, after the pilot accidentally dumped his fuel.

1979 Donna Summer teamed with Barbra Streisand and rolled onto the best-seller's list with "No More Tears (Enough Is Enough)" (#1). It was Donna's fourth chart topper in two years.

Dusty Springfield

295

October

#1 Song 1989: "Miss You Much,"
Janet Jackson

Born: Celia Cruz, 1924; Manfred
Mann (Manfred Lubowitz), 1940; Steve
Cropper, 1941; Elvin Bishop, 1942;
Kathy Young (Kathy Young & the
Innocents), 1945

1958 Elvis Presley's soon-to-be double-sided smash, "One Night"/"I Got Stung," was released today. "One Night" reached #4 while "Stung" rose to #8. It took RCA a year to convince Presley the A-side was good enough to be issued.

1958 Buddy Holly's last formal recording session included "It Doesn't Matter Anymore" and "True Love Ways." It was done at Coral Records New York 80th Street studio.

1965 Bill Black was the stand-up bass player for Elvis Presley in the exciting early years of Presley's career. He was fired when he asked for a raise above the $100 a week he was getting, but went on to have hits under the name of Bill Black's combo ("White Silver Sands"). He played on all the Sun Record singles and many of Elvis's RCA cuts including "Jailhouse Rock" and Heartbreak Hotel." He died in Memphis from a brain tumor at age thirty-nine today.

1967 Lulu's "To Sir with Love," which was issued simultaneously with the release of the movie, reached #1 today and stayed there for five weeks. It became her only million-seller.

Elvis Presley

October

#1 Song 1966: "Reach Out, I'll Be There," The Four Tops

Born: Annette Funicello, 1942; Bobby Fuller (Bobby Fuller Four), 1943; Leslie West (Mountain), 1945; Eddie Brigati (The Rascals), 1946

1955 TV star Gale Storm (really Josephine Cottle) blew onto the singles charts with a cover of Fats Domino's "I Hear You Knocking" (#2). It was her first of twelve hits through 1957.

1964 The Shangri-Las arrived in London for a round of TV shows to promote their new single, "Leader of the Pack"; however, three major shows, *Ready, Steady, Go; Thank Your Lucky Stars;* and *The Eamonn Andrews Show*, all banned the group from performing the song. Despite that, the single reached U.K. #14.

1966 The Beach Boys' epic rock symphony "Good Vibrations" charted on its way to #1. It took producer Brian Wilson six months to do, involved seventeen sessions at four different studios at a then unheard of cost of $16,000.

1967 The rock musical *Hair* opened on Broadway in New York.

1969 Tommy Edwards was a soft-voiced pop–R&B artist of the '50s who had the distinction of having two #1 pop singles with the same song in different arrangements. In 1951 and in 1958, "It's All in the Game" reached the top of the charts. He had similar success with "Please Mr. Sun," first #22 in 1951, and in a new arrangement in 1958, it reached #11. In all, he had eighteen hits. He died of an aneurysm at age forty-seven today.

October

23

#1 Song 1961: "Runaround Sue," Dion & the Del Satins

Born: Charlie Foxx, 1939; Ellie Greenwich, 1940; Freddie Marsden (Gerry & the Pacemakers), 1940; Barbara Ann Hawkins (The Dixie Cups), 1943; Weird Al Yankovic, 1959

1954 Fifty-thousand–watt black radio giant WDIA in Memphis began banning all records with (what was then considered) suggestive lyrics, such as The Drifters' "Honey Love," The Bees' "Toy Bell," and the entire "Annie" series of singles by The Midnighters et al, including "Work with Me Annie," "Annie's Aunt Fannie," "Annie Had a Baby," and, what one would logically assume would be the conclusion of the series (although it wasn't), "Annie Kicked the Bucket."

1966 The first female vocal group to top the U.S. album charts were The Supremes with *Supremes A' Go Go*.

1978 Maybelle Carter was the matriarch of the famous Carter Family, pioneers of country music. The group started singing in 1927 and included Maybelle on guitar and vocals. The original group disbanded in 1943 and reorganized later with Maybelle and daughters Anita, Helen, and June (who went on to marry Johnny Cash). Maybelle died at age sixty-nine.

1987 Madonna's film *Who's that Girl?* opened in London.

October

#1 Song 1964: "Do Wah Diddy Diddy," Manfred Mann

Born: Jiles Perry "J.P." Richardson (The Big Bopper), 1930; Bill Wyman (The Rolling Stones), 1936; Santo Farina (Santo & Johnny), 1937; Ted Templeman (Harpers Bizarre), 1944

1954 Clyde McPhatter recorded with The Drifters for the last time. The only released single from the session was "Everybody's Laughing" (Atlantic). The pioneering tenor went on to have twenty-one pop hits, including "Treasure of Love," "A Lover's Question," and "Lover Please."

1960 Brenda Lee's "I Want to Be Wanted" reached #1, giving "Little Miss Dynamite" three million-sellers in a row.

1978 Keith Richards's punishment for a heroin-possession charge in Canada was a one-year suspension and an order to play a charity concert for the blind.

1987 The Monkees performed at a benefit concert at Lowry's Park Zoo in Tampa, Florida, for more than 100,000 fans.

Keith Richards

October

25

#1 Song 1975: "Bad Blood," Neil Sedaka

Born: Helen Reddy, 1941; Jon Anderson (Yes), 1944; John Hall (Orleans), 1947

Died: Johnnie Richardson (Johnnie & Joe), 1988

1960 Elvis Presley, who had been a pet lover for years, bought a monkey today, adding to his collection of mynah birds, dogs, pigs, chickens, and peacocks.

1964 The Beatles won the Most Outstanding Contribution to Music in 1963 award at Britain's annual Ivor Novello Awards.

1973 John Lennon sued the U.S. government, alleging his phone was tapped while he was fighting a deportation order.

1974 Soul singer Al Green was burned while taking a shower when his girl-friend walked in and threw a pan of hot grits over him before shooting her-self. Soon after, Green went back to gospel music, bought a church, and became its minister.

1992 A popular country music artist of the '60s, Roger Miller was particu-larly successful with novelty recordings such as "Dang Me," "King of the Road," and "England Swings." In the mid '60s, Roger earned eleven Grammys. He died at the age of fifty-six from lung cancer.

Al Green

October

#1 Song 1974: "Then Came You," Dionne Warwick & the Spinners

Born: Mahalia Jackson, 1911; David Was (Was [Not Was]), 1952

Died: Wilbert Harrison, 1994; Hoyt Axton, 1999

1958 Bill Haley & the Comets played the first rock 'n' roll concert in Germany at the West Berlin Sportspalast. Seven thousand fans rioted, and the minister of defense declared that Haley was promoting nuclear war by engendering fanatical hysterical enthusiasm among German youth.

1962 The first Motown revue began in Washington, D.C., at the Howard Theater. The tour ran for three months and included only acts from the Motown stable, like The Supremes, "Little" Stevie Wonder, Smokey Robinson & the Miracles, The Temptations, Marvin Gaye, Mary Wells, Martha & the Vandellas, The Marvelettes, and The Contours.

1963 A year and twenty-two days after Bob Dylan played before only *fifty-three* people at the Carnegie Hall Annex, he played to a sell-out crowd at Carnegie Hall.

1991 Bill Graham's name is synonymous with concert promotion and '60s rock 'n' roll. Raised in Nazi Germany, the Russian Jew escaped to America and built a concert empire, first with San Francisco's Fillmore West followed by New York's Fillmore East. He discovered such acts as The Jefferson Airplane, Janis Joplin, Santana, and The Grateful Dead. Graham was flying from a Huey Lewis concert when his helicopter hit a tower, twenty-five miles outside of San Francisco. He was sixty years old.

1992 Judy Collins, Carly Simon, Lucy Simon (Carly's sister), Lesley Gore, Odetta, Maureen McGovern, Cissy Houston, and The Roaches recorded "America the Beautiful" and "Michael Row the Boat Ashore," as The Clintones for torchlight parades across America to promote the Women Light the Way for Change cause on October 28.

October

#1 Song 1979: "Rise," Herb Alpert

Born: Floyd Cramer, 1933;
Simon LeBon (Duran Duran), 1958

1945 Margaret Whiting's "It Might as Well Be Spring" swept onto the best-seller's list, reaching #6. It became her first of thirty-six hits through 1967.

1958 Simon LeBon, lead singer of the top-selling band Duran Duran, was born today. The band was named after a character in the Jane Fonda film *Barbarella*. They scored twenty hits between 1982 and 1995, including "A View to a Kill" and "Hungry Like a Wolf."

1960 Ben E. King began his solo career after leaving The Drifters when he recorded four songs today, including "Spanish Harlem" and "Stand by Me."

1962 Elvis Presley's "Where Do You Come From" charted and reached his lowest Top 100 position ever, stalling at #99. It mattered little as it was the B-side of "Return to Sender," which stormed its way to #2 where it stayed for five weeks. The #1 for those exact same five weeks was The Four Season's "Big Girls Don't Cry."

1975 Bruce Springsteen appeared on the covers of *Newsweek* and *Time*.

Ben E. King

October

#1 Song 1978: "Hot Child in the City," Nick Gilder

Born: Wayne Fontana (The Mindbenders), 1945; Telma Hopkins (Dawn), 1948

1945 Wayne Fontana, lead vocalist for Wayne Fontana & the Mindbenders, was born today. The band, originally called The Jets, formed in 1961. The Mindbenders were named after a British film making the rounds at the time. Their biggest hit was "The Game of Love" (#1) followed by "A Groovy Kind of Love" (#2); by the time "Groovy" hit the charts, however, Wayne had already left for a solo career.

1957 Elvis Presley made his first performance appearance in Los Angeles at the Pan Pacific Auditorium. In a show that prompted headlines like: "Elvis Presley Will Have to Clean Up His Show—Or Go to Jail" Elvis, unimpressed, simply stated, "Well, if I don't dance tonight, maybe I don't have to take a shower tonight."

1964 The Beach Boys performed in the T.A.M.I. Show, a stage extravaganza that included Lesley Gore, The Supremes, The Rolling Stones, and James Brown, among others. The show was videotaped at the Civic Auditorium in Santa Monica, California, for British movie release and American TV.

1978 The Barbra Streisand and Neil Diamond hit collaboration on "You Don't Bring Me Flowers" was not their first performance encounter. In fact, they sang together at Brooklyn, New York's Erasmus Hall High School in the choir during the '60s.

October

#1 Song 1966: "96 Tears," Question Mark & the Mysterians

Born: Fanny Brice, 1891; Eugene Daughtry (The Intruders), 1939; Denny Laine (The Moody Blues), 1944; Kevin DuBrow (Quiet Riot), 1955

1944 Denny Laine, original lead singer of The Moody Blues, was born today. He sang on their first hit, "Go Now," before leaving to eventually join Paul McCartney and Wings.

1955 The first R&B show held at Carnegie Hall in New York featured Etta James and The Peaches, The Five Keys, Gene & Eunice, The Clovers, and Big Joe Turner.

1961 The single The Beatles recorded on June 22, "My Bonnie"/"The Saints," was released in Germany on Polydor. The group was renamed "The Beat Brothers" for that single because their name sounded too much like "Peedles," which was German slang for male genitalia.

1971 Duane Allman was the trail-blazing guitarist who led The Allman Brothers into Southern country-rock history. With brother Gregg, they formed The Hour Glass, which became The Allman Brothers Band. Duane died in an accident when he lost control of his motorcycle while trying to avoid a big rig. He was twenty-four.

1983 In an apparent bad year for the record business, Dolly Parton's duet with Kenny Rogers, "Islands in the Stream," became #1 today and turned out to be the only platinum-selling single of the year.

October

#1 Song 1971: "Maggie May," Rod Stewart

Born: Grace Slick (Jefferson Airplane), 1939; Timothy B. Schmit (The Eagles), 1947; Otis Williams (The Temptations), 1939

1954 The Chordettes hit the Hot 100 with "Mr. Sandman" (#1), their first of fourteen hits through 1961.

1960 Tony Sheridan joined The Beatles onstage at the Top Ten Club in Hamburg, Germany, for a jam session which ended with a seventy-minute version of "What'd I Say."

1961 Joey Dee & the Starliters "Peppermint Twist" was released. It reached #1, adding greater legitimacy to the "Twist" craze.

1971 Melanie leaped onto the singles survey with "Brand New Key," a runaway #1. Misinterpretations of its overtly innocent lyric caused the song to be banned by numerous radio stations.

2000 Steve Allen was the first successful late-night talk show host. He also introduced numerous cutting-edge artists with his prime-time TV show, including Elvis Presley and Bob Dylan. Steve was also a top songwriter, who penned more than 5,000 tunes, such as "This Could Be the Start of Something (Big)." He died in a car crash at age seventy-eight today.

Melanie

October

31

#1 Song 1964: "Baby Love," The Supremes

Born: Russ Ballard (Argent), 1945; Bernard Edwards (Chic), 1952

1954 Elvis Presley (prior to his hit status) met The Jordanaires for the first time, backstage at the Ellis Auditorium in Memphis. The quartet had been singing backup for Eddy Arnold at the time. Elvis told them he hoped he would be able to have them sing on his records someday. Two years later, when he joined RCA, they became the backup group on hundreds of Presley recordings.

1963 The Beatles returned to London to face hundreds of screaming teenage girls on the roof of a building at Heathrow Airport. Coincidentally, Ed Sullivan was passing through the airport just in time to observe the chaos. He was so impressed, he decided to book the group for his show even though they were totally unknown in America.

1970 Michelle Phillips, formerly of The Mamas & the Papas and just divorced from Papa John Phillips, married actor Dennis Hopper. The happily married couple lasted through eight days of wedded bliss.

1988 Debbie Gibson held a seance at a Halloween party, in an attempt to contact Liberace and Sid Vicious (not necessarily in that order).

November

Born: Phil Terry (The Intruders), 1943;
Dan Peek (America), 1950

1955 The Keynotes recorded their second single, "I Don't Know," for Apollo Records at New York's Beltone Studios. The song was the basis for Dion & the Belmonts 1958 hit and career starter, "I Wonder Why."

1965 Petula Clark was offered the chance to co-star in the film *Paradise Hawaiian Style* with Elvis Presley but turned it down.

1969 The hit "Raindrops Keep Fallin' on My Head" was recorded by B.J. Thomas only after songwriter Burt Bacharach was turned down by Bob Dylan.

1986 Sippie Wallace (Beaulah Thomas) was a gospel singer turned blues vocalist of the '20s who was influential among such later-day artists as Bonnie Raitt. Sippie was best known for recordings like "Bedroom Blues" and "Up the Country Blues." She died the day she was born while on tour in Germany at the age of eighty-eight!

Petula Clark

November

#1 Song 1974: "You Haven't Done Nothin'," Stevie Wonder

Born: David "Jay Black" Blatt (Jay & the Americans), 1938; John "Jay" Traynor (Jay & the Americans), 1941; Keith Emerson (Emerson, Lake & Palmer), 1944; k.d. lang, 1961

1962 Little Richard played the Star Club in Hamburg, Germany, with The Beatles. Paul McCartney, enamored with Richard's talent, asked him to teach the young Beatle his singing style.

1963 Dion performed "Donna the Prima Donna" on England's *Ready, Steady, Go* and then left because he was irritated by the audience dancing around him despite still having another song to sing.

1968 Mary Hopkin's hit "Those Were the Days" peaked at #2 for three weeks, unable to dislodge her label mates The Beatles' "Hey Jude" from #1. Mary went on to record the song in Hebrew, Italian, French, Spanish, and German. By early 1969, the worldwide sales topped 8 million copies.

1982 Elton John began a tour of the U.K. encompassing forty-two shows.

1995 With no business or musical training, Florence Greenberg, a housewife from New Jersey, started one of the premier indie-record companies of the '60s, Scepter Records. She discovered The Shirelles ("Will You Love Me Tomorrow") and Dionne Warwick and had hits with B.J. Thomas, The Kingsmen, Chuck Jackson, and numerous others. She died of a stroke at age eighty-two.

Little Richard

November

#1 Song 1962: "He's a Rebel," The Crystals

Born: Brian Poole (The Tremeloes), 1941; Lulu, 1948; Adam Ant (Adam & the Ants), 1954

1956 The Cadillacs' "Rudolph the Red Nosed Reindeer" (#11) was released. It began the official holiday season, but didn't chart until ten days after Christmas.

1958 The Crescents were on their way to a recording audition when they were involved in a head-on car crash. Miraculously, no one was hurt and they proceeded to the audition, which led to the quintet signing with Pittsburgh's Calico Records, where they changed their name to The Skyliners. They went on to have such hits as "Since I Don't Have You" and "This I Swear."

1972 Carly Simon married James Taylor in her New York apartment. That evening, she joined him onstage to share the news with the audience.

1977 Elton John, having collapsed onstage twice before, announced his retirement from live performances. He would be back onstage within fifteen months.

1991 Mort Shuman was half of the tremendous writing team of (Doc) Pomus and Shuman, who wrote '50s and 60's hits like "Teenager in Love" (Dion & the Belmonts) and "Little Sister" for Elvis Presley. He also wrote Presley's "Surrender." Mort moved to France, where he became a successful artist and writer. He died of liver failure at fifty-three.

November

4

#1 Song 1972: "I Can See Clearly Now," Johnny Nash

Born: Harry Elston (Friends of Distinction), 1938; Delbert McClinton, 1940

1963 The Exciters, known for their 1962 hit "Tell Him," released their newest single, "Do Wah Diddy," which would only reach #78. The song would go on to be a quintessential part of the British invasion less than a year later as "Do Wah Diddy Diddy," when it reached #1 by Manfred Mann.

1963 The Beatles appeared for a Royal Command Performance of the Queen Mother and Princess Margaret at the Prince of Wales Theatre in London along with eighteen other acts, including Tommy Steele, Buddy Greco, Marlene Dietrich, Pinky & Perky, and the Prince of Wales Theatre Orchestra. They performed seventh on the bill, playing "From Me to You," "She Loves You," "Til There Was You," and then John Lennon introduced "Twist & Shout" with his now legendary bit of sarcasm, "In the cheaper seats, you clap your hands. The rest of you, just rattle your jewelry." After the group met the Queen Mother, she was quoted as saying they were "most intriguing."

1978 Prince's single "Soft and Wet" became his chart debut, reaching only #92 on the pop Top 100.

1986 The Monkees revival culminated in seven albums breaching the *Billboard* charts Top 200, all at the same time.

1989 Elton John became only the third artist to score fifty chart singles in England. The others were Elvis Presley and Cliff Richard. Elton did it with "Sacrifice."

Elton John

November

#1 Song 1966: "Last Train to Clarksville," The Monkees

Born: Ike Turner, 1931; Art Garfunkel, 1941; Gram Parsons (The Flying Burrito Brothers), 1946; Peter Noone (Herman's Hermits), 1947; Mike Score (Flock of Seagulls), 1957; Bryan Adams, 1959

1947 Peter Noone, lead singer of the pop group Herman's Hermits, was born today. One of England's most successful bands in the colonies, Herman's Hermits had eleven Top 10 hits in just two years and nineteen chart singles in their three-and-a-half-year American invasion (1964–1968). They're best known for "Mrs. Brown You've Got a Lovely Daughter," "I'm Henry VIII, I Am," and "There's a Kind of a Hush."

1958 After only three singles together (including the pioneering soul single "For Your Precious Love"), Jerry Butler & the Impressions separated.

1960 Nicknamed the "Singing Fisherman," Johnny Horton spent some time as one in Alaska and went on to become a top country-pop artist best known for his story songs "Battle of New Orleans" and "North to Alaska." The last place he and fellow singer Hank Williams played in before they died (eight years apart) was The Skyline Club, near Houston. Ironically, Horton was married to Williams's former wife, Billy Jean Eshlimar, at the time of his death. He was killed in a head-on car crash in Milano, Texas, by a drunk driver. Johnny was only thirty-five.

1988 Talk about draught coupled with longevity, The Beach Boys reached #1 with "Kokomo" twenty-two years after their last #1, "Good Vibrations," hit the top.

1988 Taylor Dane ascended the Hot 100 with "Don't Rush Me" (#2), her fourth Top 10 single in a row.

1989 Staff Sgt. Barry Sadler had the unlikely distinction of becoming a hit-making Green Beret during the Vietnam War when his recording of "The Ballad of the Green Berets" became a #1 million-seller in 1966. After a leg injury forced the Army medic stateside, he became an Army recruiter and recorded the song originally as part of a recruiting campaign. He was reportedly assassinated in Central America today, while providing medical care to the poor.

November

6

#1 Song 1971: "Gypsys, Tramps & Thieves," Cher

Born: Jim Pike (The Lettermen), 1938; P.J. Proby, 1938; George Young (The Easybeats), 1947; Glenn Frey (The Eagles), 1948

1961 The Chantels' only up-tempo hit, "Well, I Told You" (#29), was issued today.

1965 The historic Fillmore West theater opened with Jefferson Airplane and The Grateful Dead performing.

1968 The Monkees' movie *Head* premiered.

1971 Elvis Presley performed at the Cleveland Public Hall Auditorium in Ohio. A local announcer, Al Dvorin, would immortalize a phrase: after the King's performance, the audience refused to leave in hopes Elvis would take another bow; he said, "Elvis has left the building."

The Grateful Dead

November

#1 Song 1970: "I'll Be There,"
The Jackson 5

Born: Mary Travers (Peter, Paul & Mary),
1937; Dee Clark, 1938; Johnny Rivers, 1942;
Joni Mitchell, 1943

1960 The Heartbeats' perennial "A Thousand Miles Away" charted for the second time (#96 pop) in four years.

1965 Capitol Records was not so politely prodded by The Beatles into discontinuing promotion for the single "Boys." They felt that it was not typical of their current sound. Wes Farrell, the writer of the song, was, needless to say, greatly disappointed.

1969 Ike & Tina Turner were the opening act on a Rolling Stones U.S. tour that started in Denver.

1987 Sixteen-year-old Tiffany topped the charts with "I Think We're Alone Now," a chart hit for Tommy James & the Shondells made four years before she was born.

November

8

#1 Song 1969: "Wedding Bell Blues," The 5th Dimension

Born: Patti Page, 1927; Chris Connor, 1927; Bonnie Bramlett (Delaney & Bonnie), 1944; Roy Wood (Electric Light Orchestra), 1946; Bonnie Raitt, 1949; Ricki Lee Jones, 1954; Leif Garrett, 1961

1956 After pop vocalist Kay Starr rejected a new song, it was given to Patsy Cline, who reluctantly recorded it today at Bradley's Barn in Nashville. She commented, "It's nothin' but a little ol' pop song." Patsy's version of That "little ol' pop song," "Walkin' After Midnight," reached #2 country and #12 pop in early 1957.

1957 Elvis Presley's third film, *Jailhouse Rock*, opened across the nation. It would become the fourteenth most popular film of the year and one of Presley's most enduring motion pictures.

1969 The Supremes' swan song, "Someday, We'll Be Together," was the last of the group's twelve #1s; however, it was technically not The Supremes at all. Diana Ross wound up recording the song with the vocal backing pros The Waters and Johnny Bristol on bass.

1992 Barry Manilow performed before 94,000 people in the Ultra Football Stadium in Manila.

1999 Gwen Gordy Fuqua, who convinced her family to stake brother Berry Gordy the $800 he needed to start Motown Records, died in San Diego. Fuqua, former wife of Moonglows leader Harvey Fuqua, started Motown's artist development department, guiding the careers of acts like The Supremes and Temptations. She was seventy-one.

Barry Manilow

November

#1 Song 1974: "You Ain't Seen Nothing Yet," Bachman Turner Overdrive

Born: Tom Fogerty (Creedence Clearwater Revival), 1941

1961 Beatles manager-to-be Brian Epstein saw the group for the first time at a Cavern Club (Liverpool) lunch hour performance.

1963 "Louie, Louie" by The Kingsmen, the greatest party record ever issued, charted today on its trip to #2 for a six-week stay. The Kingsmen's version was a cover of Richard Berry & the Pharaohs 1956 single based on Ricky Rivera & Rhythm Rockers' "El Loco Cha Cha Cha." Lead singer Jack Ely was reportedly so "falling down" drunk when he did the vocals that the indistinguishable lyric caused controversy and investigations all the way up to the FBI. The day after the Kingsmen recorded it for $50. After hearing another local band, The Wailers, performing it, Paul Revere & the Raiders recorded "Louie Louie" in the same studio. The Kingsmen's recording gained initial attention when a Boston disc jockey played it and called it the worst record he'd ever heard. When the governor of Indiana called it "pornographic" [see February 1], it took off nationally. By the way, as if the middle-of-the-road gods where conspiring against the garage rockers, the #1 records that kept "Louie" from the top were "Dominique" by The Singing Nun (three weeks) and the Polish pop star, Bobby Vinton's "There! I've Said It Again" (three weeks).

1963 Joan Baez charted with "We Shall Overcome" (#90), her first of nine Hot 100 singles through 1975.

1967 The debut issue of *Rolling Stone* magazine hit the newsstands.

1990 The reunited Go-Go's performed on David Letterman's *Late Night Show*.

November

10

#1 Song 1979: "Heartache Tonight," The Eagles

Born: Greg Lake (Emerson, Lake & Palmer), 1948; Donna Fargo, 1949

1945 Peggy Lee rode onto the best-seller's list with "Waitin' for the Train to Come In" (#4), her debut hit of a career thirty-four winners through 1969.

1948 Greg Lake—vocalist, guitarist, and bass for Emerson, Lake & Palmer—was born today. The classical rock trio formed in 1969 and brought some tremendous avant-garde music to the masses during the early '70s, including "Lucky Man" and "From the Beginning."

1958 LaVern Baker's "I Cried a Tear" was issued. It became her biggest hit (#6) of twenty charters between 1955 and 1966.

1965 Bill Graham rented the Fillmore Auditorium in New York for $60 and then proceeded to become the premier music promoter of the rock era. His first concert featured The Jefferson Airplane and The Grateful Dead.

LaVern Baker

November

#1 Song 1978: "MacArthur Park,"
Donna Summer

Born: LaVern Baker, 1929; Jesse Colin
Young (The Youngbloods), 1944

1957 Elvis performed for servicemen and the public at the Schofield Barracks, Pearl Harbor, Hawaii. It would become his last public performance before joining the Army.

1969 Jim Morrison of The Doors was arrested after annoying a flight attendant on a trip from Los Angeles to Phoenix to see the Rolling Stones.

1972 A year and thirteen days after The Allman Brothers Band's Duane Allman died in a motorcycle accident, the band's bass player, Berry Oakley, was killed when his motorcycle collided with a bus three blocks from where Duane died.

1978 Donna Summer's disco version of the 1968 Richard Harris hit "MacArthur Park" climbed to #1 and stayed for three weeks.

1999 The RIAA (Recording Industry Association of America) named The Beatles the best-selling act of the twentieth century. The Fab Four were the only act in history to have five diamond albums (sales of ten million each) and sold more than 106 million albums in the U.S. alone. Elvis Presley had the most gold and platinum albums. The King was the century's top-selling rock artist with 77 million units sold, including eighty gold and forty-three platinum in the U.S. The Eagles had the century's best-selling album with 26 million in sales for *Their Greatest Hits 1971–1975*. Garth Brooks was the century's top-selling male artist with 89 million records, and Elton John's "Candle in the Wind" single was the top single of the century, tallying more than 11 million units in the U.S. Also, Barbra Streisand was named the most successful female artist of the century. Streisand sold more than 62 million records during the previous thirty-eight years.

November

#1 Song 1968: "Hey Jude,"
The Beatles

Born: Jo Stafford (The Pied Pipers), 1920; Ruby Nash (The Romantics), 1939; John Maus (The Walker Brothers), 1943; Brian Hyland, 1943; Neil Young, 1945

1955 Elvis Presley was named the "Most Promising Country & Western Artist" in *Billboard* magazine's annual disc jockey poll.

1955 Dorothy Collins's novelty "My Boy Flat Top" charted, en route to #16. Dorothy was one of the stars of TV's *Your Hit Parade*.

1955 Sultry songstress-actress Julie London stormed onto the best-seller's list with "Cry Me a River" (#9), the only hit for the wife of Sgt. Joe Friday (Jack Webb) of TV's *Dragnet*.

1970 The Doors played their last concert with Jim Morrison in New Orleans. The group then recorded the *L.A. Woman* album, and Morrison subsequently moved to Paris, where he died.

1970 Elton John played The Fillmore West with The Kinks.

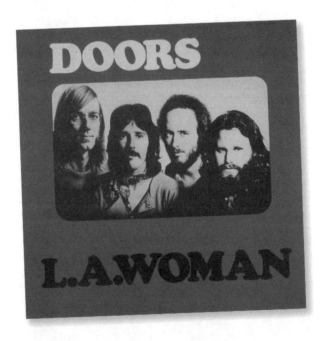

November

#1 Song 1976: "Tonight's the Night," Rod Stewart

Born: Jeanette "Baby" Washington (The Hearts), 1940; Annette Kleinbard, a.k.a Carol Connors (The Teddy Bears), 1941

1954 The Moonglows' first hit, "Sincerely" (Chess Records #20 pop, #1 R&B), and The Moonlighters'—their alter ego—"Shoo Doo Be Doo" (Checker Records) were released the same day. For a time, their agents would book them into unsuspecting clubs as two groups! Also released today were collectors' rarities: The Flamingos' "Blues in a Letter" (Chance, $400), The Orioles' "Runaround" (Jubilee, $40), and The Platters' "Shake It Up Mambo" (Federal, $40)

1959 One of the most famous album covers ever issued appeared today with Elvis Presley in his gold lamé suit along with the compilation *Elvis Gold Records, Vol. 2: 50,000,000 Elvis Fans Can't Be Wrong*.

1961 The Tokens were on the verge of going into record producing instead of singing when "The Lion Sleeps Tonight" (RCA #1) charted, becoming one of the biggest hits of all time.

1966 Paul McCartney created a backdrop at the Saville Theater in London for a performance by The Four Tops.

1987 Sonny & Cher sang "I Got You Babe" together for the first time in ten years on *Late Show with David Letterman*.

November

14

#1 Song 1960: "Georgia on My Mind," Ray Charles

Born: Freddie Garrity (Freddie & the Dreamers), 1940; Cornel Gunter (The Coasters), 1938; Stephen Bishop, 1951

1952 The first British pop chart was published in the *New Musical Express*. The Top 6 were by American acts, with Al Martino's "Here in My Heart" at #1.

1960 The Shirelles (formerly known as The Poquellos), with writer Carole King playing drums, had their soon-to-be standard "Will You Love Me Tomorrow" released today.

1981 Australia's version of a British invasion in America occurred when four of the Top 10 singles were from Down Under, led by technical Aussie Olivia Newton-John's "Physical" (#3). The others were Little River Band, Air Supply, and Rick Springfield.

Olivia Newton-John

November

#1 Song 1980: "Lady," Kenny Rogers

Born: Petula Clark, 1932; Clyde McPhatter (The Dominoes, The Drifters), 1933; Little Willie John, 1937; Anni-Frid Lyngstad (ABBA), 1945

1957 Patsy Cline won *Billboard*'s Most Promising Country & Western Female Artist of 1957 award.

1932 Gifted vocalist Petula Clark was born today. Though well known in America for more than twenty hits, including "Downtown," "My Love," and "Don't Sleep in the Subway," she's also an accomplished actress, having appeared in more than twenty British films. Her chart career started in 1954 with "The Little Shoemaker" and spanned four decades. Ironically, her last U.K. hit in 1988 was a remix of her first U.S. hit "Downtown" (1964).

1956 Elvis' first motion picture, *Love Me Tender*, debuted six days ahead of its national release at the Paramount Theater in New York City. The now famous forty-foot photo of Presley adorned the top of the marquee for the film's entire run.

1986 The Bangles hit #3 in England with "Walk Like an Egyptian," a song rejected by Toni Basil.

1986 Madonna's single "True Blue" peaked at #3 in America.

November

16

#1 Song 1959: "Mr. Blue," The Fleetwoods

Born: Garnett Mimms (The Enchanters), 1937; Winfred "Blue" Lovett (The Manhattans), 1943

1960 Patsy Cline, recently signed to Decca Records, began recording her first session for them, including her standard "I Fall to Pieces."

1963 ABC, NBC, and CBS all filmed part of The Beatles show and the hysterical audience at the Winter Gardens in Bournemouth, England. *Life* magazine photographer Terence Spencer showed up at their hotel after the show, but The Beatles didn't. Consequently, they blew the front cover that would have appeared on January 3, 1964. Spencer recalled, "The Beatles must be the only people in showbiz ever to have turned down a *Life* cover."

1969 Janis Joplin was charged with two counts of using vulgar and obscene language during a show at Curtis Hall in Tampa, Florida.

1974 John Lennon's "Whatever Gets You Through the Night" became his only solo U.S. #1. Piano and backup vocals were done by Elton John.

1998 J.D. Sumner was the glorious bass vocalist for The Blackwood Brothers, one of gospel music's great groups through the '50s and early '60s. He joined The Stamps Quartet in 1965. By 1972, they had become one of Elvis Presley's backup groups (along with The Jordanaires). J.D. died of a heart attack at age eighty-three.

November

#1 Song 1962: "Big Girls Don't Cry," The Four Seasons

Born: Gordon Lightfoot, 1938; Gene Clark (The Byrds), 1944; Bob Gaudio (The Four Seasons), 1942; Dino Martin Jr. (Dino, Desi & Billy), 1953; Ronnie DeVoe (New Edition), 1967

1958 Brenda Lee's Christmas classic "Rockin' Around the Christmas Tree" was first released today and has been a holiday radio and sales staple for more than forty years. In 1960, it actually reached #14 pop.

1968 Dion appeared on *The Smothers Brothers Comedy Hour* on CBS-TV.

1973 Ringo Starr's third solo album titled *Ringo* was the charm as it debuted today on the U. S. charts, rising to #2. Technically, however, it wasn't a solo album because all four Beatles appeared on it.

1984 Madonna's "Like a Virgin" reached the singles survey today on its way to #1. It was the first of eleven #1s for the sexposé expert.

1984 Jules Bihari was the founder of the legendary West Coast R&B labels Modern, RPM, Flair, and Kent Records. The labels were at their peak during the '50s with recordings by The Cadets, The Jacks, John Lee Hooker, Etta James, B. B. King, and Jesse Belvin, to name just a few. The Hungarian Jew, originally from Oklahoma, died at the age of seventy-one today.

November

18

#1 Song 1957: "Jailhouse Rock," Elvis Presley

Born: Hank Ballard (The Midnighters), 1936; Graham Parker (Graham Parker & the Rumour), 1950; Kim Wilde, 1960

Died: Junior Parker, 1971

1950 Patti Page's career-maker, "The Tennessee Waltz," danced onto the best-seller's list, rising to #1 and taking root there for thirteen weeks.

1958 The unprecedented Elvis Presley popularity reached a new high when an EP titled *Elvis Sails* was released today, eventually selling more than 60,000 copies. It contained nothing more than Elvis's farewell press conference before leaving for Germany and the Army, along with other Presley interviews.

1989 Two '60s vocal groups, The Shangri-Las and The Three Degrees, went to court in a dispute over who owned their respective names. The Shangri-Las won, but The Three Degrees court ruling granted their name to former manager Richard Barrett.

1990 Milli Vanilli were ordered to return their Grammy award when it was discovered they had not actually sung on their hit records. When confronted about the recording, Milli Vanilli member Rob Pilatus said, "Everybody asks me if I sing on this record. Even my mother asks me. Fabrice and I think we are big talents. We can sing as good as any other pop star in the Top 10."

November

#1 Song 1966: "You Keep Me Hangin' On," The Supremes

Born: Dave Guard (The Kingston Trio), 1934; Hank Medress (The Tokens), 1938; Warren "Pete" Moore (The Miracles), 1939

1955 Doing a remote broadcast on the Louisiana Hayride from Gladewater Texas High School, Elvis performed Bill Haley's "Rock Around the Clock," along with his "Baby Let's Play House" and "That's All Right."

1955 Carl Perkins recorded "Blue Suede Shoes" at Sun Studios in Memphis.

1964 The Supremes became the first all-girl group to reach #1 in Britain when "Baby Love" hit the coveted top spot.

1966 While on a flight from Kenya to London, Paul McCartney envisioned the idea for the *Sgt. Pepper's Lonely Hearts Club Band* album. His thoughts were to create an album with a group of false identities instead of it being just another Beatles album.

1979 Chuck Berry left prison after a stay for tax evasion.

The Supremes

November

#1 Song 1982: "Up Where We Belong," Joe Cocker and Jennifer Warnes

Born: Tony Butala (The Lettermen), 1940; Norman Greenbaum, 1942; Duane Allman, 1946; Joe Walsh (The Eagles), 1947

1954 Known as Little "Miss Sharecropper," LaVern Baker (born Delores Williams) had her debut disc, "Tweedlee Dee," released today. It reached #4 R&B and #14 pop, while beginning her string of twenty-one hits through 1966.

1956 Elvis Presley attended a special pre-release screening in Memphis of his first film, *Love Me Tender.* It's reported Elvis's mother cried upon seeing her son's on-screen character die.

1961 The Crystals' debut single, "There's No Other" (#20), charted as the first of their eight hits.

1967 The Beatles' "I Am the Walrus" single was banned on BBC Television and Radio, because the BBC felt that there was a drug connotation in the song, even though they couldn't find one.

November

#1 Song 1960: "Stay," Maurice Williams & the Zodiacs

Born: Lonnie Jordan (War), 1948; Steve Ferguson (NRBQ), 1949; Livingston Taylor, 1950

1960 Gene Pitney's first single under his own name, "I Wanna Love My Life Away," was issued (#39). He recorded in 1959 as Billy Bryan and in a duo as Jamie of Jamie & Jane. He went on to have twenty-four hits between 1961 and 1969, including "Only Love Can Break a Heart," "It Hurts to Be in Love," and "(The Man Who Shot) Liberty Valance."

1967 The Who's classic album *The Who Sell Out* was released.

1981 Olivia Newton-John's "Physical" topped the singles charts today and remained there for ten weeks.

1987 Produced and written by Michael Bolton, Cher's "I Found Someone" charted today on its way to becoming her first Top 10 hit (#10) in eight years.

Michael Bolton

327

November

22

#1 Song 1975: "Fly, Robin, Fly"
Silver Convention

Born: Jamie Troy (The Classics), 1942;
Steven Caldwell (The Orlons), 1942,
Steve Van Zandt, 1950

1961 Elvis Presley's two-sided hit-to-be "Can't Help Falling In Love" (#2)/ "Rock-A-Hula Baby" (#23) came out today. Both were in the *Blue Hawaii* film that also opened nationwide and would become one of Presley's biggest film hits, spanning two years (#18 in 1961 and #14 in 1962).

1968 The Beatles album, a.k.a. *The White Album*, was issued in England. The two-record set included such highlights as "While My Guitar Gently Weeps," "Back in the USSR," "Dear Prudence," "Blackbird," "Revolution 1," "Glass Onion," "Ob-La-Di, Ob-La-Da," "Rocky Raccoon," "Happiness Is a Warm Gun," and "Helter Skelter."

1976 Jerry Lee Lewis was arrested for driving drunk when he drove his Rolls Royce into a ditch.

1980 Heart reached the best-seller's list with "Tell It Like It Is" (#8), their biggest hit to date.

1988 Janet (Ertel) Bleyer was a member of the barbershop-group-turned-pop The Chordettes. They had fourteen hits in the '50s and early '60s, including "Lollipop" and "Mr. Sandman," on Cadence Records owned by her husband and bandleader, Archie Bleyer. She died in her hometown of Sheboygan, Wisconsin, at age seventy-five.

Heart

November

#1 Song 1963: "I'm Leaving It Up to You," Dale & Grace

Born: Ruth Etting, 1907; Betty Everett, 1939; Bruce Hornsby, 1954

1899 The first Jukebox was installed at The Palace Royal Hotel in San Francisco, California.

1960 Elvis Presley's film *G.I. Blues* debuted nationally. Another Presley success, it would finish the year at #14.

1962 The Beatles auditioned in London for the BBC-TV's *Light Entertainment*. They played a short set and were notified by mail four days later that they'd been rejected.

1974 Disco Tex & the Sexolettes single "Get Dancin'" charted today, ushering in the full-fledged disco era. Though not the first disco single, the dance tune, penned by writer Kenny Nolan ("Lady Marmalade" and "My Eyes Adored You"), was the first of many hits to be broken out of disco clubs. Disco Tex was Monte Rock III (Joseph Montanez, Jr.), who was actually the owner of a chain of hair salons.

1976 For the second time in two days, Jerry Lee Lewis was arrested, this time at Elvis Presley's Graceland when he emphasized his desire to see the King by pulling out a loaded Derringer!

November

#1 Song 1973: "Photograph," Ringo Starr

Born: Donald "Duck" Dunn (Mar-Keys), 1941; Lee Michaels, 1945; Bev Bevan (Electric Light Orchestra), 1946

Died: Freddie Mercury (Queen), 1991

1956 The Dell Vikings recorded nine songs, including "Come Go with Me," all a cappella. Instrumentation was later added. In early 1957, "Come" went on to be the first Top 10 pop hit (#4 pop, #2 R&B) by a racially mixed rock 'n' roll vocal group. The quintet consisted of three black and two white members at the time.

1958 The soul era began with the release of The Fiestas' "So Fine" (#11 pop, #3 R&B), a cover of The Sheiks 1955 single.

1961 The Beatles performed at the Casbah Coffee Club, West Derby, Liverpool, with Rory Storm & the Hurricanes, Gerry & the Pacemakers, and Faron Young & the Flamingos. A British singer, Davy Jones (still five years away from fame with The Monkees), did two songs backed by The Beatles.

1972 Don Kirshner's *Rock Concert TV* debuted, featuring Chuck Berry; Blood, Sweat & Tears; and Alice Cooper.

November

#1 Song 1967: "Incense & Peppermints," Strawberry Alarm Clock

Born: Percy Sledge, 1940; Amy Grant, 1960

25

1961 After twenty-nine chart singles together, The Everly Brothers' career was put on hold by Uncle Sam when the duo was inducted into the Marine Corps Reserves at Camp Pendleton in California for a six-month stay.

1964 Elvis began wearing a Jewish "chai" symbol around his neck, presumably after learning he was part Jewish on his mother's side.

1965 In order for The Beatles to do some undisturbed Christmas shopping, London's famous department store Harrod's opened for three hours and the foursome ran amok.

1982 Aretha Franklin and Gladys Knight performed in the Jamaica World Music Festival at the Bob Marley Performing Center in Montego Bay. They played before an audience of more than 45,000.

Aretha Franklin

November

26

#1 Song 1983: "All Night Long," Lionel Richie

Born: Tina Turner, 1938; John McVie (Fleetwood Mac), 1945

1962 The Beatles' "Please, Please Me" was recorded.

1963 After a performance at the Regal Cinema in Cambridge, England, John Lennon was asked by a reporter, "How long do you think The Beatles will last?" Lennon replied, "About five years."

1968 Cream appeared at The Albert Hall in London for their farewell concert.

1990 Wilson Phillips won the Hot 100 Single category at the 1990 Billboard Music Awards with "Hold On."

Cream

November

#1 Song 1971: "Theme from *Shaft*," Isaac Hayes

Born: Jimi Hendrix, 1942

1954 Colorado-born Jaye P. Morgan charted with "That's All I Want from You" (#3). It was her initial hit followed by nineteen more through 1960.

1954 Sarah Vaughan reached the coveted hit list with "Make Yourself Comfortable" (#6), her biggest single of thirty-three hits.

1969 Janis Joplin and Tina Turner sang together at The Rolling Stones concert in Madison Square Garden.

1971 The nine-member, female-dominated vocal group The Hillside Singers, featuring Lorri Marsters Hamm, bounced onto the Hot 100 with "I'd Like to Teach the World to Sing" (#13). The hit was known more for its worldwide exposure as a Coca-Cola commercial than for its hit status.

1993 Celine Dion powered her way onto the charts with "The Power of Love," the first #1 in America for the French Canadian. She would have three more by 1999.

November

28

#1 Song 1987: "(I've Had) The Time of My Life," Bill Medley & Jennifer Warnes

Born: Berry Gordy, Jr. (founder of Motown Records), 1929; Gary Troxel (The Fleetwoods), 1939; Randy Newman, 1943

1964 The Shangri-Las' "Leader of the Pack" hit #1. Taking sound effects to the extreme, engineer Joe Veneri brought his "Harley Chopper" into the studio and put in the record's trademark revved-up engine sound right in the booth.

1960 Elvis Presley's "Are You Lonesome Tonight?" reached #1 nationally and spent the next six weeks in the top spot.

1970 George Harrison made his American chart debut with "My Sweet Lord," which went to #1.

1992 Thirty-six years after The Five Satins' original legendary hit, Boyz II Men's remake of "In the Still of the Nite" charted, soaring to #3 pop (#4 R&B). The feat was all the more impressive in the rap era as the Boyz sang the recording a cappella.

1992 Prince's thirty-ninth chart single was simply named "7." Coincidentally, that is how high it went on the national pop charts.

Boys II Men

November

#1 Song 1969: "Come Together/Something," The Beatles

Born: John Mayall, 1933; Chuck Mangione, 1940; Denny Doherty (The Mamas & the Papas), 1941; Felix Cavaliere (The Rascals), 1944; John Wilson (Sly, Slick & Wicked), 1949

1963 The Beatles' 45 "I Want To Hold Your Hand"/"This Boy" was issued in England on Parlophone. The record created a historic first in the U.K. when advance sales surpassed the million mark before it was even released.

1969 Following on the heels of his #1 million-seller "Suspicious Minds," Elvis Presley's "Don't Cry Daddy" debuted on the Top 100 and would eventually reach #6.

1969 Serge Gainsbourg and Jane Birkin charted in America with the French song "Je T'Aime...Moi Non Plus" (#58), a sexual recording banned on many stations worldwide, yet it managed to reach #1 in England.

1986 Cyndi Lauper's "Change of Heart" charted, eventually reaching #3.

2001 George Harrison died today. He was the guitarist and vocalist with the most popular band of all time, The Beatles. After they split up in 1969, he had #1 solo success with "My Sweet Lord," "Got My Mind Set on You," and "Give Me Love," among his sixteen post-Beatles chart singles. He died of lung cancer at the age of fifty-eight.

November

#1 Song 1985: "Separate Lives," Phil Collins and Marilyn Martin

Born: Dick Clark, 1929; Noel Paul Stookey (Peter, Paul & Mary), 1937; Rob Grill (Grassroots), 1944; Shuggie Otis, 1953; June Pointer (The Pointer Sisters), 1954; Billy Idol, 1955

1956 The Jive Bombers recorded their immortal "Bad Boy" (#36 pop, #7 R&B). For lead vocalist, thirty-nine-year-old Clarence Palmer—who had been performing since the 1920s—the hit ended a thirty-year drought!

1963 A near mobbing was averted after The Beatles' show at the Empire Theater in Sunderland, England, when they escaped from the theater by dashing from the stage into the fire station next door, down the fire pole to a waiting fire engine. (No report on whether they donned helmets and fire-proof coats during their escape.)

1991 Bette Midler's album *For the Boys* charted (#22), becoming her thirteen of fifteen hit albums between 1972 and 1993.

1996 Tiny Tim (Herbert Khaury) was the most unusual pop star to come out of the '60s. Singing in falsetto and playing a ukulele, he built a following by reworking songs of the '20s and '30s. A curiosity to many, he became a celebrity when he had the hit "Tip Toe Through The Tulips" in 1968. He married seventeen-year-old "Miss Vickie" on Johnny Carson's show in front of a viewing audience of more than 40 million. He died of a heart condition while performing "Tip Toe" at a women's club in Minneapolis.

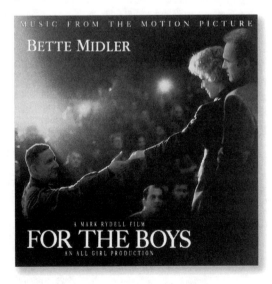

December

#1 Song 1958: "To Know Him Is to Love Him," The Teddy Bears

Born: Billy Paul (The Blue Notes), 1934; Lou Rawls (Pilgrim Travelers), 1935; Sandy Nelson, 1938; John Densmore (The Doors), 1944; Bette Midler, 1945; Gilbert O'Sullivan, 1946

1956 Pat Cordell & the Crescents' "Darling Come Back" and The Youngsters' "Xmas in Jail" were released. The Crescents (minus Pat) went on to become The Elegants of "Little Star" fame. Pat's father didn't want her touring with a group of highly active, testosterone teen boys and his decision ended her musical career.

1958 After publisher Al Nevin played a demo of "The Diary" by Neil Sedaka to RCA's Steve Sholes, the A&R man signed Sedaka as an artist.

1960 Twenty-four-year-old Bobby Darin married sixteen-year-old actress Sandra Dee in a secret ceremony in Elizabeth, N.J. They met three months earlier on the set of the film they both starred in *Come September*. The same day, one of Darin's former girlfriends pined away by debuting at New York's Copacabana for a two-week engagement. The heartbroken miss was Connie Francis.

1966 The Young Rascals made their performance debut in England at the Scotch St. James Club on the strength of their recent hit, "Good Lovin'." A new fan, Paul McCartney, showed up to see them perform.

1990 Rod Stewart's unlikely pairing with Tina Turner in a duet resulted in a remake of Marvin Gaye and Tammi Terrell's "It Takes Two," which topped off at #5 in Britain today. It was never released in America as a single.

December

#1 Song 1967: "Daydream Believer," the Monkees

Born: Tom McGuinness (Manfred Mann), 1941; Rick Savage (Def Leppard), 1960

1957 Because of a last-minute cancellation by Little Anthony & the Imperials, newcomers Danny & the Juniors performed their new single "At the Hop" on Dick Clark's *American Bandstand.* A month later, the record was #1.

1963 During an appearance by the fledgling Beatles on a local British TV show, the show's producer was overheard stating his concern that, "The show won't be aired for a couple of months. Let's hope they're still popular then."

1967 When The Monkees' *Pisces, Aquarius, Capricorn & Jones Ltd.* LP reached #1, it became the fourth Monkees album of the year to do so, setting a record for new releases.

1972 Carly Simon stormed onto the hit list with "You're So Vain," a single that spent three weeks at #1 and included the backing vocals of Mick Jagger.

1995 Mariah Carey, singing lead for Boyz II Men, reached the best-seller's list with "One Sweet Day," a recording that spent an incredible sixteen weeks at #1, making it the #1 hit of the rock era.

The Monkees' Pisces, Aquarius, Capricorn & Jones Ltd.

December

1948 Ozzy Osbourne was born today. The counterculture rocker was the vocalist for the '70s heavy-metal band Black Sabbath, who originally called themselves Earth. After leaving the band, he dueted with Lita Ford on the hit "Close My Eyes Forever." What started out as some TV producer's twisted parody of a reality show turned into a massive cult-like phenomenon when Ozzy and his family expletived their way through a weekly TV visit to their home in 2002.

1958 The Skyliners recorded their timeless classic "Since I Don't Have You" (#12 pop, #3 R&B) at Capitol Studios in New York City.

1965 The Beatles started what would become their last tour of Great Britain in Glasgow, Scotland, along with The Moody Blues. The same day, their single "Day Tripper"/"We Can Work It Out" was issued in England as was the album *Rubber Soul*.

1968 Elvis Presley's Christmas TV special (his first TV special) aired on NBC-TV and captured 42% of the audience, making it the number one-rated show of the year. Though it was billed as a Yuletide show, it only contained one seasonal tune, "Blue Christmas." It has long been considered his comeback show. Premiered on the special, Elvis's "If I Can Dream" single was a major contributor to his comeback, reaching #12, his highest-ranking single since 1965.

1988 Choreographer-turned-singer Paula Abdul charted with "Straight Up," a dance tune that zoomed to the top spot, becoming the first of her six #1s in less than three years.

December

#1 Song 1971: "Family Affair," Sly & the Family Stone

Born: Freddie Cannon, 1939; Chris Hillman (The Byrds), 1942; Dennis Wilson (The Beach Boys), 1944

1948 Oklahoma-born Kay Starr found her way onto the best-seller's list with "You Were Only Foolin'" (#16), her first of forty-two hits through 1962.

1956 When Elvis Presley dropped by Sun Studios in Memphis to see old friends Carl Perkins, Jerry Lee Lewis, and Johnny Cash, who were working on a Perkins recording, an even more historic session took place. Dubbed "The Million Dollar Quartet" recordings, with an LP featuring a picture of all four, only three actually recorded as Cash, who had been nagged into going shopping by his wife, left before the tape started rolling.

1976 The Carpenters received twenty-one gold records while visiting London. Unfortunately, they had to leave them behind at the airport because they were too heavy to take on as excess baggage.

1988 Roy Orbison played his final show at The Front Row Theater in Highland Heights, Ohio.

1993 Frank Zappa was a musician and artist who took on classical, avant-garde, rock and doo-wop in an ever-changing career. He was the leader of The Mothers of Invention and their doo-wop alter ego, Ruben & the Jets. Although never a Top 40 favorite, he did record more than fifty albums. He died of cancer at the age of fifty-two.

December

#1 Song 1960: "Are You Lonesome Tonight," Elvis Presley

Born: Little Richard, 1932; J.J. Cale, 1938; Andy Kim, 1946; Jim Messina (Loggins & Messina), 1947

1953 The Harptones' standard "A Sunday Kind of Love" was released. It was their first of twenty-nine singles between 1953 and 1982.

1968 Graham Nash left The Hollies. Within a year he would be part of the future supergroup Crosby, Stills & Nash.

1987 Ex–Go-Go member Belinda Carlisle stormed to #1 with "Heaven Is a Place on Earth." Helping to promote the single was a video directed by actress Diane Keaton.

1990 Aretha Franklin was honored by the National Academy of Recording Arts and Science (NARAS) with a Living Legend Award.

Crosby, Stills & Nash

December

6

#1 Song 1969: "Na Na Hey Hey Kiss Him Goodbye," Steam

Born: Len Barry (The Dovells), 1942

1968 Janis Joplin made her last appearance with Big Brother & the Holding Company as their tour ended in Hawaii.

1975 Donna Summer's sex-saturated single "Love to Love You Baby" (#2) became her first of thirty-two charters today, spanning sixteen years through 1991.

1969 The Rolling Stones held a free concert at Altamont Raceway in Livermore, California, but, unlike Woodstock four months earlier, Altamont was a deadly affair as an eighteen-year-old was beaten to death by the supposed security, a coven of Hell's Angels. The all-star bill also included Jefferson Airplane; Santana; Crosby, Stills, Nash & Young and The Flying Burrito Brothers.

1988 Rock great Roy Orbison died at his mother's home of a heart attack. He was fifty-two. Bruce Springsteen at Orbison's induction into the Rock and Roll Hall of Fame said: "I want to write words like Bob Dylan that sound like Phil Spector but with singing like Roy Orbison, but nobody sings like Roy Orbison."

Roy Orbison

342

December

Born: Harry Chapin, 1942; Tom Waits, 1949

Died: Richard Taylor (The Manhattans), 1987

1957 George Harrison saw The Quarrymen play for the first time and stated to the effect that he was impressed by John Lennon's trendy clothes and side-burns. "He was a terribly sarcastic bugger right from day one," George noted.

1963 The Beatles were guests as the panelists for the BBC's *Juke Box Jury* before an audience of their Northern Area Fan Club. Their usual wisecrack-ing selves, they rated each record as a hit or a miss:

Elvis Presley's "Kiss Me Quick"

> George: "If he's going back to old tracks, why not release "My Baby Left Me?" It'd be a number one. Elvis is great, his songs are rubbish."
>
> Ringo: "Last two years Elvis has been going down the nick."
>
> Paul: "What I don't like about Elvis are his songs. I like his voice. This song reminds me of Blackpool on a sunny day."

1985 With her mother, Cissy, singing backup vocals, Whitney Houston jumped onto the hit list with "How Will I Know," an eventual #1.

December

8

#1 Song 1973: "Top of the World," The Carpenters

Born: Johnny Otis, 1921; Sammy Davis, Jr., 1925; Jerry Butler (The Impressions), 1939; Jim Morrison (The Doors), 1943; Greg Allman (The Allman Brothers Band), 1947

1956 The Schoolboys' two-sided classic "Please Say You Want Me"/ "Shirley" (#13 pop, #15 R&B) was released, as were The Flamingos' "Would I Be Crying," The Jaguars' "The Way You Look Tonight," and The Moonglows' "I Knew from the Start." "I Knew" was written by songwriter Ben Weisman, who wrote for The Harptones, The Teenagers, The Larks, and fifty-seven songs for Elvis Presley.

1957 The Platters appeared on *The Ed Sullivan Show*.

1961 The Beach Boys signed their first recording agreement with Candix Records.

1980 John Lennon was gunned down by a madman outside his New York apartment who, earlier in the day, had sought and received Lennon's autograph. Lennon, of course, was the leader of the immortal Beatles from 1962 through 1970, when they disbanded. His numerous solo successes include "Imagine" and "Whatever Gets You Thru the Night." He was forty when he died.

1990 Celine Dion swept onto the charts with "Where Does My Heart Beat Now" (#4), her first of nineteen hits.

The Beach Boys

December

1955 Elvis played both a high school (with Johnny Cash) and club in the same evening in Swifton, Arkansas.

1957 On the strength of their *American Bandstand* performance on December 2, Danny & the Juniors' "At the Hop" was picked up by ABC Paramount from the small Philadelphia label Singular and went on to sell more than 2-1/2 million copies.

1967 The Doors' Jim Morrison, who spent almost as much time being arrested as performing, was taken into custody for breach of the peace in New Haven, Connecticut.

1981 Legendary Orioles lead singer Sonny Til died of a heart attack at fifty-one. He formed the group in Baltimore, originally calling them The Vibranairs in 1948. The pioneering R&B group had eleven hits between 1948 and 1953, including the immortal ballad "Crying in the Chapel." An influence on hundreds of later groups, they were inducted into the Rock and Roll Hall of Fame in 1995. Til died from diabetes at age fifty-six.

1978 Elton John's first album without writing partner Bernie Taupin's lyrics, *A Single Man*, peaked at #15 in America.

December

10

#1 Song 1966: "Good Vibrations," The Beach Boys

Born: Chad Stuart (Chad & Jeremy), 1943; Jessica Cleaves (Friends of Distinction), 1948; Ralph Tavares (Tavares), 1948

1949 Twenty-one-year-old Antoine "Fats" Domino recorded his first million-seller, "The Fat Man." He went on to sell more than 65 million records in a six-decade career.

1965 The Jefferson Airplane with Signe Anderson and The Great Society with Grace Slick both performed at the inaugural concert at Bill Graham's Fillmore Auditorium in San Francisco, California.

1967 Otis Redding was a '60s soul legend who parlayed an emotional, gruff, and growling style into hits like "Tramp" and "Try a Little Tenderness." In a career that saw him have almost a third of his chart records after his death (ten) as before his demise (twenty-one), he recorded his biggest hit, "(Sitting on) The Dock of the Bay" three days before he was killed in a plane crash today at age twenty-six.

1979 The Knack's Doug Fieger spent his royalty check to buy Giant Hall of Famer Willie Mays 1963 Bentley Continental.

1994 The Beatles, who had a long history with BBC Radio, had recorded many songs for the British broadcasting service. Fifty-six of those from 1962 through 1965 were packaged into *The Beatles Live at the BBC* album, and twenty-five years after they broke up, this collection entered the British charts today...at #1.

December

#1 Song 1961: "Please Mr. Postman,"
The Marvelettes

Born: Willie Mae "Big Mama" Thornton,
1926; David Gates (Bread), 1940; Brenda Lee,
1944; Jermaine Jackson (The Jackson 5), 1954;
Nikki Sixx Ferranno (Mötley Crüe), 1958

1957 Jerry Lee Lewis wed his thirteen-year-old cousin Myra Gale Brown,
while still married to his wife, Jane Mitcham.

1960 Aretha Franklin made her New York performance debut at the Village
Vanguard in Greenwich Village singing not gospel or rhythm and blues, but
standards.

1964 Sam Cooke was a '50s and '60s pop and soul legend who began
singing gospel with The Highway Q.C.s and then the immortal Soul Stirrers.
He went solo in 1957 and scored forty-three pop hits, including "You Send
Me," "Cupid," and "Chain Gang." Cooke was killed
today in a seedy Los Angeles motel by manager Bertha
Franklin after Cooke was reportedly attempting to
rape a young woman there. He was thirty-three.

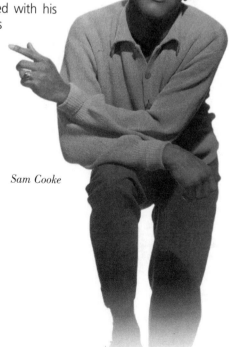

1982 Sammy Hagar, formerly of the rock bands
Montrose and Van Halen, charted with his
biggest of thirteen solo singles
when "Your Love Is Driving Me
Crazy" hit the Top 100 today on
its way to #13.

Sam Cooke

December

12

#1 Song 1970: "Tears of a Clown," The Miracles

Born: Frank Sinatra, 1915; Connie Francis, 1938; Dionne Warwick, 1940; Terry Kirkman (The Association), 1941; Grover Washington, 1943; Paul Rodgers (Free), 1949

1964 The Righteous Brothers' wall-of-sound winner "You've Lost that Loving Feeling" charted,. reaching #2. The harmony included The Ronettes and Cher. Bobby Hatfield of the Brothers wasn't sure about the record's possibilities, asking co-writer Phil Spector, "What do I do while he [Bill Medley] is singing the whole first verse?" Spector's blunt response was, "You can go directly to the bank!"

1965 The Beatles played their last concert in Britain at The Capitol Theatre in Cardiff, Wales.

1968 The Rolling Stones filmed their *Rock 'n' Roll Circus* TV show, which they later decided to shelve.

1985 Ian Stewart was a founding member of The Rolling Stones who started playing keyboards as a member of Rory Storm & the Hurricanes, Ringo Starr's early band. Downgraded to playing offstage because his stout size didn't fit the Stones slender image, he was nevertheless on most of the band's albums and was referred to as the "sixth Stone." He died in his doctor's office in London today of a heart attack at age forty-seven.

1988 Madonna signed a two-year deal with Columbia Pictures to do five films.

December

#1 Song 1969: "Na Na Hey Hey Kiss Him Goodbye" Steam

Born: Ted Nugent (Amboy Dukes), 1948; Jeff "Skunk" Baxter (The Doobie Brothers), 1948

1947 The Ravens' first release on National, "Write Me a Letter," became the first R&B record to breach the pop Top 25, reaching #24.

1969 Mariska Veres and her band, Shocking Blue, hurtled onto the Hot 100 with "Venus," the first Dutch group #1 on the American hit list.

1986 Jackie Wilson's debut hit of 1958, "Reet Petite," reentered England's charts twenty-eight years after first appearing and two years after Wilson died.

1986 Madonna's "Dress You Up" reached #5 in England, becoming her eighth Top 10 hit of the year in the U.K.

Ted Nugent

349

December

#1 Song 1959: "Heartaches by the Number," Guy Mitchell

Born: Charlie Rich, 1932; Joyce Vincent Wilson (Dawn), 1946; Patty Duke, 1946

1952 The rarest R&B record of all time, "Stormy Weather" by The Five Sharps (Jubilee), was issued today. Only two or three 78-rpm copies are known to exist and the estimated value, if auctioned, would be more than $20,000! A 45-rpm copy has never been seen, but if it existed, the value would be astronomical.

1964 The Left Banke's Mike Brown met Rene Fioden at a recording session in New York. The meeting inspired him to write the hit "Walk Away Renee."

1966 In one of RCA's most overt pursuits of plunder, it issued Elvis Presley's "Tell Me Why," a nearly nine-year-old unreleased recording, as a single today. They must have known what they were doing. Elvis fans bought more than 400,000 copies even though it only reached #33 on the charts.

1968 The Beatles' *White Album* debuted on the U. S. charts reaching #1 and staying there for nine weeks.

1996 In one of the most unlikely vocal pairings in recorded history, Elton John and opera star Luciano Pavrotti dueted on "Live Like Horses," which reached #9 in England today. It was never issued in America.

The BEATLES

The Beatles'
The White Album

December

#1 Song 1979: "Babe," Styx

Born: Alan Freed, 1922; Cindy Birdsong (The Bluebelles, The Supremes), 1939; Dave Clark (Dave Clark Five), 1942; Carmine Appice (Vanilla Fudge), 1946; Harry Ray (Ray, Goodman & Brown), 1946; Steve Lundy (Force M.D.'s) 1965.

15

1968 Grace Slick appeared wearing blackface during The Jefferson Airplane's performance of "Crown of Creation" on *The Smothers Brothers Show.*

1973 Melanie's version of The Shirelles' "Will You Love Me Tomorrow" (#82) became her last of nine charters that started with "Lay Down (Candles in the Rain)" in 1970.

1979 Jackie Brenston inadvertently became a part of music history. The sax player was a member of Ike Turner's Kings of Rhythm in 1951 when they recorded "Rocket 88" at Sam Phillips's Sun Studios in Memphis. When the record came out, it read "Jackie Brenston and his Delta Cats," which wouldn't have been that big a deal except it went to #1 and has been considered the first rock-'n'-roll record by many. Ike and the band felt they didn't get any recognition and soon parted ways with Brenston. He died today of a heart attack at age fifty-two.

1985 "Do They Know It's Xmas" by Band Aid entered the British charts at #1 & became the biggest U.K. single in history, selling three million copies. The recording was made to raise money for famine relief for the people of Ethopia and included mostly British rock stars, including Paul McCartney, Phil Collins, Sting, Boy George, U2, Duran Duran, George Michael, Spandau Ballet, Paul Young, Frankie Goes to Hollywood, Heaven 17, Banarama, and James Taylor, among the 36 artists. The record reached #13 in America.

December

16

#1 Song 1957: "Jailhouse Rock"
Elvis Presley

Born: Tony Hicks (The Hollies), 1943;
Benny Anderson (ABBA), 1946

1960 Maurice Williams & the Zodiacs (formerly The Gladiolas of "Little Darling" fame) appeared on *American Bandstand*, performing their soon-to-be #1 "Stay," which at 1:50 became the shortest #1 hit ever. Also appearing were The Viscounts and Fabian.

1962 Bob Dylan, still a year away from his first hit album and three years from his first hit single, embarked on his inaugural European tour, starting in London.

1964 Colonel Tom Parker finalized a deal for Elvis Presley's involvement in two motion pictures with United Artists. The films would be *Clambake* and *Frankie and Johnny*.

1978 Originally a member of The Soul Satisfiers (1971), Gloria Gaynor attacked the singles survey with "I Will Survive," a #1 anthem for women and the sixth of her seven hits from 1974 through 1979.

1983 The Who disbanded; however, they would regroup in 1986 for the Live Aid Concert.

Gloria Gaynor

December

#1 Song 1983: "Say, Say, Say,"
Paul McCartney and Michael Jackson

Born: Tommy Steele, 1936; Arthur
Neville (The Neville Brothers), 1937; Eddie
Kendricks (The Temptations), 1939; Paul
Butterfield, 1942; Wanda Hutchinson (The
Emotions), 1951

1961 Elvis Presley's *Blue Hawaii* became the first rock 'n' roll LP to top the charts for twenty or more weeks.

1962 The Beatles made their first TV appearance on Britain's *People & Places*, performing "Love Me Do." They were paid a total of $56.

1982 Karen Carpenter made her last performance at Buckley School, Sherman Oaks, California, a show attended by her godchildren.

1983 Former vocalist with the group Blue Angel, Cyndi Lauper ascended the charts with "Girls Just Wanna Have Fun," an eventual #2. It was her debut single and first of fourteen hits through 1995. Not bad for a girl who started out working at a racetrack walking horses.

1999 Jazz great Grover Washington, Jr. died. The saxophonist passed away after taping a performance for CBS's *The Saturday Early Show*. President Bill Clinton, who had played sax with Washington in 1993 after a White House jazz concert, said of him, "Grover Washington was as versatile as any jazz musician in America, moving with ease and fluency from vintage jazz to funk and from gospel to blues and pop. I will miss both the man and his music."

December

18

#1 Song 1961: "The Lion Sleeps Tonight," The Tokens

Born: Chas Chandler (The Animals), 1938; Keith Richards (The Rolling Stones), 1943

1943 Keith Richards, lead guitarist for The Rolling Stones, was born today. Considered by many as the world's greatest rock-'n'-roll band, the quartet was inducted into the Rock and Roll Hall of Fame in 1989 and is still touring through 2003.

1969 Tiny Tim married "Miss Vickie" on Johnny Carson's *Tonight Show.*

1971 Jerry Lee Lewis's marriage to his thirteen-year-old cousin ended in divorce after thirteen years.

1971 One-hit wonder Beverly Bremers's "Don't Say You Don't Remember" ascended the singles survey on its way to #15. When her recording career waned, the Chicago born singer-actress went on to win numerous song festivals, including the Korean Song Festival and the American Song Festival with co-writer Jackie English.

1982 Janet Jackson's "Young Love" reached the hit list today (#64), becoming her first of thirty-six charters through 1999.

December

#1 Song 1964: "Come See About Me," The Supremes

Born: Phil Oaks, 1940; Maurice White (Earth, Wind & Fire), 1941; Zal Yanovsky (The Lovin' Spoonful), 1944; Alvin Lee (Ten Years After), 1944

1955 Carl Perkins recorded his immortal "Blue Suede Shoes" at Sun Studios.

1964 *Cashbox* magazine reviewed The Who's first single "I Can't Explain" six weeks before it was released in their home country although it gave the nod to its B-side, saying in part, "The Who, a new English group, bows on Decca with a wild-sounding affair that could bust loose. It's a blues-styled hand-clapper, tagged 'Bald Headed Woman.'"

1974 George Harrison debuted on the U. S. album charts with his first non-instrumental solo album, *All Things Must Pass*, which was #1 for seven weeks.

1975 While still a member of the group The Faces, Rod Stewart's solo album *Atlantic Crossing* was certified gold in America.

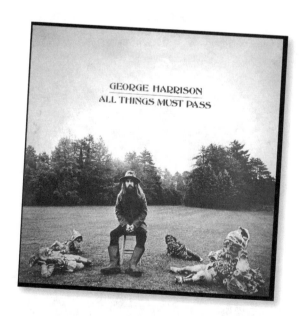

December

#1 Song 1969: "Leaving on a Jet Plane," Peter, Paul & Mary

Born: Bobby Colomby (Blood, Sweat & Tears), 1944; Peter Criss (Kiss), 1947; Anita Baker, 1957

Died: Bobby Darin, 1973

1963 The Beatles were voted the World's Best Vocal Group and Britain's Best Vocal Group, according to the British tabloid *The New Musical Express*.

1957 Elvis Presley's Christmas present from the U.S. Army was his draft notice. He was served at his home in Memphis.

1973 Bobby Darin (Walden Robert Cassotto) was a consummate entertainer who sang pop, rock 'n' roll, and folk. He had forty-one pop charters between 1958 and 1973, including "Splish Splash," Dream Lover," and "Mack the Knife," which spent nine weeks at #1. Darin died of a heart condition today brought on by childhood rheumatic fever. He was thirty-seven.

1980 Jackie English—known for only having songs recorded by such black artists as George Benson, Ronnie Laws, Patrice Rushen, and Eloise Laws, among others—finally had a record by a white artist when she charted with "Once a Night" (from the movie *Hopscotch*). The white artist was herself.

1986 The Bangles' "Walk Like an Egyptian" became their biggest hit, topping the charts for the first of four weeks.

Bobby Darin

December

#1 Song 1968: "I Heard It Through the Grapevine," Marvin Gaye

Born: Frank Zappa, 1940; Ray Hildebrand (Paul & Paula), 1940; Carla Thomas, 1942; Carl Wilson (The Beach Boys), 1946

1957 Elvis Presley visited the mansion of Tennessee Governor Frank Clement and with little prompting performed with a local quintet of black convicts, The Prisonaires of "Just Walkin' in the Rain" fame who were regular entertainers at Clement's home and all inmates at the Tennessee State Prison. Lead singer Johnny Bragg, who had known Presley from his early days of recording at Sun Studios, traded leads with Elvis until the early hours of the morning. You could say it was an evening with "The King" and "The Con."

1968 The Brooklyn Bridge's debut disc, *Worst That Could Happen*, charted on its way to #3. The lead singer was Johnny Maestro, formerly of The Crests, while the background vocalists in "The Bridge" were the former members of The Del-Satins, the uncredited group on Dion's eleven hits from "Runaround Sue" to "Come Go with Me" (1961–1963).

1969 Diana Ross & the Supremes made their final TV appearance together when they performed "Someday We'll Be Together" on *The Ed Sullivan Show*.

1974 Rod Stewart signed with Warner Brothers after a dispute between Warners and Polygram as to who controlled his solo recordings since he was still a member of the British rock band The Faces.

December

#1 Song 1962: "Telstar,"
The Tornadoes

Born: Robin and Maurice Gibb
(The Bee Gees), 1949

1949 The Gibb twins, Robin and Maurice, were born today. Along with brother Barry, they became the world-famous Bee Gees, having their first hit, "New York Mining Disaster 1941," in 1967. They went on to have more than forty hits through four decades with some of the '60s and '70s best-loved songs, including "I Started a Joke," "How Can You Mend a Broken Heart," "Jive Talkin'," "Night Fever," and the classic "Stayin' Alive." They amassed nine #1s, six of them in a row from 1977 through 1979.

1958 Frankie Ford's eternal rocker "Sea Cruise" was released, eventually reaching #3.

1974 John Lennon hit the American charts with the single "#9 Dream," which coincidentally went to #9.

1979 Pat Benatar (Patricia Andrzejewski) rocked onto the hit list with "Heartbreaker," her first of seventeen hits through 1988.

1984 Madonna streaked to the top of the charts with "Like a Virgin." It perched there for six weeks.

December

#1 Song 1957: "You Send Me," Sam Cooke

Born: Little Esther Phillips (Esther Mae Jones), 1935; Eugene Record (The Chi-Lites), 1940; Jorma Kaukonen (Jefferson Airplane), 1940; Tim Hardin, 1941; Eddie Vedder (Pearl Jam), 1966

1964 Brian Wilson (The Beach Boys) suffered a nervous breakdown during a flight from Los Angeles to Houston. He gave up performing and was replaced for gigs by studio musician Glen Campbell & later ex–Rip Chords member Bruce Johnson.

1966 Britain's music TV show *Ready, Steady, Go* broadcast for the last time.

1967 The Beatles album *The Magical Mystery Tour* charted in the U.S., eventually rising to #1 where it stayed for eight weeks.

1972 Hawaiian-raised Bette Midler hula'd her way onto the singles survey with the 1958 Bobby Freeman hit "Do You Wanna Dance" (#17). It was her first of eighteen hits through 1991.

1994 The Beatles double album *Live at the BBC* charted, on its way to #3 in America. It was culled from fifty-two BBC shows. Thirteen days earlier it reached #1 in England.

December

#1 Song 1977: "How Deep Is Your Love," The Bee Gees

Born: Dave Bartholomew, 1920; Lee Dorsey, 1924; Jan Akkerman (Focus), 1946

Died: Nick Massi (The Four Seasons), 2000

1954 R&B balladeer Johnny Ace died after playing Russian roulette backstage at the Houston City Auditorium. He was twenty-five.

1957 Elvis Presley formally requested a deferment from the Army by sending a letter to the Memphis Draft Board, so he could finish work on his film *King Creole*. Between the power of Paramount and the prestige of Presley the government felt compelled to roll over. The draft board responded only two days later.

1964 The Beatles performed at the Hammersmith Odeon in London, doing two shows a night for their annual Beatles' Christmas Show. Also on the bill were The Yardbirds, Freddie & the Dreamers, Georgie Fame, and Elkie Brooks.

1974 Carly Simon, Joni Mitchell, Linda Ronstadt, and James Taylor enjoyed Christmas Eve by singing Christmas carols door-to-door in Los Angeles.

1999 Zeke Carey, leader of The Flamingos of "I Only Have Eyes for You" and "I'll Be Home," fame died today. The Flamingos were considered by many fans and historians as the greatest vocal group of all time. Zeke, born January 24, 1933, was sixty-six.

2000 Nick Massi was the bass singer for the rock 'n' roll quartet The Four Lovers, who, later with the addition of Bob Gaudio (from The Royal Teens), became The Four Seasons. Nick sang on most of their hits, including "Sherry" and "Big Girls Don't Cry." He died of cancer at sixty-five.

December

#1 Song 1972: "Brand New Key," Melanie

Born: Chris Kenner, 1929; O'Kelly Isley (The Isley Brothers), 1937; Jimmy Buffett, 1946; Barbara Mandrell, 1948; Annie Lennox (Eurythmics), 1954; Robin Campbell (UB-40), 1954

1954 The DeJohn Sisters jumped onto the best-seller's list with "(My Baby Don't Love Me) No More," an eventual #6 hit.

1954 The Penguins classic "Earth Angel" charted en route to #8. It is considered to be the most popular R&B oldie of all time.

1965 The Mamas & the Papas classic "California Dreamin'" was released.

1971 Melanie's "Brand New Key" reached #1 and stayed there for three weeks. She originally wrote the song as a simple ditty for use in between songs at concerts. It took her all of fifteen minutes to write it.

1976 Karen Lawrence and The L.A. Jets charted with "Prisoner" (#86). The obscure tune was later a hit for Barbra Streisand when music publisher Jay Warner placed the song with Streisand and it became the title song from the film *Eyes of Laura Mars*, reaching #21 as "Love Theme from *Eyes of Laura Mars* (Prisoner)."

Jimmy Buffett

December

#1 Song 1970: "My Sweet Lord," George Harrison

Born: Abdul "Duke" Fakir (The Four Tops), 1935; Phil Spector (The Teddy Bears), 1940

1960 Brenda Lee's "Emotions" (#7) was released.

1964 Red Bird Records made the unusual move of releasing two singles by The Shangri-Las at the same time, and both "Give Him a Great Big Kiss" (#18) and "Maybe" (#91), a remake of The Chantels hit, charted today.

1964 The Beatles had their sixth #1 when "I Feel Fine" topped the charts. It was also their twenty-ninth hit, in one year!

1964 "Let's Lock the Door" by Jay & the Americans charted, en route to #11. It was their fourth of eighteen hits in eight years. During the group's career, they had two lead singers named Jay: original lead Jay Traynor for the first few hits and Dave Blatt, who changed his name to Jay Black. Coincidentally, both were born on the same day, November 2, but Black was three years older (1938 to 1941).

December

#1 Song 1969: "Someday We'll Be Together," Diana Ross & the Supremes

Born: John "Buddy" Bailey (The Clovers), 1931; Mike Pinder (The Moody Blues), 1941; Mick Jones (Foreigner), 1944; Tracy Nelson (Mother Earth), 1944; Karla Bonoff, 1952

1964 The Supremes made their TV debut on *The Ed Sullivan Show*.

1975 The Four Seasons charted with "December 1963 (Oh What a Night)". It went to #1, becoming their first chart topper since 1964's "Rag Doll." "December" had an unusual rebirth when a dance remix of the song charted nineteen years later in 1994 (#44).

1963 The Rolling Stones appeared on the British TV show *Ready, Steady, Go!*, singing the song Lennon and McCartney had written for them, "I Wanna Be Your Man." Also on the show was Little Stevie Wonder.

The Rolling Stones

December

28

#1 Song 1959: "Why,"
Frankie Avalon

Born: Roebuck "Pops" Staples
(The Staple Singers), 1915; Johnny
Otis, 1921; Dorsey Burnette, 1932;
Edgar Winter, 1946

1957 Jackie Wilson, The Five Satins, The Ravens, and The Hollywood Flames performed at Chicago's Regal Theater.

1963 Lesley Gore's fourth Top 5 charter in a row, "You Don't Own Me," began its run up the Hot 100 today, en route to #2. It became an anthem for both women and gays in coming decades.

1968 The third major rock-pop festival and first on the East Coast was held in Miami, Florida. Known as The Miami Pop Festival, many of the acts were really folk artists, such as Buffy Sainte-Marie, Richie Havens, and Ian & Sylvia. The rock and pop were represented by The Turtles, The Grateful Dead, Chuck Berry, Joni Mitchell, The Box Tops, Iron Butterfly, Joe Tex, and Marvin Gaye.

1974 George Harrison's *Dark Horse* album hit the U. S. charts on its way to #4. It was the ex-Beatles fourth Top 5 album in five years.

1983 Beach Boy Dennis Wilson, the only real surfer in the group, drowned while swimming off of his boat moored in Marina Del Rey, California. He was thirty-nine.

George Harrison's
Dark Horse

December

#1 Song 1958: "The Chipmunk Song," The Chipmunks

Born: Ray Thomas (The Moody Blues), 1941; Jerry Gross (The Dovells), 1942; Patti Drew, 1944; Marianne Faithfull, 1946; Yvonne Elliman, 1951

1946 Wispy-voiced Marianne Faithfull was born today. Discovered by Rolling Stones manager Andrew Loog Oldham, Marianne's biggest chart success was "As Tears Go By" in 1964.

1956 In his first year of pop chart success, Elvis Presley registered seventeen singles on the Top 100, the last being his audition song at the age of ten, "Old Shep."

1962 The Crystals charted with "He's Sure the Boy I Love" (#11). Unfortunately, as with their previous hit, "He's a Rebel," it wasn't The Crystals singing on the record, but Darlene Love & the Blossoms, thanks to the decision-making shenanigans of producer Phil Spector.

1973 Olivia Newton-John hit the Top 200 with *Let Me Be There* (#71), her second of seventeen chart albums between 1971 and 1992.

1980 Tim Hardin was a folk-rock musician who added touches of jazz to set his style apart though he became more well known for writing songs that became successful for others, such as "If I Were a Carpenter" (Bobby Darin, The Four Tops) and "Reason to Believe" (Rod Stewart). He died while overdosing on a combination of morphine and heroin.

December

1950 Billy Ward & the Dominoes (with bass Bill Brown on lead) recorded their mega-hit "60 Minute Man," which went on to spend three-and-a-half months at #1 (R&B) in 1951 (#17 pop).

1957 Alan Freed's Brooklyn Paramount Christmas Show extravaganza featured The Moonglows, Heartbeats, Dells, G-Clefs, and Three Friends.

1957 The Diamonds' tenth hit, "The Stroll," charted giving rise to the popular dance of the same name.

1957 The McGuire Sisters bounced onto the national singles survey with "Sugartime," ultimately spending four weeks at #1.

1995 The Beatles seventy-first American Top 100 45 entered the charts today. "Free As a Bird" was originally a demo from 1977 by John Lennon that had new vocals and instrumentation by the surviving Beatles. The eighteen-year-old recording reached #6, becoming their last of thirty-four Top 10 hits.

Bo Diddley

December

#1 Song 1967: "I'm a Believer," The Monkees

Born: Andrew Summers (The Police), 1942; John Denver (The Mitchell Trio), 1943; Burton Cummings, 1947; Donna Summer, 1948

Died: Rick Nelson, 1985

1960 "There's a Moon Out Tonight" by The Capris charted, eventually reaching #3. The group had given up two years earlier and disbanded, only to regroup when the record hit the charts.

1961 The Beach Boys' first live performance was at the Ritchie Valens Memorial Concert at the Municipal Auditorium in Long Beach, California. They earned $300.

1961 Janis Joplin made her first public singing engagement at the Halfway House, Beaumont, Texas.

1966 Certain upper-crust places in London were still no place for a Beatle without a tie. George Harrison, Brian Epstein, Eric Clapton, and others were not allowed into Annabel's Night Club because George was tieless, so they brought in the New Year at the Lyon's Corner House Restaurant instead.

1970 The worst-kept secret in rock 'n' roll was officially announced today. The Beatles had broken up.

1975 Elvis Presley did a rare New Year's Eve performance at the Silverdome in Pontiac, Michigan. He then flew home to Memphis to ring in the new year watching old Monty Python episodes in his bedroom with his entourage. The show itself earned him the largest one-night gross ever received by a solo artist, $800,000.

1982 Bette Midler and Barry Manilow appeared as "Baby New Year" and "Father Time" respectively at a New Year's Eve concert at the Universal Amphitheater, Universal City, California.

About the Author

Jay Warner is a six-time Grammy-winning music publisher, recipient of the Heroes and Legends Foundation "Pioneer" Award, and first publisher to be entered into The Congressional Record for his contributions to the music industry. He has turned his meticulous passion for information into a distinct and separate career as an author and music historian with a series of best-selling books and his definitive series of Music-Cals™, the mini book in a day-by-day format.

As a music publisher Warner has represented writer-artists as diverse as Bruce Springsteen, Barry Manilow, and Rick James, and has published more than 100 Top 40 hits, including "Blinded By the Light" (Manfred Mann), "Born to Run" (Bruce Springsteen), "Up, Up and Away" (The 5th Dimension), "By the Time I Get to Phoenix" (Glen Campbell), "Midnight Train to Georgia" (Gladys Knight & the Pips), "Groovin'" (The Rascals), "Party All the Time" (Eddie Murphy), "In My House" (Mary Jane Girls), "Love Is All We Need" (Mary J. Blige), and many more.

In 1978 Jay wrote the first in-depth text on publishing, songwriting, and copyright law in layman's terms, *How to Have Your Hit Song Published* (Hal Leonard). Twenty-five years later, it is in its fifth printing, is still the definitive text on the subject, and has never been out of print.

In 1993 Warner's encyclopedic work *The Billboard Book of American Singing Groups, A History 1940–1990* was published to rave reviews as the ultimate resource on the subject.

In 1997 Warner's *Billboard's American Rock-n-Roll in Review* continued his streak of entertaining references. His *Just Walkin' in the Rain* (the true story of a convict quintet, a liberal governor, and how they changed Southern history through rhythm and blues) shook up the establishment in 2001 with a mind-boggling best-seller that is now an acclaimed documentary and a soon-to-be motion picture.

Jay lives in Los Angeles with his wife, Jackie, and favorite four-legged friends, Napoleon and Sunny.

Acknowledgements

To my biggest believers: my father, Bob, and my mother, Ray; my uncle Archie "Willie" Friedberg; my aunt Sydelle and uncle Hymie Sherman; Sam Shatzman; my cousins Michael, Jerry, and Deanna; and my loving and loyal wife, Jackie. May your spirit, faith, and love forever guide me, and may God always bless you.

I'd also like to thank a few long-standing supporters who have given of themselves truly out of friendship: Dennis Wolfe, Sam Atchley, John Wilson, Barry Petermen, Phil Kozma, Chas Peate, Peter Foldy, Stu Nadel, and Peter Shadis. I feel rich indeed to know you and wish you everything I wish for those I hold most dear.

Lastly I want to thank the entire Hal Leonard organization, whom I have been privileged to know and work with for more than twenty years, especially Keith Mardak, Jeff Schroedl, John Cerullo, Belinda Yong, and Larry Morton. I appreciate your belief in my work. You're a class act.